ENIOLA ALUKO

Eniola Aluko is a former England footballer, with over 100 caps and 33 goals to her name.

Her club sides include Birmingham City, Charlton, Saint Louis, Chelsea and Juventus where she has won three English league titles, four FA cups, the Serie A title and the Coppa Italia. She also represented Great Britain in the 2012 Olympic Games.

Eniola was the first female pundit on *Match of the Day*. She is a national newspaper columnist and an ambassador for UN Women UK.

She holds a first class honours degree in law.

ENIOLA ALUKO

They Don't Teach This

With Josie Le Blond

VINTAGE

1 3 5 7 9 10 8 6 4 2

Vintage
20 Vauxhall Bridge Road,
London SW1V 2SA

Vintage is part of the Penguin Random House group of companies
whose addresses can be found at global.penguinrandomhouse.com

Penguin
Random House
UK

First published in hardback by Yellow Jersey Press in 2019
First published by Vintage in 2020

penguin.co.uk/vintage

A CIP catalogue record for this book is available from the British Library

ISBN 9781529112856

Printed and bound in Great Britain by Clays Ltd, Elcograf S.p.A.

Penguin Random House is committed to a sustainable future
for our business, our readers and our planet. This book is made
from Forest Stewardship Council® certified paper.

MIX
Paper from
responsible sources
FSC® C018179

Eternal gratitude and glory to the Most High for He who is in me has always been greater than He who is in the world.

Eternal love for my family, friends and mentors - Thank you.

'*Little children, you are from God and have overcome them, for he who is in me is greater than he who is in the world.*'

1 John 4:4

'*Learning is the only thing the mind never exhausts, never fears and never regrets*'

Leonardo Da Vinci

COURSE SCHEDULE

PROLOGUE

A whistle blew. I sprinted forward, squinting against the slanting sun as the players fanned out across the pitch. My gut fizzed in expectation. We were one point away from winning the league. I could almost feel the cold, glinting silverware under my fingers. The next ninety minutes would wash away years of disappointment. No second place this time. This time, we would lift the trophy.

Everyone here on this bright autumn afternoon was as certain as I was. This was our game. On the sidelines a cluster of TV cameras was trained on the pitch, here to capture our title victory. In the stands a large away crowd waved and cheered. Even our opponents seemed resigned to our win. Way down in fifth place, Manchester

City had nothing to play for. They had even rested some of their key players. This was going to be a routine win. I had visualised it all. I would score, I would win, and I would lift the trophy.

The whistle blew once more. A free kick to City inside our half. All eyes followed the ball as it arced in towards our goal. Our keeper Marie Hourihan stormed out of the scrum and leapt, arms outstretched, as a midfielder barrelled in from the left. The players collided with a sickening crack and plummeted to the ground. Marie stayed down, clutching her head in her white gloves. Paramedics jogged on to the pitch and bundled her into an ambulance as the news ran like a shiver through the team: it was a broken collarbone.

I fought a rising wave of nausea. Marie was more than our last line of defence; she was the foundation of our morale. Eleven minutes in, this game, our game, had taken a nightmarish turn. The backline looked on, glum and shell-shocked, as a substitute keeper warmed up and stepped on to the pitch. Losing our keeper had hit us hard. All our bravado was evaporating into the pale afternoon air.

Sensing we were shaken, our opponents sent a timid, probing shot long and low across the pitch. The ball bounced slowly at the edge of the box and somehow in over our sub keeper. I stared in horror from the other end of the pitch as we struggled to register the goal. Our defence was still reeling when they attacked again. A sky-blue shirt raced down the wing and cut back to a striker who, in one flowing movement, controlled the ball on her chest and volleyed it up into the top corner. A second gut punch within minutes of the first.

I gazed around my teammates. There was no fire or fight in their eyes, only numb shock. Up front, it would fall on me to stop the freefall into despair. We wrested back control in the second half and, pushing hard, got one back. Now it was close again; we only needed a draw. The title was just one goal away. It was down to me to claw this back.

The minutes slid away. I gave it everything I had, but their defenders closed in, a determined, grim back line. In the last minute, we took a corner. My throat tightened and my vision swam as I stood on the goal line, waiting for our final chance. The ball looped in, there was a desperate scramble, and their keeper emerged triumphant, clutching it in her gloves. The whistle blew and I collapsed on to the field, sobbing, as my world crumbled around my ears. I was inconsolable.

Slumped on the pitch that day in 2014, I still had a lot to learn. That defeat shook me to my core. It shattered

my love of football and even made me question my faith in God. I felt humiliated. I felt like a failure. To climb all season to the top of the table and fall short at the last minute, on the last day, by just one goal. It was too much to bear.

People tried to comfort me. There was always next year, they said. I'm sure they meant well, but the thought of going back out there, climbing back up the table, and getting close enough to win, close enough to fail, made my stomach squirm. What if we lost again? I wasn't sure I could take that crushing disappointment a second time.

But I didn't quit. I got over it, and in doing so, I learned one of the hardest lessons of my life. The following year, when at last, not one, but two trophies came, I understood: it was the defeat that had driven us not only to win, but to exceed even our own expectations. That humiliating loss gave us an edge over the other teams, it was the extra fuel that propelled us over the finish line to claim both the title and the FA Cup. Our failure was the foundation of our success.

Since then, I've learnt to embrace failure, when it comes. It didn't happen overnight, I still get disappointed, that's only human. But I'm never inconsolable like I was that day, because I know that if I fail, a lesson will surely follow. I began to see that failure, disappointment and challenges shouldn't be feared. They are opportunities, necessary steps along the winding road to success. They are life's best teachers.

And there was a lot to learn. As a kid, I was taught to behave a certain way by my parents, coaches, teachers, and preachers. They gave me a set of a guiding principles and morals to live by. But out in the real world, things were different. Life was much messier than I had been taught to expect. I found myself in situations no one had taught me how to deal with. Situations that no one could have prepared me for in advance. These were lessons I had to learn on my own. Lessons they didn't teach.

They don't teach you what to do when you lose your job thousands of miles from home. Or how to deal with a loss so devastating it makes you question your faith. They don't teach how to perform under pressure, or deal with criticism, or fight for change, or stand up to a mighty organisation when it tries to crush you. They don't teach what to do when you are lost and alone in a team, or when the newspapers print half-truths about you. They don't teach how and when to tell your truth.

And they don't teach women how to break through the glass ceiling, or what women of colour experience as a more impenetrable concrete ceiling. As a black woman, I've spent my whole life learning how to break free of the limitations others impose upon me. I've learned that it is OK to be first, to be a pioneer. They said I can't, I said I'll do it anyway. I played football at the highest level, qualified as a lawyer, and analysed the game I love on TV. I've had great mentors, coaches and professors help me along the way. Still, none of them could prepare me to face many of my highest and lowest moments. No one taught me how, life did.

Like everyone else out there, I've had to figure these lessons out on my own, by going through it. I've failed at times, I've got things wrong, had to go back and try again. And through each failure, I've grown, learned, and come out better equipped for the next challenge life has thrown at me. And all the successes, all the trophies, all the victories, were made all the sweeter by the obstacles I had to overcome along the way.

Life has been a series of these lessons learned from experience, each one of them hard-won and precious. I want to share them, these lessons they don't teach. I hope they are useful; I hope they resonate with what you might be facing in your own life. This is my story. It starts with a failure, because failure is the best teacher, the best lesson, and they don't teach this.

Class 1:

Heaven's Number 9

Suddenly it all made sense. I wasn't alone any more. I didn't need to apologise for being

the girl who was good at football.

CHAPTER ONE

The ball flew across the grey sky and fell ahead where darker clouds gathered, threatening rain. It landed and bounced, long and low, towards our makeshift goal. We sprinted after it, down the slope, throwing up piles of cut grass behind us as we went. I reached the ball first and kept running.

I looked up. Ahead, a boy squatted between two jumpers, his legs far apart, his hands spread in anticipation. We locked eyes and his face screwed up in challenge. Out of the corner of my eye I sensed someone gaining on me. The other boys shouted from behind.

'Go on, Eddie, shoot!'

Not yet, I wasn't there yet. I darted forward, dribbling, eyes glued to the ball at my feet. Two shapes were closing in on me now from behind, one from the left and one from the right. I glanced up. A bit nearer, and I'd get a clear shot. A foot lunged in to tackle from the right and I swerved hard to the left. I broke into a sprint, tapped the ball ahead, manoeuvring around a crushed coke can trodden into the grass. I looked up; I'd shaken them off. I'd only have a second. The boy shifted back and forth in goal.

I swung my leg back and kicked the ball hard at the goal. The keeper lunged too late. The ball flew at chest height between the jumpers, past the keeper's outstretched hand, and bounced cheerily down towards the bottom of the field. The keeper landed, scowling, and sprawled on top of the near jumper-post. I yelled and jumped and celebrated like I'd seen Manchester United's Ryan Giggs do on TV. I spun around to face the others, beaming wide, ready to receive the glory.

It didn't come. Instead, a series of sharp, hollow barks echoed off the concrete buildings. The sound zigzagged across the field. I froze, my chest tightened, and my knees buckled. I dared myself to look up. At the far end of the field, where the grass gave way to the estate, stood a large, black Rottweiler. The dog shifted on its front feet, straining against its lead. Each bark exposed a flash of yellow fangs, and its eyes were fixed on the ball, which had come rolling to a stop nearby. Struggling on the other end of the cord was a girl of about ten. She glared at us from under her black hoodie.

Each bark made me want to run, but I stood still. I couldn't risk the others laughing at me. I turned my head and looked up the slope towards home. There was our building, up where the field met the main road. And there, at the small kitchen window of our ground floor flat, the dark outline of my Mum, Sileola, busy at the sink. I took a deep breath. She was there. Apparently unfazed by the Rottweiler, the keeper had fetched the ball, and the game had restarted. The dog wasn't letting up. Another round of barks rebounded off the buildings and I bolted up the slope towards home. Mum looked up and opened the kitchen window.

'Eni, Sone!' she called. 'Come in now. Dinner's ready.'

These are my earliest memories, kicking a ball around with the local kids and my little brother, Sone, and being petrified of that Rottweiler. I can't have been more than five years old, which would have made Sone only three. We grew up together on a sprawling council estate in southern Birmingham. I'm proud that both of us started playing football on the street. There's a kind of grit you can only get from learning how to beat defenders while dribbling around broken glass and coke cans. We come from estate football. No adults, no referees. Jumpers for goalposts.

Football filled a lot of gaps growing up. Mum arranged childminders, but we often had the freedom to entertain ourselves. That almost always meant playing outside. Our building was the last in a row of three multi-storey blocks along the Redditch Road that backed on to a sloping field. The open space drew all the kids from the large estate on the other side, especially the football players. A game was always going on, right there, outside our bedroom window. It made sense we would join in.

The other kids struggled with my Nigerian name. A boys' name, Eddie, was easier for them, and it stuck. I had started at Broadmeadow Junior, a primary school in a neighbouring district about two miles east of where we lived. At school I was Eniola, or Eni; on the estate, I was Eddie. Mum was always taken aback when our friends rang our doorbell and asked if Eddie and Sone were coming out to play. I just wanted a boy's name that sounded a bit realistic. I cringe about it now, but back then I liked it. I felt like I belonged, like I'd been accepted.

It also helped that I could play. Playing football on an estate, we learned to play with whoever turned up. I soon realised I could outrun any of the other kids and if I was already out front with the ball no one had a hope of catching me. That was my starting point, speed. From there I started building other skills, picking up tricks from the others to outsmart and get past defenders. A sudden stop, a sharp turn, a misleading dip of a shoulder. I learned to dribble the length of the pitch, weaving and dodging anyone who tried to stop me. At the end of the run, I'd score. It was the same then as now. My goals have always been about running ahead, using my speed and slotting past the keeper, just as I did on the estate. It became second nature, flowing, easy. I found I could look down the pitch and map out a path to goal. Then, before anyone could stop me, I'd be at the other end of the field, shooting.

That's how it all started, but football was never a conscious decision for either me or Sone. No one taught us how to play. The rules seeped in on their own, through our eyes, ears and feet. At the beginning, there was no one to show us, coach us, or push us on. My dad, Daniel, had played when he was younger. He was probably good enough to have gone professional, but he chose a career in oil and politics instead. I guess our natural football ability came from him, but growing up we barely saw him – Dad spent most of his time in Nigeria. Football didn't come from Mum. She played squash for her health, but she was never really wired for competitive sports. All the passion, the skill, the interest, it came from us. Sone and I were born with a football instinct. God made us that way, with the game inside us

It took me a little while to understand this, that God created me as a footballer, with this talent. It was masked at first because God also created me as a woman, and I grew up in a world that was still struggling to accept female players. I would face a lot of resistance before I realised it didn't matter what the world said. I was God's creation, I was female, and I was a footballer. It didn't matter if the world found it hard to accept me as a striker at first. I could be God's number 9, heaven's number 9. I didn't need society's say so, I was born to do this.

But that came later. In the early days, football helped me feel accepted. The better Sone and I got, the more popular we became on the estate. Everyone wanted us on their team. At any given time, wherever we were, it was a safe bet that a kind of chaotic game would form around us. Sometimes we were a huge crowd of players, sometimes just a handful. We could always count on our core friendship group of about six kids. Sone was the youngest, the others were around my age. One boy, our ringleader, was a few years older. I was the only girl. There weren't any other girls around, apart from the owner of the Rottweiler, and I wasn't about to make friends with her. The girls on the estate weren't interested in what the boys were playing. And I wasn't into whatever it was they were doing. I only wanted to play football, and that made me one of the lads. So, I did anything, everything, the boys did.

That was until, one by one, the other kids got bikes. Beautiful, alien-looking, dirt BMXes, with thick tyres, long handle bars, and high saddles. Our friends went everywhere on them, and Sone and I couldn't stand being left behind. Mum wanted us to be happy, and I wanted to be cool like the other kids on the estate. It wasn't easy, but she made the bikes a priority, and in the winter, when I turned seven and Sone turned five, we each got a BMX bike for our birthdays.

It was like we had been given wings. On wheels, our territory stretched further, to the outer limits of the estate. We began to wonder how far we could ride in a day. We got to scheming, planning adventures into the unknown, beyond the reach of adults. We settled on Lickey Hills, a huge country park about four miles to the west of the estate. From the top of the hills, on good days, you could see for miles around. There, we would have space to test out what our new bikes could do. Our plan was to ride there, bike around for a bit and get back before anyone noticed we were gone. We knew we wouldn't be allowed to go if we asked permission, so we didn't ask.

We had a childminder to look after us before Mum got home from work. We were always outside anyway, playing football or riding our bikes, so it was easy to give her the slip. One day, we waited until she wasn't looking, and then we headed out with the others. We rode our bikes across the field and through the estate, in what we guessed was the direction of Lickey Hills. This was long before mobile phones and GPS – we had only a vague idea of where we were going, we were riding on instinct. We didn't get far. Somewhere beyond the estate, past the golf course and the playing fields, we got lost in the back streets. It was a while before we realised we had been going in circles. We gave up and turned back for home, but nothing looked familiar. A lump of dread rose in my throat; maybe we'd never get home. At last, after trying a different turning, we emerged at the playing fields. Relief washed over us, and we pedalled as fast as we could back through the estate.

We must have been gone much longer than we thought, because when we got home, we found Mum in a full-blown panic. She was standing outside our building, scanning the field. The childminder stood next to her; both their faces were pinched with worry. Mum's face softened for an instant when she saw us riding up the slope, then it hardened again. She was furious. She and the childminder had been searching the whole estate for us, calling our names and asking if anyone had seen us. Not knowing where else to turn, Mum had even alerted the police. Another few hours and they would have filed missing person's reports. We were in big trouble.

I learned my lesson. That was the last time we left the estate on our bikes. It didn't matter, though, we had enough to keep us busy right outside our front door. If Sone and I weren't playing football, we were watching matches on TV or lost in shared daydreams, reliving goals, or brooding over the details of painful defeats. We were Manchester United fans. Like the rest of the world, Sone and I loved maverick striker Eric Cantona and winger Ryan Giggs. To us, United were unbeatable. It seemed like every year the club won either the Premier League or the FA Cup. That year we got bikes, United won both, their first Double. That clinched it for us. Mum saved up again to buy us both full United kits.

The following season, the club's crown began to slip. Cantona was given a lengthy ban for kung-fu-kicking a supporter, and United were almost entirely dependent on new signing Andy Cole up front. Cole had won the Golden Boot the previous season, but it wasn't the same without Cantona. Suddenly United, the club that always won, couldn't be sure of either trophy. The Premier League title race came down to the wire, with United chasing Blackburn Rovers. On the last day of the season, Sone and I sat down to watch Match of the Day with United needing a win against West Ham. It was 1–1. All they needed was that one chance, that one goal, to claw back victory. Cole was working hard, but he kept missing chances. When the final whistle went, Sone and I were in shock. This wasn't the United we knew. We were used to celebrating.

United were due to face Everton in the FA Cup final the following weekend. Sone and I counted the days, hoping we could save face. United always won something. I couldn't remember Everton ever winning anything. That Saturday, Sone and I dressed in our kits and sat in front of the TV, glued to the pre-match build-up, desperate for the game to begin. If disaster was in the air, we weren't about to admit it. United were starting without all three of their top scorers. Cantona was still banned, Cole was cup-tied, and right winger Andrei Kanchelskis was injured. At kick off we were anxious, but neither of us really believed Everton could beat United.

It happened so fast, in the thirtieth minute. Everton broke like lightning down the middle. On the edge of the area, right back Matt Jackson cut inside and closed in on our goal. Sone and I were on our feet in front of the TV.

'No!' I yelled above the swelling roar from the Everton fans.

Jackson squared the ball to Graham Stuart.

'No, no, no!'

Stuart shot and we held our breaths. The ball hit the crossbar and plummeted down hard, bouncing in front of the goalmouth. There was no time for relief. Centre forward Paul Rideout bolted in and headed the rebound home. We froze, a shocked silence fell in the lounge. On screen, Rideout sprinted towards the corner, his arms raised in victory. A lump grew in my throat. Sone looked up at me, his face screwed up in pain. I shook my head.

'It's early,' I told him. 'There's still time.'

United were hungry for an equaliser in the second half. Every chance had us back on our feet and shouting at the TV. But there was no Cantona, no Cole, or Kanchelskis. There were no creative masterstrokes, no flashes of brilliance, and nothing broke though. Time sped up. The closing minutes of the game ticked down like seconds. My eyes filled with stinging tears. They couldn't lose. This was Manchester United, the winners.

On the final whistle, the United players collapsed on to the pitch. We collapsed too on to the lounge floor. The disappointment was too much to bear. We had been expecting a celebration, and we had been humiliated, again. On screen, the Everton players hugged each other. In the stands the fans jumped and sang their victory. It felt like they were jeering at us. I let out a sob and set Sone off too. By the time Mum came in to see what was wrong, we were both in floods of tears.

It was a bitter lesson. For the first time, I understood that even the best player, the best team, had to lose, sooner or later. But losing didn't matter. It was what you took from a loss that counted. The following season, Manchester United were back on form, and became the first club to win both trophies twice, the double Double. I understand now that it was losing the year before that spurred the players on, that made the wins all the sweeter. Defeat had made them stronger.

Later that year, I watched captivated as Cantona celebrated an iconic goal against Sunderland. He stood rooted to the spot, collar up, turned to the crowd and gave the world a look that let them know he was the king. I thought about the buzz of sprinting down the pitch, weaving through defenders and finding the net. I knew I could be that kind of striker. The kind that makes the difference between winning and losing.

CHAPTER TWO

The thumping woke me up. Dull, heavy knocking from somewhere above my bedroom ceiling. Then muffled shouts. A man's voice. Then a clattering sound, more yelling. I lay in bed, eyes wide, listening. A door opened and slammed, and the voices grew louder. After a while, the noises stopped, and the building fell silent. I lay awake, listening for a while, then I drifted back to sleep.

In the morning we were up early, as usual. Mum's shifts began at seven thirty and she had to battle morning traffic to get to the hospital on time. We were still too young to be left alone, so a childminder came in most days to take us to school. Sometimes, when our usual minder was sick, Mum would pay the lady who lived upstairs to look after us. She was friendly and good with kids and we liked her. On the days our neighbour had to go to work herself, she would take us down the road to her mother's place for her to drop us instead. It wasn't ideal, nothing was in those towers, but it worked somehow. We always made it to school.

That morning, we were up, dressed, and had finished breakfast, but there was no sign of the childminder. Mum was pacing the kitchen, looking at her watch. Six twenty. It was getting late. Mum pulled on her coat and shoes and sat down on the edge of the couch, her bag on her lap, ready to go as soon as the minder appeared.

Five minutes passed, then ten. I could see Mum was getting anxious, she hated being late. She worked as a nurse at what was then Dudley Road Hospital to the west of the city centre. It was about a thirty-minute drive away, but during rush hour the journey could take up to an hour. Mum stood up and went to the front door to check for any sign of the minder. But when she grasped the handle, she got a shock. The door was jammed shut. She double-checked the lock, tried the handle again, pulled harder. But the door wouldn't budge.

A knock at the kitchen window made us all jump. Mum went to the sink, peered out from the brightly lit kitchen into the early morning gloom. The shape knocked again on the glass. Mum opened the window. Outside stood a police officer, holding out his badge.

'Hello?' said Mum, scanning the man's badge and uniform. 'What's going on?'

'You can't come out now,' said the officer, sticking his head through the window and looking around the tiny flat. He nodded at us, then looked back at Mum. 'The stairwell is an active crime scene.'

'What do you mean?' said Mum. 'I have to get out. I need to go to work.'

The officer shook his head.

'I'm afraid not,' he said. 'You'll have to wait. We had to block your door until we're done. We'll let you know when you can come out.'

He was gone before Mum could reply. She turned back to us, sighed heavily, and looked at her watch.

'This is crazy,' she said. 'I'm going to be so late.'

She walked to the door and tugged the handle.

'Give us fifteen minutes,' came a voice through the door.

We watched Mum pace in front of the door, tutting and sighing and checking her watch every few minutes. There was a knock on the door. Mum grabbed the handle, then paused and looked back at us on the sofa.

'Stay where you are,' she said.

Mum opened the door, stepped outside and closed it behind her. We waited. After a minute she came back, followed by our childminder, who had been waiting outside to get in. Both of their faces were drawn and serious. Mum sat down heavily on the couch and beckoned to Sone. He climbed up alongside her. She put her arm around him. All her urgency was gone.

'It appears a man has killed himself in the hallway,' she said. 'Just outside the door.'

I stared at her. Mum looked at me and shuddered, as if trying to shake an image from her mind.

'He's still out there,' she went on quietly. 'They've covered him in plastic, but he's still there.'

My mouth dropped open. I struggled to process what Mum had said. A man had killed himself. There was a dead body outside our door. He was still there, hanging from the bannister.

'The police are outside dealing with it. They'll take the body away and then you can go to school,' said Mum. She turned to speak to the childminder to reassure her, before asking Sone and I if we would be OK.

I nodded, but couldn't speak, not yet, it was too horrible. Mum hugged us both, nodded at the childminder, and found her way out. The body was gone by the time we came out to go to school. The hallway was full of police, taking photos and covering the stairs and floor in a thin layer of white powder. They stopped work to let us tiptoe through. We had to duck under yellow tape to get out of the building.

All day at school, I tried hard to block out what had happened. But I felt uncomfortable coming home to the eerie hallway. The entrance to our home was never the same for any of us. We were never sure exactly what had happened, but Mum told us the rumours she had heard from some neighbours.

Apparently, the man who killed himself was known to our neighbour who occasionally took us to school. The night that he died, he had appeared at her door, asked to stay the night. The neighbour refused and turned him away, only for him to return claiming that he had nowhere to go. Eventually she opened the door a crack to throw him a sheet to sleep with. The man had tied the sheet to the bannisters, fixed the other end around his neck, and thrown himself off the stairs. His body came to rest in the stairwell, hanging, almost directly opposite our front door.

The story was deeply shocking. The neighbour had always seemed entirely ordinary, even slightly nerdy. She was prim, proper and very house-proud. Nothing could have hinted that, as the rumours went, she had been dabbling in prostitution. As for the suicide, it was difficult to shake off the morbid feeling left behind by the stranger's desperate final act. For Mum, the incident was like an alarm going off. It was all light years away from her own privileged upbringing in Nigeria. This was the sign that we had to leave our flat as soon as possible. After all, it had always only been a stopgap.

It turned out that leaving a council property wasn't all that easy. Mum wanted to buy somewhere, but she would need savings to put a down payment on a mortgage. Even so, mortgage advisors took one look at her current address and wrote Mum off the moment she sat down. For the next year or so, she channelled her energy into buying a new property.

She found us a three-bedroom, semi-detached house a short walk along the main road from the estate. We were all very excited to move. The new house felt big after living in a flat and the building was in a better state, too. It was warm, dry, and solid, and at first, we all felt a lot safer. It felt like we were moving up in life.

The best thing about the new house was that we could still play football every day. Now, instead of playing on the field, our friends from the estate would come to us. We had a long stretch of garden out the back where we could kick a ball around, so every day the kids would call on us in the new house. The only problem was they would also come uninvited, when we weren't there. We would often come home to find a crowd playing in our back garden. We loved it, but Mum wasn't so sure. She worried how many people knew how to get into our garden. Not long after we moved in, the police knocked on our door. They were looking for one of the older kids. Apparently, he had been seen jumping over the fences into our back garden to hide. They didn't say why they were looking for him, and we didn't hear if he was ever caught, but the police visit was a reminder that we might have left the estate, but the estate hadn't left us.

Not long after we moved, we joined a new church. Elim, a Pentecostal church in south-west Birmingham, was housed in a spacious, red-brick building on the intersection of two suburban back streets. The old church interior had been gutted and replaced with modern fittings. The floor was carpeted in mint green, and the worshippers sat on rows of matching chairs facing a raised stage. There, behind a modest glass lectern, the pastor gave his sermons. Music was very important at our church. We sang modern worship songs accompanied by an amped-up band, complete with keyboard, bass, and guitar. In the far corner, behind a Perspex screen, there was even a full-size drum kit. The lyrics were projected on to a screen at the back. At times, it felt a bit like being at a pop concert. There was always joy and love in the room.

I joined the church youth group. We studied the Bible, made music, and at the end of the service we re-joined the adults to sing. The rules we learned in church reinforced the lessons we had been taught at home. We were to show others respect, compassion and forgiveness, and never to judge or condemn. Most important was the golden rule: love others as you love yourself. Over time, I developed a simple and strong faith. It made sense that God had created me and watched over me. It gave me comfort to know that he loved me for who I am. The Bible said I belonged to God, that I was one of his children. I was with him, and he was with me. That belief made me stronger. And that strength would be tested soon enough.

The nightmares began not long after we moved in. They always began the same way. It was dark, I saw our street from above. Parked cars shone in the light from the moon. There was our red-brick house, the chimney, the sloping roof, the pebbledash wall, and the bay window. There was the long rectangle of our back garden, lined at the bottom by a flimsy wooden fence. Then, the view changed, and I was on the path that led behind the row of gardens. A figure was sneaking along the path ahead of me. He stopped outside our gate and I saw him more clearly. A man, hood up, scarf wrapped around the bottom of his face, rattling the garden gate. The gate broke off its hinges, and the figure scurried silently through the garden and up to the back door. He pulled out a crowbar, wedged it into the door frame and prised out the lock. The door fell open. The man was inside, running through the house, up the stairs, turning the handle of our bedroom door. I'd wake up, crying out, covered in sweat.

The first time I had the dream, Mum came in to see what the matter was. She sat on the side of my bed and listened as I told her what I'd seen.

'It's a warning from God,' I said. 'Someone wants to get in here.'

'What a horrible dream,' she said. 'It's OK, Eni. Nothing's going to happen. But let's pray now.'

I shook my head. I was convinced God was speaking to me in my dreams.

'It's a message,' I said. 'In the Bible a lot of the messages come in dreams.'

Mum said a prayer asking for God's protection, but I couldn't get back to sleep. The images from the dream whirled around my head like a carousel. They were so real, like photographs. Our house from above, the gate flying off its hinges, the back door swinging open. I couldn't shake the shock of the lock breaking, how quickly the man could enter our territory.

I had similar dreams every few weeks during those first months in the house. Christmas approached and they stopped. I began to feel safer, like things were going better. Mum bought a tree and wrapped a few presents to put underneath. One night, just before Christmas, we came home to find the back door had been forced open. All the presents were gone.

It was a shock and Sone and I cried at first. We had no doubt who had done it. We knew them, the people from the estate, there was nothing more we could do. As for the presents, we knew Mum had tried. We swallowed our disappointment as best we could and went to bed.

I lay in bed, wide awake, waiting for sleep, wondering if the dream would come again. It was shock more than anything that kept me awake. Not shock that someone had broken in, but that the dream had come true. I knew this had been coming all along, I had been given warnings. I closed my eyes and gathered all my strength, I needed to send an urgent message. I mouthed a prayer for my family.

'Please God,' I whispered. 'Protect us. Keep us safe. Watch over us. Deliver us from evil.'

CHAPTER THREE

The ball bounced hard on the AstroTurf and flew down the left wing towards me. I took it on the chest, dribbled forward and glanced up. Three defenders, closing in ahead. I swerved to avoid the first and pivoted left, putting my arm out to block as a second came in to tackle. I wanted to steer left, outrun him, but this was indoor seven-a-side, there was no space for that. I'd have to improvise.

I angled the ball towards the waist-high wooden kickboard that lined the pitch. The defender spun on his heels and ran after it. I sprinted past him, meeting the ball as it rebounded off the board ahead and cut in at an angle towards their goal. The board trick worked perfectly. One of my teammates couldn't have given me a better cross. I shot before the keeper knew what had happened. The ball slammed into the upper right corner of the goal. I turned and ran, both arms raised in the air, heart thumping, grinning wide. Another goal, my third of the day. I was on fire, I was invincible.

'Get her off,' a man shouted. 'She's not allowed in here anyway.'

I stopped and looked around. It was loud in the hall. There were several tournament games going on at once. Maybe I'd misheard. Maybe I'd picked up something from beyond the curtained nets that separated the pitches. Play restarted, and I focused on the ball, feeling for chances to intercept. The other team's midfielders passed, quick and short, back and forth between them.

'Why is a girl on this team?'

A different voice this time. Sneering, taunting, from the side of the pitch.

'Girls can't play,' said the voice. 'This is a boys' tournament.'

At this, cheers erupted from the onlookers around the nets. Blood rushed to my face, I slowed to a walk and hung my head. They had to be talking about me, I was the only girl here, but I had no clue what they were talking about. This was a school football tournament. No one had ever said it was only for boys. This competition was a big deal for our school team. I was proud we had made it here, to Aston Villa, to play against schools from all over Birmingham.

I shook my head, tried to shake the voices out of my mind. I knew what they were saying was rubbish. At nine years old I'd already had enough of arguing with adults, even coaches, who thought women shouldn't play football. I was the team's top scorer; I had every right to be here. It didn't matter to me who I was playing with or against. I was good enough to play with anyone. Why were they making such a fuss? We were only playing football.

I ran after the ball, faster and faster, until the shapes of the onlookers blurred, and their voices sounded muffled and far away. The ball bounced hard again, bringing the echoing hall back into focus. The other team's centre midfielder made a sloppy pass and I got the ball. I raced down the left wing as their defence melted away. The keeper darted out to tackle, but I dodged around him and shot into the open goal. I didn't smile. Instead I clenched both fists in protest.

'Get her off!' came the voice again.

I stopped dead and scanned the nets. I found him. There, among the parents and coaches standing along the nets lining the pitch, stood a middle-aged man. He was shouting at the top of his voice, his hand raised towards me. His face was red and sweaty with the effort.

'It shouldn't be allowed!' he yelled again.

'It's not fair,' a parent next to him joined in. He sounded almost manic. 'Why is she here?'

And then it clicked. These men, these adults at least four times my age, didn't have a problem with me because I was a girl, but because I was good. Because I was the one attracting attention. Because our team was winning, and I was the best on the team. They were just proud dads who wanted their little boys to win and couldn't stand them being beaten by a girl. They thought it wasn't fair, so they wanted to erase me, delete me, from the game. It was their only way out.

But then another thought hit me and sent panic to my core. These men were adults, they had power. Enough to stop me playing, if they wanted to. What would I do, what would I be, without football? Football was in me. It was me, and I was it. On the estate, at school, I was the girl who played football. When I played, I was happy, and I was used to making other people happy by playing. These men wanted to take that away from me.

The last minutes of the game were approaching. I hardly noticed. Our team had won, but I felt as if I had lost everything. I jogged back down the wing to watch the other side seek a last-minute consolation goal. I scanned the nets again. The red-faced men were still staring at me. They wanted to make sure I knew I wasn't welcome here. They wanted me to feel like a freak, an alien invader. They wanted me gone. The final whistle blew, I hung my head and walked slowly off the pitch. On the way out, I had to pass my coach. He was arguing with some parents at the exit to the enclosed pitch. They fell silent when they spotted me.

'Great job today, Eni,' said the coach, patting my shoulder as I went past.

I looked up and tried to force a smile, but I was too upset. I felt the stares of the other kids and their parents on my back as I trudged, alone, towards the women's toilets to get changed.

By the time I got home, my mind was made up. I never wanted to go through that again. The taunts, the rejection, it wasn't worth it. Maybe the red-faced men were right. I knew as well as anyone there was no future for girls in football. It didn't matter how good I was. There was nowhere to go. I would have to accept that. No one was going to reward me for scoring goals, they were going to fight me every step of the way. Well, they could have it their way. I was out.

When I told my mum about the men and what they had said, she looked up from the papers she had been working on.

'I know you're the only girl on the team, but you can't let them stop you,' she said.

I shook my head.

'Of course, you'll play football,' she said. 'You're in the school team. You just played in a tournament, they said you did really well.'

'No, I'll play something else,' I said.

I struggled to tell her how unwelcome I'd been made to feel.

'I've had enough,' I said. 'That's it.'

'OK, if you say so,' she said, not sounding convinced.

Football had never been something Mum had made me do. She had fostered and nurtured the talent she saw in both me and Sone. But the drive came from us, from me. I was the one that would pack my kit, get my boots on, and tell her where I needed to be dropped off for the next game. Now all that was gone, I had lost my motivation. It wasn't worth having to battle them all just to be allowed on the pitch. I still played for fun, with Sone and our friends from the estate. They didn't care I was a girl. To them, I was a good player and that's all that mattered. The games carried on at school, too, but my heart wasn't in it. What was the point?

Of course, things were different for Sone. Around this time, he was taking his first steps towards becoming a professional footballer. Aged six, he joined the under-11s team of local Sunday League club Kings Heath Concorde. The following season he was scouted by Birmingham City FC for the under-9s academy team. Training was twice a week and focused on developing young players' skills. Sone was being inducted into the system. If all went well, he'd be on track to land a professional training contract in a few years.

Sone and I played the same football. We were both fast, had mastered the same tricks, we were both top scorers. He was left-handed, which some said made him a more creative player, whilst I had the slight edge on scoring goals. We were both good enough to go professional. The only real difference was our sex. I had to accept it was the way things were. Being a girl, I'd have a different path. The women's game had been growing fast since the Football Association had launched the Women's Premier League after taking over governance in 1992, and there were now a fair few semi-professional and professional clubs. Some of them even had girls' youth training schemes, but none of us had a crystal ball. It seemed women's football couldn't offer me a professional future. I tried to make my peace with it, step back from it, close the door in my mind.

Not long after the seven-a-side tournament, my junior school PE teacher took me and Mum aside for a chat. He told us a charitable trust had selected Broadmeadow for its inner-city school sponsorship scheme. One pupil was to get regular after-school tennis coaching, all expenses paid. Was I interested? I was intrigued. I reckoned I could do it; I had played tennis in school before. I enjoyed it, and I was fast, with a powerful forehand. My teacher seemed to think I was good enough. We agreed to take up the offer.

Tennis training was twice a week, after school. Mum was now a nurse advisor for a pharmaceutical company, which meant she often had to travel around the Midlands. It made it difficult for her to take us to all my training and matches, so she shared the responsibility with other parents. Logistically, it made sense that Sone came along with me. While he waited, he started knocking around with a racket. Seeing Sone's speed, coordination, and skill, the tennis coaches offered to take him on as well. We started playing each other and both fell in love with the game. Before long, it became almost as big an obsession as football.

And, unlike football, it felt like there could be a future in it for me. That summer, an American teenager burst on to the international tennis scene. She was just seventeen, and still a touch goofy, with braces on her teeth, hooped gold earrings, and white, red and blue beads braided into her hair. I watched spellbound as unseeded Venus Williams battled her way through the US Open, only to be beaten in the final by the world number one, Martina Hingis. Venus was stronger than any woman I'd ever seen. She played with a revolutionary power surging through her arms and legs. A few months later, in the Australian Open, she faced her younger sister Serena. From there, the Williams sisters climbed the world rankings together, smashed through barriers, and carved themselves a place in history.

I was captivated. These players looked like me. They were black, they were girls, and they were setting the world on fire with their game. Until then, my race had never really come up as an issue. We didn't speak about it much at home. The boys on the estate were all white, and they had never treated us any differently because of the colour of our skin. But seeing the Williams sisters right there in front of me, the embodiment of black success, something stirred. It was reinforcement that I, too, could succeed, and it came at exactly the right time.

Everyone, wherever they come from, needs role models that look like them. These black female athletes were showing me the way. To me, their rise looked like a path. Where football had shown me only dead ends and locked doors, tennis beckoned me forward. If I followed the Williams sisters, no one could tell me the game wasn't for people like me. If I worked hard, maybe I could become the British Venus. I pictured myself on Wimbledon's centre court. I even started wearing beads in my hair.

It wasn't to be. I was good at tennis, but not good enough. I would practise against Sone, and he began to beat me more and more often. We were both fast and agile, with power and good reactions, but it was clear to everyone Sone had the edge. As in football, his left-handed play was more creative, and crucially, he had the temperament for long, drawn-out matches. Sone could keep his cool whatever happened. He started getting picked to play in county teams. It was a different story with me.

One match in particular put the lid on my tennis career. I was playing against a girl named Evey. We were quite evenly matched, and I went in feeling I could win. The first game began well. I won the first three points and I was forcing her to run across the court with every return. I won the game, and the next two. I was on track to win the first set. Then, in the fourth game, I began to make unforced errors and miss shots I should have reached. I was handing her points. It annoyed me; I was better than that. I could feel the frustration building in my chest.

Second game, my serve. I took a deep breath, I'd show her. I bounced the ball on the court and threw it above my head, reaching up to follow it with my left hand. I bent my legs, leaned back, lifted my right arm and whipped the racket, smashing the ball forward. Straight forward. It flew over the net and bounced on the wrong side of the centre service line. Fault. I cried out and threw my racket on to the court. I took out another ball and bounced it, breathing deep. I tried to forget my mistake, but the fault sat like a dead weight on my chest. I threw the ball above my head and smashed it as hard as I could. It slammed into the net. Double fault.

That was it, I'd had enough. I wanted the match to be over, but we hadn't even finished the first set. It was all I could do to carry on playing. I fell apart, forgot everything I'd been told. The rest of the match I played with my gut, overplaying every ball, recklessly smacking through to the baseline, hoping for a winner each time. Every point I lost made me play more wildly. The frustration closed like a hand around my throat. I was deliberately tanking the match. By the second set I was in tears. At last, it was over. I smashed my racket down on to the court and stormed off.

It would have been different if I'd been destined to play tennis. I could have learned how to control the frustration. But I just wasn't as good as I wanted to be. The feeling on court was smothering, nothing like playing football. Nothing compared to the feeling of carving out a path to goal and scoring. Football was what made me happy, it was my driving force. I still played whenever I could, not hoping for a career, just for that buzz. In my last season at primary school, I scored fifty goals in sixteen games for our team. If I'd been male, the scouts might have snapped me up.

That autumn, aged eleven, I moved up to Woodrush High, a mixed secondary school in Hollywood, an affluent district of south Birmingham out towards the countryside. The school had great sports facilities, two football pitches, and a floodlit AstroTurf, but I was no longer allowed to play in the same team with the boys. The PE teachers saw I was a good player and promised to run a girls' football team for the first time. A few other girls joined, but it was slow-going, and more than ever I missed having a real outlet for my talent. I was lost.

Around this time, faith began to play a bigger role in my life. I was baptised into the church, and as I got older, the things we learned there started to reach me on a deeper level. I was drawn to teachings that spoke of acceptance.

They helped me find a path when everything felt stacked against me. Especially in football. I knew I'd been put on earth to play. As I got older, I began to understand I owed my skills to a higher power. God wanted me to play, so I played for him. And with him on my side, I prayed I could overcome anyone who didn't want me on the pitch.

My prayers were soon answered. News got around my new school that I was good, and I was invited to try out for a local team. It was the under-16s team of Leafield Athletic Ladies, a Sunday League club not far from the school. The trial would be at their ground, joining one of their training sessions. I was excited to show the coaches what I could do. I arrived and was given a yellow shirt and a pair of black shorts. In the changing rooms I looked at the shirt, felt the circular club badge between my fingers. This wasn't like the school kits I'd played in before. This was official.

Out on the pitch, listening to the coach, I snuck glances at the other players' faces. It was the first time I'd seen a women's team up close. Here they were, at last. Girls who played football, who took football seriously, and were being taken seriously. It was a revelation. I could feel a weight falling from me. My whole life – on the estate, in my school team – I'd been the odd one out. But these girls were all like me. They'd been through it too. I hopped silently from foot to foot. I couldn't wait to play.

We warmed up and went straight into a game. The coach put me on the left wing. I got the ball and sprinted with it as fast as I could. I felt the atmosphere change. The coach had seen I had something, the other players too. Ten minutes in, our side were awarded a free kick and the coach signalled I should take it. I walked over to the spot and placed the ball on the ground. It was a tight angle, but it was close enough to shoot. I had to score; I knew I could.

I weighed up the angle, waited for the wall of players to settle. I decided I'd aim for the top left corner. I took four long steps back and stood, hands on hips, focusing as I drew breath. I would score, I could see it. I visualised the flight of the ball into the back of the net. The whistle blew and I ran up, planted my left foot next to the ball, and hit it with the inside of my right foot. The players jumped. The ball curled over their heads, past the keeper's outstretched hand, and sank into the top corner. I clenched my fists and beamed. I had scored for a club while wearing an official kit, and it felt amazing.

Suddenly it all made sense. I wasn't alone any more. I didn't need to apologise for being the girl who was good at football, the girl who could beat the boys. There would be no more taunts, no more questions. At last, I'd found a place to play the game that God had put me on earth to play. I jogged back towards the halfway line, raised my eyes, and whispered thanks to heaven.

I realised then, for the first time, that I had been looking for acceptance and validation in the wrong places. I couldn't control whether the other kids, or their parents, thought it was acceptable for a girl to play football. I would have to seek validation elsewhere, from my creator, from God. It was God who had made me a woman, and it was Him who had made me a footballer. Knowing that gave me purpose, and it gave me permission to break out of society's mould, and just play. I would have to wait for the world to accept me as a striker. In the meantime, I would be heaven's number 9.

Learning this lesson was only the beginning; my search for acceptance was far from over. I would spend another two decades figuring it out. Along the way, I would waste time looking for endorsement in the wrong places, often from the people around me, and have to learn all over again that the way others saw me was beyond my control. The eureka moment came much later, during a testing time playing for England. Life taught me then that true validation could only come from within, that only I could give myself permission to be the person God made me.

Class 2:

Embrace The Hyphen

The world right now seems to want to put everyone into one of two piles:

US

and *THEM*

It's up to all of us to reject that.

CHAPTER FOUR

I was born into the white heat of a Lagos afternoon. The sun flooded through the maternity unit's sixth-floor windows, bathing Mum's delivery suite in a pool of burning light. The air-conditioning units were on full blast, but the cold air didn't make the experience any less intense.

Two navy-uniformed Nigerian midwives flitted around Mum's bed. The elder of the two, a middle-aged matron, radiated calm and experience. The other, a younger nurse, busied herself with the beeping monitors. The nurses had seen it all before, but Mum hadn't. At a little over twenty-two years old, she was giving birth for the first time.

Mum concentrated on her breathing, waiting for the building pain of the next contraction.

'Hell,' she moaned, as the pain rose again. 'This is crazy. Goodness, I can't bear it. I'm in agony!'

The matron raised her finger and shook her head. 'No, no, no,' she said. 'Don't say that again. Let's have no more craziness or hell here. Everything is good. No more words like crazy and hell here. You're fine.

Mum would have to watch her mouth. There were beliefs to consider, superstitions to think of, even here, in this place of medical science. Here, even figures of speech could be dangerous, as if saying something out loud would call it into being and jeopardise her child's destiny.

Mum calmed her mind in anticipation of the next wave of pain. She wasn't in agony, she told herself, she was safe, she was in good hands. I arrived at last, wrinkled and screaming. The younger nurse handed me to the matron, who smiled at Mum encouragingly.

'Well done,' she said. 'Welcome to the lovely baby.'

Mum lay back on her pillow, smiling, relieved it was all over, as the midwives took me away to wash and dress.

Mum often says my birth made me strong-willed. Whenever I'm determined, hard-headed, or unyielding, she recalls how the nurses encouraged her to focus on the positive rather than her agony and suffering. Mum still believes that what a mother says during the birth of a child hangs over that child's life like a halo.

I was born in Nigeria, but I didn't stay there for long. When I was seven months old, Mum had to leave the country. Her mother, my grandmother, was seriously ill and needed to go to the UK for private medical care. She couldn't go alone, so Mum agreed to go with her. That summer, the three of us left for London, where my grandmother would be treated at a facility in St John's Wood. The next months were a blur of appointments, consultations and waiting rooms, nappies, bottles and babygros. It was a tough time, but the two women supported each other and got through it somehow. After three months, my grandmother returned to Nigeria and Mum and I stayed in London. Mum had hoped her mother could come back for further treatment, but she was too weak. My grandmother passed away in Nigeria not long afterwards, leaving me with only a vague memory of a rain song she used to sing to me as a baby.

My grandmother's illness planted the seed of my life in Britain, but she wouldn't have wanted me to make too much of that fact here. A few days after I was born, when Mum first took me to see her, the subject of my name came up. Mum told my grandmother she wanted to give me two traditional Yoruba names: Eniola, meaning 'person of wealth,' and Enitan, which means 'person with a story'. My grandmother shook her head at this last suggestion.

'No, not Enitan,' she said. 'The baby will have her own story. We don't want it to be the story of my illness in any way.'

It moves me now to think that, in a way, my grandmother saw far beyond herself, into the future. That she anticipated that one day, I would have a story to tell, and be telling it here in this book.

Before Mum had a chance to plan to go back to Nigeria, Dad joined us in London, cementing our move to the UK. Suddenly there were lots of reasons for us to be in Britain. Dad wanted to study, and he had business contacts in London. Dad's sister, my aunt, had been living in Ireland with her family, and was also planning a move to the UK after her husband, a surgeon, landed a new job. Dad found a big semi-detached house in West London, where all seven of us could live together: me, Mum, Dad, my aunt and uncle, and my two young cousins, Tayo and Deji.

Life in Britain was tougher than Mum was used to. She and Dad both came from affluent, privileged Yoruba families, the largest grouping in south-western

Nigeria. Yoruba people have a strong cultural identity and share a common language. Religion and spirituality play important roles in Yoruba life, and both my parents were raised as Christians in the Anglican tradition. Their religion wasn't the only thing they had in common. Both their fathers worked in academia: Dad's father was a famous economist and professor and Mum's father was a renowned university registrar. Mum and Dad met through their parents and hadn't been married long before I came along.

In London, they had to start again from scratch. Dad started on a post-grad course, but it was harder for Mum. In the UK no one cared about Mum's biochemistry degree or her middle-class upbringing. That first winter, after my grandmother returned to Nigeria, Mum took a cleaning job as a stop-gap and set her sights on training to become a nurse. My little brother Sone arrived the following February, two days before my second birthday. Once Sone was a few months old and I had joined a play group, Mum started her nursing course. It was a lot to juggle, studying while looking after a baby and a toddler, but she worked hard to provide a foothold for me and my brother in this new country. Mum aspired to greater and better things. One day, she vowed, we would have it easier.

London wasn't short on opportunities, but it was expensive and a lot of hassle. Dad found the figures weren't adding up and began thinking about how to reduce costs. Dad's parents had studied in Birmingham for a year when he was younger, and they put him in touch with an old friend of theirs, a retired professor. Dad visited him and came back reassured that life in England's second city was good, and above all, it was affordable. Dad found us a two-bedroom house in Kings Norton, south of Birmingham city centre, for less than half what he had been paying in London.

Mum wasn't overjoyed at the move. Leaving London meant she would have to disrupt her nursing course only six months in. It wasn't her choice to make, so she resigned herself to making the best of it. In Birmingham, she applied for another college and worked doubly hard to make up for lost time. She started again for a second time and redoubled her efforts to put down roots in the UK.

Dad never settled in Birmingham. His plan to secure management of a petrol station dealership fell through and he returned to London to retain the opportunities he had found there. Besides, it seemed, he felt out of place and missed having a Nigerian network around him. A few months after we moved, Dad announced he was returning to Nigeria. It was then that Mum put her foot down. She had had enough of moving, she was going nowhere until she finished her course. And that's how it happened: Mum stayed in Birmingham, and Dad returned to Nigeria.

And so began a new life for Mum, Sone and me, a life that would see me raised with one foot in two countries. It was an upbringing that gave me a hyphenated identity. I would be neither solely British, nor solely Nigerian. I would be both, I would be British-Nigerian. It was a balancing act; one I would spend my whole life learning how to navigate.

The set-up wasn't easy for Mum. She faced the daily struggle of being a single parent and trainee nurse, alone in a foreign country with two kids under the age of four. But we had each other, and Mum dedicated herself to working us into a better position.

Mum never saw challenges like I do. I tackle problems head on, Mum is the kind to solve things quietly, privately, steadily. Barriers should be skirted around, conflicts muddled through with minimum upset. So that's exactly what she did. She pushed on, day by day, sticking to her routine, working with what she had. She studied hard and focused all her hopes on the nursing job she would get once she graduated. She drew confidence from the sense that she was advancing, bit by bit.

Unfortunately, there are some challenges in life that have to be tackled head on. Like paying the rent. Before he left, Dad had managed to give the landlord one month's rent in advance along with the deposit and, somewhat optimistically as it turned out, promised to send help once he got to Nigeria. That turned out to be wishful thinking on his part. Trainee nurses get a tiny stipend and it was difficult for Mum to keep up the payments alone. The months drifted on, until one day, the landlord appeared at the door. He wanted to sell the house, he said, and gave Mum notice to leave.

Mum had no experience of finding a place to live, let alone in a foreign country. In the end, the landlord reported the matter to the council, and our young family were gently moved into alternative accommodation. And so we arrived, happy and relieved, on the verge of an estate, in a ground-floor maisonette, surrounded by fields crying out for a game.

CHAPTER FIVE

Shortly after we moved to the estate, Sone and I visited both sets of grandparents in Akure, Ondo State. I have dim memories of the back garden of Dad's parents' house in the state capital. There, Sone and I spent hours playing under the shade of mango and papaya trees, chasing lizards off their basking spots on concrete slabs.

But Grandpa, ever the academic, didn't want me to play all day. He was impressed that, not yet four, I was already reading, and so he decided to take me along to the neighbourhood play group to learn with the other kids. This was an aspirational kind of nursery, and at the end of my four-week stay, I took an assessment with the other toddlers. It wasn't unusual at the time for nurseries to have such assessments that formed a basis for streaming. I came top of the class in English and Grandpa was very proud.

We also visited Mum's father at his home a few miles away. Like my late grandmother, he was musical, and had a church organ in his living room that fascinated me. He sat me on his lap and pressed my fingers against the keys as he pushed the pedals with his feet underneath. In that short visit, he passed on a love for the piano that remains with me to this day.

My first clear impressions of Nigeria came much later. I didn't visit the country again until I was twelve, in 1999. In the intervening years, instead of us going to him, Dad would come to stay with us in the UK. I had to accept Dad being away as the way things were.

Growing up, I didn't give Nigeria all that much thought. We were all focused on life in the UK, and I'd never known any different. Nigeria was the place Dad lived, the place Mum was from, the place I was born. Beyond that, it was a bit of a mystery. Sometimes, I'd hear Mum speaking to Dad or other relatives and friends on the phone in Yoruba and I'd sit and listen, captivated by the rhythm of the rolling vowels.

'*Bawo ni, sho wa?*' I'd hear her say when she picked up the phone. 'How are things?'

As time went on, I picked up enough words and phrases to follow Mum's conversations. Mum was impressed and complimented my natural understanding of the language, but though she encouraged me, there wasn't ever time for formal lessons. It wasn't until I was twelve that the chance came along to try out my Yoruba for real.

Since returning to Nigeria, Dad had been busy building a career in politics. Nigeria was going through some big changes at that time. The country was transitioning from military to civilian rule, from a dictatorship into a fledgling democracy. Nigeria had tried this switch twice since gaining independence from Britain forty years before, but power had repeatedly lurched back into military hands.

This time was going to be different, and Dad wanted to be a part of it. It helped that Aluko was already an established name in Nigerian politics. Dad's father, my grandpa, Sam Aluko, was a well-known economist with lifelong links to the establishment. In February 1999, Nigeria held elections for a new National Assembly and Dad won a seat on the Senate, the new upper house. At the age of thirty-five, he was to become one of the youngest senators in the country. It was an amazing achievement.

Nigeria's new government was to be sworn in during a ceremony that May, and Dad told Mum he wanted us all to be there with him for the event. We visited him at his home in Abuja, the new Nigerian capital. We would be there for about twelve days, enough time to attend all the official events and the inauguration.

Returning to Nigeria was a big step. Abuja was a planned city that had barely existed at all before Mum left Nigeria. Since then, it had risen from the hilly savanna, the nation's shining new seat of government.

Nigeria had changed, and so had Mum. She was a mother of two now, and a businesswoman running a healthcare business that she began in the spare room of our family home in Birmingham. She had gone through tough times and come out flourishing on the other side. By the time we were set to leave for Nigeria, she was about five months pregnant with my sister Olivia. She was showing to anyone looking closely, but she preferred to keep it as quiet as possible, it wouldn't do to make a fuss. She was able to travel during this stage in her pregnancy, but still she would have to take it easy on the journey. As the eldest, I felt protective of her and wanted to look out for her while we were away.

We landed in Abuja one morning in late May, bleary-eyed after a seven-hour flight from Heathrow and a connecting flight via Lagos. Dad met us at the airport with his driver. In the car on the way back to his house, I sat glued to the window, squinting out into the early morning haze. I couldn't remember ever being anywhere like this before. Nigeria was greener than I had imagined. Between the brash roadside advertisements, the streets were lined with high palms and rambling bushes.

After a little while, Dad turned back to look at us from the front seat of the car. 'Welcome to Abuja,' he said, and pointed through the windscreen.

The road split ahead and in the centre stood a huge white arch shaped like a letter 'H''. Printed in giant letters across the central bar were the words 'YOU ARE WELCOME', below the two unicorns of the Nigerian crest. Suspended between the two prongs of the city gate fluttered a large green and white Nigerian flag.

The traffic grew heavier as we entered the city on a wide highway. Vendors wandered through the slow-moving vehicles, selling newspapers, gum, clothes and toiletries. I gazed up through the window as we rolled past an enormous golden-domed mosque with a turret at each corner. It seemed like the only finished building in the whole city. The skyline was crowded with cranes and the roadsides choked with chaotic scaffolding. We turned off the highway and on to winding streets dotted with large gated houses. We came to a stop outside high, whitewashed walls topped with barbed wire. A guard opened the metal gate with a clank and the car rolled inside. So, this was where Dad lived.

That night, after we had settled in, Mum and Dad spoke to us over dinner. Our schedule for the week was filled with family reunions and events. First on the agenda was to meet with my grandparents, who were also in Abuja for the inauguration. We were in any case well mannered, but this was the first time Sone and I would be putting our knowledge of Yoruba culture and Nigerian values into practice. It was nerve-racking, as if we were preparing for a test the next day.

'Make sure you greet Grandma properly,' Mum began.

She looked at me. 'Don't say "hi" to anyone casually unless they are your friend,' Mum went on. 'You say "good afternoon". OK?'

Sone and I nodded in agreement.

Gestures and language, especially greetings, are very important in Yoruba culture. Traditionally, men and women show respect to elders or family members by kneeling or bending to the floor. We had been taught a modern version, a curtsey for girls, and for boys, a dòbále, a gesture of respect to elders in which they bow low with their upper body and place their right hand on the floor.

'Also, Eni,' said Mum gently, 'Grandma might not fully understand about you playing football. So, if she asks about sport, it would be easier if you told her you played tennis instead.'

I stared at her. Not this again.

'OK?' she said firmly.

I looked at Dad, and he nodded. There was no room for doubt. I lowered my eyes to the table.

'OK,' I said grudgingly.

Grandma and Grandpa were set to come to Dad's house the following afternoon. They arrived in formal Nigerian attire. They were kind and smiled and asked us questions about our lives in the UK. They knew Britain well; they had studied there in their youth. Both spoke calmly and carefully, especially Grandpa, who radiated gravitas.

I could tell right away that Grandma had traditional views on what was appropriate behaviour for girls. In her eyes, playing sport wasn't a pastime for a lady, and she was convinced all well-heeled girls should strive to be ladylike. In Nigeria, in conservative circles, ladies didn't play football, they studied and increasingly they were leading the way in traditionally male-dominated fields like engineering and medicine. Girls were expected to choose a feminine sport, something with class and grace. Tennis, for example, was ideal. Grandma had swum competitively when she was younger but had given up after the age of sixteen. Ladies swimming past that age were considered a little too liberal in her time.

Football wasn't something that Grandma understood. All that running around in the mud, all that shouting and kicking. No, it wasn't a game for women. Besides, like a lot of people her age, Grandma had never seen a woman playing football, not on TV, not at the Olympics. Certainly it wasn't fitting for the daughter of a senator.

The crunch moment came not long after our conversation began. Grandpa was asking Sone about playing football with the Birmingham City youth side, when Grandma turned to me.

'And how is your tennis, Eni?' she said.

The whole room stiffened awkwardly. For a split second, I imagined Grandma's horror if I told her I was actually striker with an all-girls' football team. I gathered all my strength, smiled at her and nodded.

'Good, thank you,' I said brightly, and the conversation moved on to other things.

I gritted my teeth and bargained with myself. It wasn't a lie, after all, I did play tennis. I reminded myself I had done it for an easier life, but it still grated on me. Football was as much a part of me as anything else I could think of. I didn't see why I should have to edit myself for my own family. I wish now that I hadn't.

It took some time, but years later, Grandma eventually celebrated my footballing success. I see now that there's no sense in putting on a mask to make others feel comfortable. Not even for family. The rules others might want me to live by, the limitations they want to place on me, aren't my own. There is no reason for me to suffer because others want to put me in a box. It was a valuable lesson, to simply be myself and let others come to terms with who I am. If I hadn't learned that, I doubt I could ever have achieved anything out of the ordinary.

It's a lesson not only for women in sport, but for musicians, artists, or any young person wanting to pursue extraordinary talents. Families aren't always the best judge of potential. It took me some time and effort to break free of the expectations placed on me by family and friends. Only later, once success came, once I had achieved on the world stage, did they come to terms with my path. I wish I could go back and tell my twelve-year-old self: pursue your own greatness, and trust me, they'll be proud eventually.

That evening, the sun sank fast, and a warm, steady wind brought red dust in on the air. We piled into Dad's car and drove down to the opulent government quarter for the first of many flashy gala dinners held for Nigeria's new politicians and their families. Dinner was a dazzling array of stews, mounds of pounded yam, okra soup, and spicy red jollof rice. Afterwards, there was music, dancing, and socialising.

I was unnerved at how superficial and showy it all felt. In Abuja, it seemed, everything was about money, and the city's upper-middle class was out in force. Most of the men wore colourful, knee-length *agbada* robes with wide sleeves and caps. The women wore *gele* head ties, painstakingly wrapped in elaborate shapes from stiff material, along with blouses and wrap-around skirts. There seemed to be a lot of weight placed on outward appearances. Clothes mattered, they displayed status, connections, and place in line.

Sone and I mingled with the other politicians' children. Many of them had also flown in from abroad to see their parents' big day, some from the US, others from Britain. Sone and I didn't have much in common with them, aside from our politician fathers, and I felt awkward and out of place. This was a far cry from the humility of our house in south Birmingham.

The nights dragged on like this, a series of showy events, every one of them the same. I found it testing to play the role of a senator's daughter. Whenever I opened my mouth, one of the adults would remark on my British accent. I tried to shrug it off and told myself I am who I am. Still, it niggled in the back of my mind.

As usual, it was sport that saved me. During the days, in between the events, there was a lot of spare time. Word got around that Sone and I played tennis and we were invited to play with some of the other senators' kids. We were better than them all, and easily destroyed them at doubles. Sone's strong left forehand even earned him the nickname 'senator junior' among the ground staff. As for me, smashing the ball through to the back of the court had never felt so good.

The day of the inauguration came around. The ceremony was to take place in the new National Assembly Complex, a stately white building with a green dome that had been built specially to house Nigeria's new government. The sun was climbing high by the time we left the house. We had been issued with access passes to get us into the building. Our car dropped us at the main entrance, and we joined the crowds streaming towards the security scanners. There was a buzz in the late morning air. This was Nigeria's day.

Mum approached a security officer and showed him our passes, hoping he would show us into the building and usher us to our seats. But the officer just waved indifferently in the direction of the crowd.

'That way,' he said.

As we got closer to the entrance, the crowd got thicker, until at the top of the wide steps, we came to a stop. We couldn't get any further. Several hundred people stood jammed shoulder to shoulder, jostling and chatting loudly to one another in the heat. I stood on tiptoe but couldn't see the door. The crowd was getting restless.

Suddenly, the throng surged forwards. I lost sight of Mum and was surrounded by tall men in robes, yelling and waving their hands around wildly. I got an elbow in my gut at the same time as someone shoved me from behind. I looked back and scowled, but the man behind pushed me forward again. The crowd carried me towards a set of double doors, where the crush grew denser as people battled, one-by-one, to get inside. Either side of the doors stood a cluster of bored-looking armed guards, apparently able to ignore the chaos around them.

The crowd had a life of its own, it moved and pulsed as one. I looked back to see where Mum and Sone were. I couldn't see them at first, then I caught sight of Mum's yellow *gele* headwrap, emerging above the throng to my left. She had been pushed to the edge of the crowd towards the staircase to one side of the door. People were crowding past her, shoving and pushing as they battled towards the entrance. My heart was beating hard and fast now. Mum could get hurt. I raised my arms above my head and began fighting my way back towards her against the flow.

'Stop pushing her!' I shouted over the churning sea of people.

The nearest strangers looked round and stared at me in surprise. A man in front tried to bat me out of the way. I raised my voice above the din. 'Are you crazy?' I yelled. 'She's pregnant.'

Another man shoved into me with his shoulder and when I pushed him back, he seemed to look right through me. The frustration was boiling over now, I couldn't bear it, the lack of consideration. I stretched out my arms in front of me and scooped people away like I was swimming breaststroke. I wasn't far from Mum and Sone, but the people kept crowding forward against me. They were like a concrete wall.

'What's wrong with you?' I yelled, trying again to push them to one side.

A woman in the crowd a few feet away turned towards me. She pulled an indignant frown and looked me up and down.

'*Ah ah which kyne girl be dis?*' she said. 'What kind of a girl is this? She shouldn't shout like that.'

I stared at this stranger in surprise, I couldn't believe it. What did they all expect me to do? Stay quiet? I forced harder against the wall of people, scrambled with both my arms to find a way through the last feet to Mum.

'Move!' I said again. 'You have to give us space. Look, we have access passes. We're the family of a senator. We need to get in.'

'Shhh, Eni, no,' Mum said, not wanting any more fuss. 'Calm down, I'm OK.'

Then the crush around me fell away and I felt a firm tap on my shoulder. I turned and saw one of the armed guards standing behind me. The crowd melted away at the sight of his rifle. He moved me aside and reached through the crowd to Mum, took her arm and pulled her through, Sone walking along behind her. The guard turned and pushed a path through the tightly packed bodies ahead, the three of us following close behind.

The guard hauled us inside through the glass door and we stumbled into the lobby, breathing hard.

We found our way into a diamond-shaped chamber with a floor that sloped downwards and ended in a wide, three-tiered desk at one end. The room was packed with people, fanning themselves and talking loudly between the wooden rows of seats. We picked our way through to some of the last free seats at the end of one aisle and sank, shaken but relieved, into the red upholstered chairs.

The inauguration of all those politicians took for ever. As I waited, bored, for a glimpse of Dad, I looked around at the other senators' wives and children and decided I'd had enough.

I didn't feel like a senator's daughter; things were much more complicated than that. I looked around the room and felt a jolt of homesickness. I knew I was born in this country, and these people were my people, but I was also Eni who grew up playing football on a Birmingham estate. I began to wonder why I couldn't be myself here.

I know now that Nigeria is so much more than what I experienced on that trip. Much later, when I went to university, I made wonderful Nigerian friends who helped me discover and connect more deeply with my Nigerian roots. I also understood that I'm not the only one to battle with these issues, with being split between two or more nations, cultures and identities. At times it has felt like I'm falling through the gap between being British and Nigerian, especially when others demand I come down on one side or the other. It was a while before I realised what a stupid question that was, like asking a mother which child she loved more.

Back then, these questions thundered around my head for the rest of our trip. I was relieved when at last, our plane taxied on to the runway and took off towards home. I sat glued to the window as we climbed higher, and Abuja's cranes, greenery and rocky outskirts grew smaller until they were swallowed up in thick white cloud. Nigeria was my country. The music, the food, the politics, the hustle, they were in me, I could feel it. Still, home was somewhere else. Home was wet grass glinting under floodlights, red-brick streets, and purple clouds heavy with rain. I couldn't wait to get back.

CHAPTER SIX

It was being called up to play for England that made me understand I wasn't officially British. Not yet, at least. Not on paper. The letter I got inviting me to my first-ever England camp instructed me to bring my passport along. That it should be a British passport was implied. I was pretty sure they didn't want to check my Nigerian document, and that was all I had. At fourteen, I was, after all, still Nigerian on paper. Mum had started the process of applying for naturalisation, but nobody could say how long it would take for us to become British citizens, and the England team wanted to see my passport now.

None of us could have seen this emergency coming. It had all happened so fast. After a year at

Leafield Athletic, I was scouted for the youth team of Birmingham City Ladies FC, the biggest women's side in the region. I was thrilled to join a big-name club, especially one on such a meteoric rise. The club had been promoted to the second division the previous year and was climbing on up the rankings under coach Marcus Bignot.

Marcus saw my potential right away. He was young, in his mid-twenties, and was himself a right-back in the first division. He had put a lot of effort into developing young talent since joining the Blues as a coach two years earlier. It made all the difference to my confidence to have his professional opinion, drive and encouragement behind me.

Birmingham was semi-professional, like most women's clubs at that time. There was little money, and training was once a week at a ground we shared with a local Sunday League side. We had little to do with the men's club, where Sone was flourishing in Birmingham City's well-established youth system. He had everything provided for free – boots, kit, equipment – whereas Mum had to pay two pounds in subs every week for me to help keep the women's side afloat. None of that mattered, though. I was just happy to be somewhere I could develop my skills.

The standard in the youth side was impressive and I was getting to play with some formidable players. One, an attacking midfielder, was electric. She was fast and tricky, with a natural creativity to her game. The pace quickened every time she got on the ball, and she could sprint as fast as I could on the attack. Her name was Karen Carney, everyone called her Kaz. She was about my age and already seemed like an old hand at the club.

We didn't know it then, but Karen and I would play together, on and off, for the rest of our careers. At the time I can't say Kaz and I were immediate allies. We weren't rivals, but there was a touch of competition as we sized each other up. It was only natural. We played similar football, skilful and fast, and were both used to being the best player on the pitch. Kaz was a quiet type and didn't say much, she had an air of steady determination and was always diplomatic. The competition was subtle, and came out in the way she played. Looking back, it makes sense that she went on to captain both Birmingham City and Chelsea, though I still tease her about the times back then when she unexpectedly lost her head.

Marcus said both Kaz and I were good enough to set our sights on playing for England. He had one player in the first team, a defender named Laura Bassett, already in the national youth team, and he was sure we had a good shot. A few months after I joined Birmingham, we were scheduled to play a tournament in Warwick and Marcus told us England scouts would be there. It seemed like good news, but beyond that I didn't give too much thought to what it meant.

The Warwick tournament was on while Dad was visiting with my grandparents. It was the first time I'd seen Grandma and Grandpa since the inauguration, and the first time they would meet my little sister, who was still only a baby. Dad was thrilled that Sone and I were now both playing for Birmingham City, and he decided he would come to watch the tournament and bring Grandpa with him. Grandma, meanwhile, was oblivious about my football career. She still wouldn't hear of me, a girl, playing football, so Mum and Dad tiptoed around the issue. If we referred to it in her presence, we said I was 'doing sport'.

Grandpa saw things differently. At the tournament he stood with Dad on the side lines, watching intently, cheering every goal. It was good having him and Dad there and I played well, creating chances and scoring a number of times. I think Dad enjoyed the back-slapping glory of having a talented kid, and from then on, he turned up for all my big games. There were times, though, that I felt his presence was more about his own fulfilment than my success. As a child he had been a talented footballer but had never been allowed to make anything of his natural abilities.

Before the last game of the tournament, Marcus took me aside and told me one of the England scouts had been commenting on me and asking a lot of questions. I grinned and felt adrenalin buzz through me as if I'd just scored, though I had no real idea what it meant or what would happen next. The final whistle blew on the tournament and I jogged over to Dad. The scout approached us while we were chatting, told me I'd played well, took my details and said he'd be in touch. That was it.

That evening, we got back to the house to find Grandma sitting downstairs with Mum, Sone and Olivia. No one said much about the tournament until later that evening, when Grandma went to bed. As soon as she was upstairs, Grandpa sat forward on his chair, his eyes shining.

'Ah, Sile, I haven't told you about the tournament, yet,' he said to Mum. 'Eni was fantastic! The best player in the whole of England!'

I beamed wide as Grandpa began reeling off all my chances, assists and goals from memory.

Dad smiled and nodded. 'Eni did very well,' he said quietly, then turned to me. 'We'll see what comes of that scout.'

*

Dad and my grandparents were gone again by the time the first letter from England landed on our doorstep. I ripped it open and scanned it.

'Mum!' I called through the house. 'England want me to go to an under-fifteens trial!'

Mum hurried into the dining room and took the letter from my hands.

'Wow, Eni,' she said, her eyes shining, her hands trembling slightly as she read the words over again. 'What an opportunity. A real blessing.'

She passed the letter back to me and I reread the words. Having the chance to play for England was a huge honour, and I was very pleased. Getting called to the trial seemed like an even bigger deal for Mum than it was for me, if that was possible. That Sunday at church, she told our pastor, Maldwyn, and his wife Ruth, that I was trying out for England. They congratulated us and asked us to dinner to celebrate. Later, Mum got the letter framed and hung it in the hallway. I think she saw it as something that rooted us, anchored us, even deeper in the UK. One of us would be representing the country.

The trial was at Loughborough University, where England had a training facility. Kaz and several others from Birmingham had been invited along too. As the date approached, Mum started to worry about what I was going to wear. Appearances have always been important to her, and this was a big occasion, so she wanted me to look smart and appear confident. I told her I'd just wear my training stuff, but she wouldn't hear of me wearing jogging bottoms. This was the England team, and I needed to show respect by wearing a suit. I didn't argue with her, it was a big day. I scanned the letter again. There were no other instructions, no dress code to go on. The week before the trial, we went shopping in town and bought a pencil skirt, a collared shirt and a suit jacket. I couldn't wear trainers with that lot, so I picked out some high dolly heels, the kind I wouldn't normally wear.

The day of the trial came, I got dressed up, and Mum drove me up to Loughborough. Parents were invited to stay for a short introductory briefing with manager Hope Powell. We pulled into the car park and I spotted a couple of other girls walking into the building with their parents. I gasped in dismay.

'Oh, God,' I said. 'Mum, look, they're all wearing tracksuits.'

She looked out of the window, but the girls had gone.

'Oh really?' she said lightly. 'No, this is a sporty university, they were probably students going to lectures.'

But I didn't buy it. I sensed disaster in the air, I was sure I was about to be humiliated. We stepped inside the building and I pushed open the door to the meeting room, my stomach doing backflips. I supressed a gasp. Thirty or forty girls sat with their parents waiting for the talk to begin, every single one of them in a tracksuit and trainers. A few faces turned to look at me and I swear I heard a murmur ripple around the room, as the girls looked round and nudged each other. Blood rushed to my face, I lowered my head and clip-clopped over to a seat in the far back corner. I sat down, mortified, wishing with every cell in my body I could disappear, or wake up and find I'd been dreaming. I shot Mum a meaningful look as she sat down next to me, but she just smiled and patted my shoulder.

I dared myself to look around the group. The girls I knew from Birmingham kept throwing confused glances in my direction. One of them caught my eye. 'Why are you wearing that?' she mouthed at me.

I looked away and shifted uncomfortably in my seat. I was relieved when, a few minutes later, Hope Powell walked into the room and launched into a business-like introduction. I didn't hear a word she said. I was too busy curling and uncurling my toes in my dolly heels. The second the talk was over, I jumped up, said goodbye to Mum and ran off to the toilet to change into my training gear. I've never lived it down since.

The trial was like a mini training camp. All the time we were being monitored by the coaches so they could whittle down the group to around eighteen players for the next England under-15s camp. We trained, played matches, and did a range of fitness tests. At one point, the coaches had us take the dreaded beep test. This measures aerobic fitness by having athletes run a series of twenty-metre spurts in time to ever-faster recorded beeps. I wasn't familiar with the format, and I didn't know it was an endurance test rather than a speed test. I was so eager to show the coaches how fast I was that I sprinted the first few easy levels. I was exhausted by the time the beeps had reached a moderate speed and the other players were just breaking a sweat. I never lived that down either.

I was sure that the beep test disaster had ruined my chances with England. But, a few weeks later, a letter arrived informing me I'd been picked for a week-long camp the following month. I scanned the letter and then took it into the kitchen to show to Mum. I began reading it out loud, then I stopped.

'Oh no,' I said. 'Mum, they want me to bring my passport. What are we going to do?'

Mum looked up from working on her staff schedule.

'Can't you take your Nigerian one?' she said.

'No, I can't,' I said, panic rising in my chest. 'How much longer until our British passports come?'

Mum frowned. She had already applied to make us all British citizens, but the paperwork, the checks, the tests, it all took a long time.

'I don't know,' she said. 'It's not a simple process, you know. They only asked for my tax records two months ago. We'll just have to wait.'

I looked at the letter again. There had to be a way around it. I kicked myself: it had never crossed my mind I would need to be naturalised as British to play for England. Currently, we had 'leave to remain', which meant we could stay in the country as long as we wanted. Not owning a British passport had never really bothered me before, it was only a formality. I felt entirely British, I'd lived in England my whole life, it was the only home I knew. Now they wanted me to play for England, and I didn't have the right bit of paper. It was embarrassing. I was so tired of being the odd one out. It had to be me, the only one called up to play for England, who didn't have a British passport. I felt a familiar despair rising, one I was coming to associate with my British-Nigerian identity.

Passports were a big deal for the Nigerian community in the UK. A red British passport was a prized possession for those that had been in the UK long enough to own one alongside the Nigerian document, known as a *green pali*. To hold a British passport was a gateway to the world.

Mum mentioned our problem to Dad, to her Nigerian friends and family. They were all adamant: there was no way I could take my Nigerian passport to the England camp. Everyone pressured her to do something, to call the authorities and try and hurry up our application, to prevent me being excluded from the team.

'Listen,' said one uncle, who liked to flaunt that he was a British citizen by birth. 'If she dares show up with *green pali*, they'll send that child straight back. She has to be *Britico* now, don't you know that?'

Mum couldn't exactly demand the authorities speed things up. My application was a little more complicated than Sone's because I hadn't been born in the UK. Things were slowed down further by a lot of back and forth clarifying the details of my entry into the country when I was a baby. Meanwhile, as the camp loomed ever closer, my mood only got gloomier.

The naturalisation process unsettled and disturbed me. It should have felt like I was being anchored in the UK; instead it made me feel uprooted, and dislocated. Every night, lying in bed, my head buzzed with questions. Suddenly I felt like an alien in my own country. I was no longer sure where I belonged, where was I from, or who wanted me. I was in limbo. If I didn't have the right piece of paper, did that mean I wasn't British yet? If I wasn't British, then what was I? I thought back to the chaos of the crowd in Abuja during my Dad's inauguration. I felt like a foreigner there, too. So, who was I?

I focused all my hopes on the British passport. Once it arrived, I was sure all these questions would be answered. Every day I'd wake up and hope the document would drop as if by magic on to the doormat. Every day it wasn't there, and the camp was another day nearer. I hassled Mum about it on an almost daily basis.

'Can't you call the passport people and get them to hurry up?' I said. 'Can't you tell them this is really urgent?'

'Listen,' said Mum, sounding both exasperated and philosophical. 'You go to the camp with whatever you have. I'll write a note explaining that we have applied for your passport. If your manager is happy with that, fine. If not, then maybe it isn't your destiny to play for England after all and you are destined to be great in a different way. The worst that can happen is that you are sent back home.'

I knew Mum was right, but I was still apprehensive, and I felt like I was back where I started, hoping for a miracle. The day of the camp came around and my passport hadn't arrived in time. In the end, I took an acknowledgement from the Home Office proving Mum had applied for naturalisation, together with a note she wrote. It was all we had. I had proof I was in the process of becoming British, and in the end the England coaches were more relaxed than I'd expected. The timing worked out in the end.

All along, Mum had said that if I was meant to play for England, I would, and that I should never apologise for who I was. She was right, of course, and it was an important lesson to learn, but the passport issue still bothered me. Everyone else on the camp had a passport. The only other player of African descent, a young defender called Anita Asante whose family was Ghanaian, had a passport. I was the odd one out, again. Looking back, I wish I'd felt more empowered in who I am, and just accepted being the only Nigerian-born player on the England team, an identity I'd only come to fully celebrate and embrace later on.

A few months later, my passport arrived along with Sone's in a special delivery package. Mum opened the envelope and emptied the burgundy books out on to the table.

'Now you can travel wherever you want,' she said, picking one of the books up and flicking through the pages.

Mum went to the drawer where she kept our Nigerian passports and placed them on the table with the others. She was relieved and happy.

Watching her, I saw for the first time what this process meant. Getting a red passport was more than a formality. It was about status. She had been an adult when she first came to the UK, and all this time she had been a foreigner in a foreign country. She worked hard to forge new paths forwards for herself and her children. She recognised opportunities, and never shirked hard work. With faith, humility and focus, she found a way to cement our lives in a new country. Her journey shows that, with the right attitude, having immigrant status never has to get in the way of a person's destiny. It's the same mentality that has driven countless immigrants to reach the highest echelons of commerce, politics, science, sports and entertainment.

'Let me look,' I said, and held out my hand.

Mum picked out my new passport and handed it over. I turned over the little red book in my hand and stroked the gold coat of arms embossed on the front. I picked out my old Nigerian passport from the pile on the table and held it in my other hand. These two documents would be with me for the rest of my life. Two passports, two nationalities, two identities.

I stared down at the green and the red book. Weighing them in my hands, I began to understand that having two identities wasn't a seesaw, or a pair of scales. I was British, and I was Nigerian. Both sides had equal weight in shaping who I was. Others would want me to choose between them. They would want to know on which side my heart, head and soul lay. Looking at the green and red books, I saw that was a false choice. I could rip myself in two trying to find an answer, or I could reject the question. I was both. I was an indivisible whole.

No one could teach me how to navigate this hyphenated identity, this balancing act. It's a lesson I'm still learning and, no doubt, will continue to learn for the rest of my life. Along the way I've met many others struggling with their own internal tugs of war, those with dual, or multi-racial identities and multi-hyphenated careers, striving to understand which they most identify with. Or those second-generation immigrants like me, African or otherwise, who feel torn between the country they were raised in and their parents' home nations. It can be tough, growing up in a diaspora community, with loyalties and focus split between two places. There's a real danger of never feeling like you belong in either.

We live in an age of mass migration, in which people move around the globe at an unprecedented rate. It's also a time of backlash and the kind of divisive rhetoric that only makes these questions of identity more complicated for those who struggle with them. It's even harder to work out the complex truth of who you are at a time when society's impulse is to separate along lines of race, identity, or heritage. The world right now seems to want to put everyone into one of two piles: us and them. It's up to all of us to reject that.

There are no easy answers, no easy lessons here. But every time I've had these conversations with others, it's helped me to realise that I'm not alone in struggling with these questions. It is in these moments when I feel the only solution is to simply embrace hyphens. To understand that we are all combinations of multiple things. That it's normal to straddle two, three, four or more identities at the same time. For me, being British-Nigerian is a tightrope I'll be on for the rest of my life. And whenever I wobble, whenever I feel like others are trying to get me to choose, to pull me in one direction or the other, I grab on to my hyphen, my balancing pole, and remember I'll always be both.

Class 3:

Choose The Most Powerful Weapon

Whatever traditional roles others expect you to perform, education is your ticket

OUT

It will give you the tools to dream of a better future.

CHAPTER SEVEN

Atticus Finch made me a lawyer. Harper Lee's *To Kill a Mockingbird* was one of my set texts for English literature at school and I was drawn to the attorney at the centre of the story. Atticus was everything a role model should be: heroic, fair and compassionate. He stood firm against ignorance, and wielded logic and the rule of law as weapons against injustice. Reading about Atticus, something clicked inside. This was what I wanted to do, too.

Suddenly, my attitude towards school shifted. Whereas football had always taken priority before I read *To Kill a Mockingbird*, now I saw the point of studying. If I wanted to be a lawyer, like Atticus, I would need to knuckle down. I would need to take my cue from Nelson Mandela, who said education is the most powerful weapon you can use to change the world. I would need to work hard to get the tools Atticus had, and then, like him, I would use them to fight injustice.

I didn't have this epiphany until my late teens. Before that, I was indifferent to school. I was in a friendship group that played up in class, left school at lunch to go to the chip shop, smoke cigarettes and come back late, or sometimes not at all. Fitting in and being accepted were still very important to me. Football was my priority, so I only ever tried smoking once, seized with the irrational fear that the nicotine would stop me being able to breath when I ran. Still, I went along with almost everything else my friends did. In school, that meant doing only the bare minimum to get by. I had a good memory and could articulate my thoughts well, so I was able to coast most of the time. But rolling with the bad crowd really wasn't me.

Then, a few months before I first read about Atticus, something happened to set me on a different path. The summer I was fourteen, Mum told me about her high-flying niece Fola. She had been a star student at the prestigious Headington boarding school in Oxford, and now, aged just twenty-eight, she had made it as a corporate lawyer in a New York firm. I had only met her once, when I was a child, but I was captivated by the idea of what she had achieved.

The urge hit me almost immediately after talking to Mum. I wanted to go to New York to visit Fola. I wanted to go on my own, as soon as possible. To me, New York meant opportunity, it meant hard work and focus. The idea landed fully planned in my head, as if it was the most obvious thing in the world. I would stay with Fola in her apartment in downtown Manhattan. Five days would do it, the school holidays were about to begin, and there were no matches on. There were flights straight from Birmingham; it would be no hassle. The plan seemed so urgent and so simple I wondered why I hadn't thought of it before. I went to find Mum to tell her about my trip.

'Can you go where?' she said, looking up from her work papers.

'New York,' I said again.

She raised her eyebrows in surprise. 'Will they let you go on your own?' she said at last. 'You're too young.'

'Mum, I want to go,' I said. 'I've checked, there are no rules against it. I have my passport, I can go.'

'Well, I guess if Fola says it's all right,' she said.

Mum called Fola, who agreed to let me stay for a few days once the holidays began. Before I knew it, I was on a plane hurtling over the Atlantic. I didn't doubt my decision for a second. This was what I needed. Looking back, I am so grateful to Mum for accommodating my eagerness to go to New York alone, to broaden my horizons and build upon my new-found inspiration. I am not sure many parents would have allowed the same. Other parents might have lacked the courage to indulge their teenager's sense of adventure or curiosity. Mum didn't, she encouraged my adventures. I never felt my wings were clipped.

Fola met me at the airport and we rode the subway back to her apartment. She was friendly and kind, but she made it clear she wouldn't have time to babysit me. She left very early the next morning for work, leaving me a key and a note telling me to help myself to food. For the next few days I barely saw her. I wandered alone through Manhattan's concrete maze, gazing up at the dizzying skyscrapers, dodging the crowds on the sidewalks. I walked north past the Empire State building, through Times Square and through Midtown to Central Park. Then I walked south down Broadway for a glimpse of the Statue of Liberty across the Hudson river.

I had never spent so much time on my own. I'd only ever gone to England youth camps without my family before, and this was a world away from that. I loved every second. Back in my cousin's beautiful apartment, I studied her lifestyle. I was deeply impressed with her high-flying job, her independence, her determination and her knowledge. Here, more real than any fictional character in a book, was a real person to aspire to. If she could do it, so could I. I made myself a solemn promise: I would quit messing around and pretending to be a rebel in school, I would study hard, become an attorney, and build for myself the life my cousin had.

On the fourth day in New York, I got a call from Mum. She sounded exasperated. My cousins on Dad's side who lived in Washington had heard I was in the US and were insisting I came to visit them, too.

'You'll go tomorrow,' said Mum firmly.

I gulped and took a deep breath. 'But Mum, I haven't got any money left,' I said.

Mum tutted down the phone.

'What?' she said, 'How can you …?' She trailed off. Then she sighed. 'I'll have to wire you some more,' she said.

I packed up my stuff and left my cousin's apartment early the next morning. I found my way to the long-distance bus station in Midtown, stopping off at a Western Union branch to pick up Mum's cash. The man at the ticket counter looked surprised when I asked for a one-way ticket to Washington D.C. I wasn't sure if it was because of my Birmingham accent, or my age, or both. I found the bus and waited on the edge of the bay for the driver to arrive and check tickets. I threw nervous glances at the other passengers, many of whom stared back at me suspiciously.

For the first time I felt painfully young and out of place. I was alone, a long way from home. The driver appeared, I climbed on to the bus, and was hit by a sharp stench of urine. I sat down towards the front, clutched my bag on my lap and avoided the other passengers' eyes as they filed on. I sat like that, terrified, for the next five hours, watching the traffic weaving on the interstate. At last, when we pulled into Washington's Union Station, I was relieved to see my cousins waiting for me.

I stayed with them at their family home in a quiet, leafy suburb less than an hour north of Washington. My cousins' upbringing had been different from mine. Their father, Dad's elder brother, was a professor at Howard University and had sent them to leading schools in the state. Now they were moving on to the next stage of their education. One was studying business and finance, the other was about to start at medical school. Listening to them talk about their plans, I felt the same excitement stir inside me as I had in Fola's apartment in New York. If football couldn't give me a future, I would have to sow the seeds of some other career. The idea rumbled around my head for the rest of the holiday.

Back at school, the teachers gave us stern talks. Things were getting serious, they said, now we were studying for our GCSEs. A lot of the other kids laughed it off, but I thought about Fola and my cousins in America. Somewhere in all this exam stuff was a future path for me, I just had to find it. I decided things were going to change. I had been moved into higher sets for some subjects, and I wasn't around my old group of friends much any more. Then, one day, I just stopped talking to them. They scowled at me in the corridors and called me a geek across the playground.

Two of the girls, who were among the few other black kids in the school, began teasing me. They were of Caribbean descent, and started calling me 'African *bhuttu*', a patois term referring to an unsophisticated African person. They tried to make me feel that because my family was African I was less than them. They said Africans were from the jungle and not as advanced as those from the Caribbean islands. They made comments about appearance, said I had big lips and unrefined hair. It was deeply hurtful.

Coming from other black people, these racial slurs were even more upsetting. For me, it was easier to be resolute and determined against bullies who were entirely different to me. But these girls looked like me, at least to the rest of the school. That they chose to highlight and make fun of our differences in heritage only made me feel more isolated. Suddenly, I felt even more at odds with my African identity. It was the only time I've experienced that kind of split between the two communities, but I know that these derogatory comments can go both ways.

At other times, the girls called me a 'coconut', a nasty term used to describe black people considered to have 'sold out', being 'white on the inside', either because they mix with white people or because they are educated and eloquent, traits some black people, both African and Caribbean, apparently consider to be exclusively white. I've always felt that this was total nonsense and a form of self-hate. It accepts the limiting stereotypes that society tries to impose on black people, telling them even how they should communicate. Even if I had tried to change the way I spoke to shake the "coconut" tag, I couldn't. I've always loved the English language in all its depth, and my communication reflected that.

These abilities and characteristics have nothing to do with race. I wanted to be educated and well-spoken because that was what I had known from my family of academics and politicians, not because I wanted to be white. Mum never let me get away with bad grammar or not speaking as clearly as I could. To this day, her corrections ring in my head when I speak. Speaking well has always just been who I am, as I'm sure is the case for many other black people out there. At the same time, I was just as happy talking in Brummie slang with my friends back on the estate. That was in me too. Language has many dimensions.

I resolved to fight all these ridiculous stereotypes and rise above them. I told myself these girls were attacking me because I had things they didn't. I had football, good grades, and the ability to mix with a wide circle of people. Things would change eventually, but I would have to work hard to break out of the moulds that others wanted to impose on me. And, if necessary, I would have to stand alone in order to do it.

I fell in with a new group of girls who were hard-working and bright. My closest friend, Laura, came from a middle-class white family and lived in a big detached house in Hollywood. I'd often go over to her place after school, but I never invited her back to our small house near the old estate. I was proud that we had moved on from the estate, I wasn't house-proud enough to invite Laura, who was used to something very different. Our house might have been bigger than others on the road and I was delighted when Mum had an extension built, but it wasn't like Laura's place, and I was too insecure to draw attention to the difference.

The change in my schoolwork was dramatic. My grades improved, especially in my favourite subjects, English and history. My English teacher, Keziah Featherstone, had a bold plan. She was trying out a new fast-tracking scheme that would see the brightest pupils take GCSE English literature a year early. Then, the following year, we would sit an early AS level. All this would mean a lot of hard work. We would study texts in half the normal time, so we would read at home, and discuss the books in class.

To Kill a Mockingbird was our first text. I was gripped from the first page, but when Scout Finch described her loving father, Atticus, a widower and dedicated lawyer, the story grabbed me on a deeper level. Atticus was defending a black man falsely accused of raping a white woman. He knew taking the case could be dangerous but felt a duty to the oppressed black man. The law said all men were equal, Atticus had to uphold that. I read his battle for justice through to its tragic end, flipped back to the first page and started again. In class, we watched the black-and-white film. By the time the courtroom scene came around, I was spellbound.

'Now, gentlemen,' said Gregory Peck, striding towards the jury to deliver Atticus's closing statement. 'In this country, our courts are the great levellers. In our courts all men are created equal. I'm no idealist to believe firmly in the integrity of our courts and in the jury system. That is no ideal to me, it is a living, working reality. I am confident that you gentlemen will review, without passion, the evidence you have heard, come to a decision, and restore this defendant to his family. In the name of God, do your duty.'

I must have watched that film fifteen times. I couldn't get enough of Atticus's courage and determination to do the right thing. It was a revelation. Here, it seemed, was something useful to do with a lifetime. Justice had to be upheld, voiceless people had to be heard. I looked for other stories of individuals fighting for justice against the odds. *One Flew Over the Cuckoo's Nest* and *The Shawshank Redemption* were some of my favourite films. These were stories crying out for an Atticus figure, someone who could fight to restore justice, some who could put things right, who believed the law could defeat the lynch mob. That was what I wanted to do. I wanted to confront injustice, to defend those who couldn't defend themselves, to address the inbalance. To do that I would need to study hard.

Much later, while facing the biggest trial of my life, I thought back to Atticus in that courtroom. By channelling my own inner Atticus, I found the strength to push on in pursuing truth, no matter what the personal cost might be to myself. Even at the time, my head full of Atticus, I recognised injustice when I saw it, clear and fast. Towards the end of that term, a boy in my class turned up to school with a different hairstyle. He was black, and had decided to wear his hair out naturally in an Afro. The other kids gave him a hard time for it, but the boy was shy, and he never fought back or stood up for himself. He just took it, looking uncomfortable, as every day the teasing got worse. The teachers finally got wind of what was going on, but to my surprise they didn't punish the bullies. Instead, they told the boy he had to wear his hair in a less conspicuous style. This only made the boy more miserable, and he started talking about leaving the school.

I couldn't believe it. The school had always been quite strict about uniform and dress codes; to me, all those little rules about haircuts and skirt lengths seemed pedantic. But suddenly putting a ban on Afros, as if it was a radical haircut, just wasn't fair, especially when there were other boys with much crazier hair around. One had long straggly hair that was dyed green and there was no ban on that. I had a burning urge to say something. And so, one lunchtime, I went to the headteacher's office and knocked on her door.

'Come in,' came the voice from inside the office.

I stepped inside and closed the door behind me. The headteacher looked up from behind her desk.

'Ah, Eniola,' she said, gesturing towards the chair opposite. 'Is everything OK?'

I sat down and took a deep breath.

'Miss,' I began. 'There's a boy in my class who has to change his hair just because he is wearing it out as an afro. But there's another boy with green hair. If that's allowed, then the boy in my class should be allowed to wear his hair naturally.'

The headmistress put her head on one side and looked at me as if she was seeing me for the first time.

'OK,' she said. 'I see your point. Leave it with me.'

I looked at her in surprise; it had been easier than I'd expected. I nodded, thanked her, stood up and walked out. The rest of that day I had a spring in my step. It felt good to try and help. I hadn't needed to stand up for the boy with the Afro, it didn't make any difference to my life, but I couldn't just let it go. The solution, in the end, wasn't exactly what I'd hoped for. The school introduced a blanket rule of short hair for all the boys, longer skirts for the girls, and long ties for everyone. It wasn't ideal, but at least it was fair.

Too many things were unfair, and most of them I could do nothing about. Towards the end of the term, a classmate was knocked off his bike by a car and killed. He was just fifteen years old. Everyone at school was devastated. I didn't know the boy well, but his sudden death hit me. It was too sad, he had been denied so much time. Again, I felt I had to do something, however small. If we could record our memories of him, I thought, it might help us deal with his sudden departure. It might feel less final. I bought a large hardback book with blank pages and handed it around so people could write down their memories of him. It was just a small gesture, but it was something.

One day, soon after the accident, the boy's parents came to school. His mother's face was pale and blank with grief. I ached with pity for her. I racked my brain, there had to be something I could do to comfort her. I found myself walking towards the woman, with no clue what I was going to say. Before I knew it, I was standing in front of her. The words came to me in that instant.

'Your son's spirit is alive,' I said, surprised at the words coming out of my mouth. 'The way you saw him that last time, crouched over, in pain, that's not where he is now. That was just his body. His spirit is free now, and it lives on.'

The boy's mum stared at me; her eyes quickly filled with tears. Then she put her arms around my shoulders and hugged me tight. I hugged her back and wondered where the words had come from.

Just before Christmas, my form tutor told me that the school was holding its annual pupil awards ceremony in the last week of term, and Mum and I were invited to attend. Neither of us knew why in advance. Pupils normally got awards for academic success, or for sport or music, so we both assumed it would be something about football, or my improved grades. Mum and I sat through the whole evening, and my name didn't come up once. Then the headmistress came on stage.

'There's just time for one last award,' she said. 'This is a very special award. We don't give it every year, only when one of our pupils does something exceptional to deserve it.' Her gaze found me in the audience. 'Eniola, would you come up here on stage?'

My mouth dropped open, and beside me, so did Mum's. I stepped up on to the stage, still with no idea what kind of award I was about to get.

'On several occasions this term, Eniola has shown great strength of character,' the headmistress said. 'She has gone out of her way to help others and speak up for them. It's my great pleasure to present her with this character award.'

From the stage, I squinted out into the audience, scanned the rows of parents and teachers until I found Mum. She was beaming with pride, her hands raised up, clapping hard. To this day, I think she's prouder of that character award than many of my football trophies. To Mum, it was proof of my upbringing in practice. For her, the qualities of being stubborn or vocal or strong-willed were only virtues if they could be used to help others.

Later, in the car on the way home, Mum wanted to know every detail of what had happened. I told her how I had gone to the headteacher on behalf of the boy with the Afro and what I had said to the poor lady who had lost her son. I told her how I couldn't bear the unfairness, and how that feeling had spurred me into action. And I told her I knew what I wanted to do with my life. I told her I was sure I wanted to become a lawyer.

CHAPTER EIGHT

I started back at school that September more determined than ever, my head full of what I could achieve if I worked hard. I was so focused my teachers didn't notice I was playing football. I had my league debut the week before school started. Birmingham City had been promoted to the top flight, then known as the National League, and I had moved into the senior team at the same time.

I scored an equaliser in our first league game, against Leeds United. It was one of those goals where you have time to think, to decide whether to shoot or take the ball around the keeper or make the wrong decision all together. I felt time slow down as I broke out, free, alone, dangerous, towards the goal. The keeper came off the line, stooping low, her arms outstretched either side of her knees. A one-on-one was the best I could have hoped for. Now she would have to decide: go down or stay tall and wait for me to shoot. It was her move against mine. I made a sharp left, as if I were about to shoot. She followed my movement and lunged. Just as her centre of balance shifted, I swerved back to the right, tapped the ball around her and shot. The keeper was left sprawling as the ball found the net. I clenched my fists as the familiar buzz filled my veins. A goal for my team, and for me, on our top-flight debut.

It was the start of a great season. Birmingham, the youngest side in the National Division, was shooting up the table. Marcus's focus on younger players like me and Kaz was starting to bear fruit and I repaid his careful mentoring with some match-winning goals. A spate of goals that winter even prompted Marcus to compare me to Everton's teenage striker Wayne Rooney in an interview with a local newspaper. Rooney had scored his stunning debut goal against Arsenal just three months earlier and now he was one of the highest paid teenagers on the planet. We were both young, fast, and scored goals. The similarities ended there, but the comparison ran for the next ten years.

We ended the season in fifth. In May, around the time of my GCSE exams, I took a trip down to London for the

FA award ceremony in a grand hotel. Marcus's efforts had seen him named Manager of the Year, and my goal tally had won me Young Player of the Year. It was a great honour, and very exciting, but I tried to keep things in perspective. I was concentrating on my exams, focusing on my academic path. Having a good season was only that, a good season. It was something to celebrate, but everyone kept reminding me that football was only a hobby and couldn't offer me a professional future.

But it didn't feel like a hobby. I was challenging for titles and my international career was taking off as well. That April I made my debut for England under-19s, in a European Championships qualifier against Ireland. I was amazed to be playing, let alone in the starting line-up. Half an hour in I got the ball on the edge of the area, saw the keeper was off her line and looped it over her. I was thrilled to score on my debut, and the 3–0 win set us on our way to qualification for that summer's Euros in Germany. At just sixteen, I had made an explosive entry into the under-19s side and staked my claim to a place in the final squad for the tournament.

Going to Germany that July felt incredible. For the first time I was going to play at a tournament abroad as a member of an England squad. I was confident, still on a high from the award and the successful season. I played in two games, scoring in a group match against Italy and starting in our semi-final defeat to France.

Being knocked out couldn't dampen my spirits. I came home buzzing from playing in an England shirt on an international stage. Before we left Germany, youth manager Mo Marley had hinted strongly that I would be picked for the England senior squad before long. I just hoped it would come in time to play in the 2005 Euros, on home soil, the summer after next. It would be a dream come true.

After such a promising summer, it was all I could do to stay focused on school, to drag myself back down to earth. But my GCSE results were strong, with two A*s, six As, one B, and a C in the fast-tracked AS in English Literature. I thought of Atticus, and of Fola, and reminded myself I had to keep going if I wanted to follow the law path. The financial stability just wasn't in the professional women's game yet; even the most famous female footballers in the world needed a day job. Still, it wasn't always easy to juggle my dreams alongside my education. There were times when I just had to put my head down and keep the faith that it would all be worth it in the end.

That September, a few weeks after the youth tournament, I started at Cadbury College, a sixth-form college less than a mile away from our house on Redditch Road, Kings Norton. I signed up for A levels in history, psychology and media studies, and an AS level in history. I would need good grades to study law at a top university, and I had my heart set on the best law departments in London. Cadbury College was a more relaxed environment than high school, and the teachers weren't as strict about attendance, provided I got my coursework in on time. I was happy there, and made dear friends, Joel and Sureeta, who went on to have hugely successful careers, in project management and artist management, and of whom I'm very proud.

A new season began, and I continued my scoring streak, netting five goals in eleven games for Birmingham before the end of November. But as the weeks went on, I began to feel like something was missing, like my progress was slowing. There were other players coming up behind me, and I needed more of a challenge, I wanted to stretch out, test what I had against the best players. I wanted to reach the top, to prove myself. I wanted trophies.

The call from Charlton Athletic couldn't have come at a better time. The coaches wanted me to come down to London to join one of their training sessions and see if I might be a fit for the team. I was intrigued. Charlton was a bigger club, hungry for challenges, for success, for silverware. In its current guise, the club was only three years old, and since forming, had narrowly missed out on a series of trophies.

That season, Charlton were on top form and were locked in a three-way title race with Arsenal and Fulham. Under manager Keith Boanas, the club had attracted some of the best players around, including senior members of the England team Fara Williams, Katie Chapman, Casey Stoney, Joanne Broadhurst and keeper Pauline Cope. Playing with them would raise my game, give me experience of the top flight, and deepen my ties to England. This could be exactly the opportunity I'd been looking for to evolve. I wanted in.

Mum drove me down to London one evening in December for the training session. The atmosphere was electric. Here was a team driving each other on, in concert, to achieve a common goal. With the title race never far from their minds, the players lifted each other up, pushed each other to limit of their abilities. I trained well, and at the end of the session, manager Keith talked to Mum and me about organising a transfer. There would be no fee, of course: Charlton was semi-professional, like most women's clubs. Still, there would be a small allowance of ninety pounds per week, and though I would have to arrange my own transport back and forth to London, the club agreed to cover my expenses.

On the way back in the car, Mum and I began working out the logistics. There was no question of turning the offer down, it was far too good an opportunity. After just one session I could already see what playing with Charlton could do for my development. But training in London twice a week while studying for A levels in Birmingham would take a lot of organisation. I convinced Mum I'd manage it, and she said she'd help however she could. It would be a challenge, but there was no other way. I was equally driven in both directions, I had to make it work.

It was a gruelling schedule. I signed with Charlton in January, the month before my seventeenth birthday, and was catapulted to the top of the table. I was thrilled to be part of it, but getting to the weekly training sessions and weekend matches was demanding. Tuesday and Thursday after college I would catch a train to Euston, then squeeze into the Tube at rush hour and head to the Eltham ground in south east London. Training finished at nine, when I would take the last train back to Birmingham and arrive into a deserted New Street Station in the early hours of the morning. Then I would grab a few hours' sleep and be up early in time for college. There was a match most Sundays, and I would do the whole thing again. Saturdays, I worked in Schuh, a shoe shop to earn some cash. I was completely exhausted all of the time. Often, when I was too exhausted after training, I'd write off my first college class the following day and stay with Keith and Pauline Cope in Eltham, or with my teammate Eartha Pond at her house near Euston.

Playing for Charlton was worth every minute. The season ended with us chasing a domestic treble. We had already won the League Cup, in a 1–0 win against Fulham. The title race with Arsenal was coming down to the wire and we would also face the Gunners in the FA Cup final at the beginning of May. The game, at Loftus Road, would be my biggest yet. Two million would tune in to watch the live broadcast. My new teammates were nervous, fighting to shake off memories of their 3–0 Cup final defeat to Fulham the previous year.

I started on the bench and watched in horror as Arsenal striker Julie Fleeting scored goal after goal. I came on in the seventieth minute, but by that time Fleeting had already scored a hat-trick. I spent the rest of the game trying in vain to break through their defence, but it was hopeless. On that day, at least, they were the better team. When, afterwards, Keith was asked for his assessment, he said two words: 'Julie. Fleeting.' Two weeks later, Fleeting delivered the final blow to our dream. Arsenal beat Fulham in the season's final fixture, stealing our league title by just one point. It was devastating to come so close only to have our glory snatched away at the last minute. We vowed the following year would be ours.

I didn't have to wait that long, though, for my next milestone. That September, I collected my first senior cap for England, at a friendly away to Holland. As hosts, England had qualified automatically for Euro 2005, but in the build-up to the tournament, the pressure was still on for me. At seventeen, I was one of the senior team's youngest-ever debutantes, and I had a lot to prove if I was going to earn a place on the final squad. Ahead of the game I was incredibly nervous. Was I too young? Was I even ready? I started the game, and every time the ball came to me, I panicked and got rid of it. I got one decent shot on goal, but I was substituted off in the second half. My fear had got the better of me on my debut. Afterwards, I worried about whether I'd done enough and waited anxiously for my next chance to play.

That term, between the usual back and forth for training, I applied for universities. My predicted grades were good enough to aim for some of the UK's top law departments. It made sense to be close to Charlton, so I applied to universities in London. By January, I had a few conditional offers. I felt confident: I would have to work hard but the grades the universities had asked for were within my grasp. The problem was finding the time to concentrate on studying. Going down to Charlton and back three times a week was all-consuming.

I was learning to drive, but with everything that was going on, it was taking a while. Just after I turned eighteen, I passed my driving test on the fourth attempt. Driving made the journeys to London easier, but it also meant I lost the study time I'd had on the train. Studying and playing football was a delicate balancing act, and any tiny shift made a huge difference. Yet an even bigger conflict was looming on the horizon. At the end of January, UEFA held the draw for the Euros, and I spotted a clash between one of my upcoming exams and an England game. I tried to put it out of my mind for the time being. There was a good chance I'd be picked for the squad, but I wouldn't know for certain until mid-May, just before my exams began.

Before that, there was the business end of the season to get through with Charlton. The stakes were high once again. We hovered at the top of the table for most of the spring, but Arsenal slipped ahead of us in the season's final weeks. By the end of April, it was clear we wouldn't catch them, leaving all our hopes resting on the FA Cup. We had reached the final for the third year running and this time we were favourites against Everton. We focused all our efforts on that one game. If we could lift the Cup, at last, it would make up for years of disappointment.

We sat with Keith in the home dressing room at Upton Park before the game and weighed up our odds. We knew we could beat Everton, but they were still a tough opponent with quality players, including our former teammate Fara Williams, who had moved there the previous summer. Three of our key players were out injured, but I was starting, and I was on good form. Before we walked out on to the pitch, Keith gave us his final words of encouragement.

'I want you to read that,' he said, pointing to a sign pinned to the dressing-room wall. We all turned our heads. The poster urged players to 'forget the memories of the past and focus on the future'. We stared at it, letting the words sink in. Keith paused, then he clapped his hands. 'We're going to make it third time lucky,' he said, grinning.

I tried to calm my excitement as we filed out of the tunnel and on to the pristine grass. The pitch was like a carpet, much better than some of the playing surfaces we were used to. The sun was shining and there were close to 10,000 fans packed into the main stand. It felt like it was going to be a good day. Both sides burst out of the blocks, forcing early chances. I was up front, seeking, hunting, feeling for chances to break free of the defence, but their centre back Lindsay Johnson was marking me tightly. Twice in the first half she took the ball off my foot as I was about to shoot. We went in at half-time frustrated, but the better team.

Then, twenty minutes into the second half, space opened in front like clouds parting for the sun. Our midfielder Emma Coss sent a through ball soaring over the heads of the defensive line. This was my chance. I sprinted, leaving Johnson and the other defenders trailing behind me. As the ball fell ahead, I saw Everton keeper Danielle Hill hesitating on her line. I didn't need asking twice. I ran on to the ball and slotted it into the far corner. The crowd roared and I peeled off towards the corner flag, beaming wide. Fireworks exploded in my chest as the buzz rose up through my legs and into my gut. My teammates caught up with me and flung their arms around my shoulders. I had scored, the Cup was now ours to lose.

Everton pushed hard for an equaliser, and we probed for a decisive second goal. But neither defence was giving an inch. Still, we had my goal, and as the minutes slid by, I dared to hope. At last, after what felt like hours, the final whistle blew. I lifted my arms in victory and ran into the centre circle. My teammates piled into me, whooping and yelling. I couldn't believe it. We had won the Cup. I had scored the winner in the Cup final.

Minutes later, giggling with excitement, we filed on to the podium for the trophy presentation. As our captain Casey Stoney lifted the Cup into the air and the red and white confetti rained down around us, I closed my eyes and said a prayer. I saw myself at seven, watching Manchester United with Sone in my living room on the estate. That loss, all losses, had been answered with this win. I opened my eyes, and saw Casey stepping towards me. Grinning wider than ever, I grasped the silver handles and raised the cup for the photographers. The buzz went into overdrive, it was the best high of my life. I had never imagined a win could feel like this. My heart overflowed with gratitude for my teammates, for Keith, who had become more like a father figure than a coach, and for the club that had recognised my potential. Now I had repaid the faith they had shown in me. At last, a win, a trophy, to plaster over all the scars of defeat.

That moment was all I had to celebrate the FA Cup win. My exams were almost upon me. The season was over, the FA Cup final was over, it was time to study as hard as I could before the Euros began. I tried to shut out football for a few days, and I told the England coaches I couldn't play a friendly against Norway at the end of that week. But let's just say it was hard to focus. I'd try to memorise all the required information, but I kept imagining scoring for my country in front of a home crowd of tens of thousands.

Then, just before my first exam, Hope Powell confirmed the final squad for the Euros. It was unreal to see my name on the list. I had done it, secured a place as part of a new rising generation of English players. Competition for places had been fierce, and Hope had tried out a wide pool of talent over the past year. I gazed at the other names on the list. I would be playing alongside England legend Kelly Smith, my old teammate Fara Williams, and current Charlton teammates Casey Stoney and Katie Chapman. Kaz, that year's Young Player of the Year, had made the squad too, along with my England youth buddy Anita Asante.

It was cruel timing. Here was my biggest chance yet to shine at football, the game I was born to play. It was a golden opportunity to be an ambassador for the women's game in my own country. To show what I could do, what women could do, on the pitch. I wanted to put every ounce of my being into my performance. But I couldn't rely on football alone. I needed an alternative future, and that rested on the outcome of these exams. I had a direction, a goal, and it was within grasp. I could get the grades, get into law school, become an attorney, build the life that Fola had.

But my footballing success made me feel light, weightless, as if I had been untethered and was floating off into the sky like a helium balloon. However seductive it seemed, I believed then that women's football would never offer me a professional career. Still, in my heart I couldn't bring myself to dismiss it as only a healthy pastime, a hobby. Here I was, about to play for England. As the days barrelled on towards the opening game, towards my first exam, my head and my heart pulled ever harder in opposite directions. It took all my strength to hold them together. I would do both, where so many other athletes hadn't. I would take my exams, and I would play at the Euros. All I had to do was keep my head down and hold my nerve.

CHAPTER NINE

The next week passed in a blur of exams and training. Hope wanted the whole squad to play together again before the tournament began, and at the end of May, between exams, I came off the bench to play in a friendly against the Czech Republic. We were already three goals up when I scored a fourth, a lob from eighteen yards. It was my first goal for the England senior team, and, I felt, a good omen for the Euros.

My teachers at Cadbury College worked a miracle and arranged last minute for me to sit my final exam, the history paper, at a sixth-form college in Blackburn. That way I could go straight from the exam to play in England's second group game against Denmark. England promised to send a chauffeured car to pick me up and take me to the stadium. The timing would still be tight: the two-and-a-half-hour exam began at nine, kick-off was at four. But there was a way. The England squad gathered in Manchester a few days before the tournament began to train. The night before the opening game, I sat in a quiet part of the team hotel lobby, studying for the history paper.

'Sorry to interrupt,' said a voice behind me. 'Can I sit down?'

I looked up from my notes to see a tall blond woman standing next to the table. I smiled at her.

'Sure,' I said, motioning for her to sit.

'I'm Misia,' she said, holding out her hand for me to shake as she sat down. 'I'm the new team psychologist. You're Eni, right?'

I nodded. She gestured at the piles of notes on the table. 'How are you getting on?'

I frowned and sighed. 'It's not easy,' I said. 'Bad timing.'

'I can imagine,' she said and smiled.

She was kind and open, and her manner made me want to talk. I told her about my upcoming exam and the clash with the game. I told her my dream of studying law, and about the grades I needed to get into the universities I'd applied to. Her eyes widened.

'Sounds a bit like being a striker,' she said, 'when everyone's relying on you to score.'

I looked at her and blinked. I hadn't thought of it like that before, but it was a lot like that. It felt good to tell someone else about the pressure I was under. Talking to Misia, I began to realise I'd been holding myself to very high standards. She made me feel more at peace: I had done all I could, the best thing to do was to try and relax into the moment.

The following day, a Sunday, we arrived early at City of Manchester stadium for the opening game of the tournament. Nerves were running high in the dressing room. We would be playing in front of 30,000 fans, the biggest audience the UK had ever seen at a women's football match. A further three million would be watching the live TV broadcast. Hope Powell briefed us once again. England were in a tough group of Scandinavian teams. First up were Finland, followed by Denmark and Sweden later in the week. Hope had started Kaz and striker Amanda Barr up front, so I was on the bench.

The action began slowly, but the fans made for a carnival atmosphere. The party really kicked off at the end of the first half when we scored two quick-fire goals. On the bench we celebrated as if we were on the pitch. By the time I came on eleven minutes into the second half, the Finns had got one back, and they were pushing for the equaliser. It was clear we needed a third goal. I forced a save from the Finnish keeper before disaster struck at the other end as Finland bundled in an eighty-ninth-minute equaliser. Suddenly, the party atmosphere turned to panic as we had just three minutes of injury time to scrape back the win. With just a minute to go, Kaz set me free in the box with a through ball and the keeper rushed out to charge down my shot. Behind me, Kaz followed up on my rebound, curling the ball into the top corner. The party was back on. We ran after her as she bolted across the pitch, yelling and swearing in victory. I still tease Kaz now about her use of colourful language. It was, and remains, an iconic goal in Kaz's career, and the celebrations were fitting. We were winning, on home turf, in front of 30,000 people, and it felt amazing.

Our next game, against Denmark, was two days later, the same day as my final exam. I was up early to force down a hotel breakfast. Then, a luxurious, chauffeur-driven Mercedes took me to a college in Blackburn to sit my history paper. The exam passed in a daze; I couldn't tell you now what it was about. Before I knew it, I was back in the car on the way to the match at Blackburn's Ewood Park.

I started on the bench again, watching anxiously as Kelly Smith battled an old injury and we failed to make the most of our chances. Fara Williams had already put us ahead from the penalty spot by the time I came on at the beginning of the second half. But even on the pitch I was still in a daze. I felt powerless as Denmark scored two late goals to turn the game on its head and grab a last-minute win. We were devastated. Hope certainly wasn't happy.

The last group game was against Sweden at the end of that week. I got to start this time, and I was feeling hopeful: we only needed a draw to qualify for the next round. Sweden, though, needed a win and they came at us from the word go. They scored from a corner after just three minutes. We spent the rest of the game chasing an equaliser. Our chances were few and far between, so I had to go hunting. Towards the end of the first half I chased down a Swedish defender, forcing her to play the ball back to the keeper. I raced after it, but the keeper reached it first. She tried to boot it to safety, but instead smashed it straight into my head. My vision went blurry and I fell to the floor. Somehow I managed to lift my head up and peek with one eye to watch the path of the ball towards the goal.

'Did it go in?' I asked the medics when they hurried over.

It didn't. The rest of the game rolled by without goals. The final whistle blew, and we slumped on to the pitch like we had been punched in the gut. The Euros were over, at least for us. We had crashed out as hosts, finishing bottom of the group. None of us spoke on the way back to the hotel. But as I packed my things up and made my way home to Birmingham, I began, amid the devastation, to feel a tiny pinprick of relief. Back at home, at last, I flung myself on to my bed, exhausted. It was all over, the season, the exams, the Euros, all of it. I could sleep for a week.

I got my A level results two months later. My grades weren't disastrous, but they were disappointing compared to my GCSEs: Bs in media and psychology and a C in history. The results weren't exactly surprising, given the load I'd been juggling for the past year, but they weren't enough to get into the top universities. I did receive an acceptance letter from Keele University. It had been so far down on my list of applications I hadn't even checked where it was. When I found out it was 200 miles from London, I ruled it out. There was no way I was moving anywhere that far from Charlton. In some ways it was a relief, it made my decision for me.

I spent the next days weighing up my options. For the first time in my life, the path ahead was open. I thought back over everything that had happened in the last months; it hardly seemed real. I had won the FA

Cup; I had played for my country at an international tournament. My football career was exploding. Maybe these disappointing grades were just a sign I should try a different path, follow my heart, and concentrate on playing. The more I thought about it, the more I warmed to the idea. There would be time to come back to education later, I could always retake my A levels and reapply to law school further down the road. Meanwhile, I could focus all my efforts on football, and see where it took me. I was one of Hope's new generation of young England players. Surely I could come back to studying once everything had calmed down.

But Mum was having none of it. When I told her my plan, her face screwed up in distaste.

'What do you mean, not go to uni right away?' she said.

'It's no big deal,' I said. 'I'll take a year out and then go.'

Mum tutted and shook her head. 'No, people always say they'll take a year out, and then never come back to it. They lose their appetite for it. You've got to keep up the momentum. There has to be a way. What about clearing?'

'But I don't want to study anywhere else,' I said, exhausted by the idea of scrambling around to find a university that would take me last minute and was also within driving distance of Charlton.

'You're being naive,' said Mum. 'It's great that you're doing well now, but what will you do later, when you can't play football any more? What will be your career path then?'

I sighed and rolled my eyes. I was so tired and I didn't see anything wrong with taking a break. That evening at training, I told the Charlton coaches about my plan. I wanted to explore all my options. If I was going to convince Mum, I would need to find a useful way of filling the time between training and games. Charlton offered me a place on a coaching course, and suggested I combine it with a part-time criminology course at one of the London colleges. They said I could start right away if I wanted. I went back to Mum with this, but she shook her head and said it wasn't for me. Deep down I knew she was right, but at least the coaching course was a way forward. It meant I would be learning something useful, and it would stop this unpleasant feeling of floating in limbo. Training as a coach seemed like a fine solution to me, but Mum wasn't letting up.

'Can't England help?' she said. 'Doesn't the team have links with Loughborough University?'

I shrugged. I knew Loughborough ran scholarships for elite athletes competing at an international level. There was an academy for England female footballers, with the best training facilities in the country. But the programme was for players who wanted to study sports science, not law.

'Let's talk to someone at England and find out,' said Mum.

'I thought for a minute. Hope wouldn't be the person to talk to about something like this. Then it came to me: Misia the psychologist would know what to do. Mum jumped on the idea, and immediately set up a meeting with her. She came back full of excitement.

It turned out Misia was herself a university lecturer, not at Loughborough but at its London rival, Brunel University. Brunel had the leading sports facilities in the country, encouraged applications from elite-level athletes and was regularly used as a training base for Great Britain Olympians. Ever since she interrupted my study session in the hotel during the Euros, Misia had been impressed at how hard I'd been studying. She promised Mum she would talk to the law department to see if they had any open spaces. It seemed too good to be true, a solid law degree at a London university renowned for its sporting tradition that was within commuting distance to Charlton.

Misia came through for us, and in mid-September Brunel offered me a place on the undergraduate law programme through clearing. Mum was overjoyed and called me in the middle of my coaching course to say I had to go to Brunel right away to sort out my admission. I was taken aback, it was all very sudden.

'I can't just leave,' I whispered into the phone. 'I'm in the middle of a child-protection course.'

But Mum wasn't giving up now. In the end, she took all my documents to Brunel herself, and sorted the whole admission process for me. That's how much she wanted it to happen. I'm very thankful to her now for her foresight in knowing that Brunel was exactly the university for me, but at the time I didn't see why she was making such a big deal out of it. She still teases me about it, asking me if I've learned anything interesting on my child-protection course lately.

Those first days at Brunel were fascinating. Everything had happened so suddenly I hadn't had time to build any expectations of what the university would be like. Brunel was modern and compact, with a large sports park and running track on the way in. Walking around the campus, it was great to see students from all over the world, as well as British students from every background. The law school was a low, red-brick building in a quiet corner of the campus. At the end of my first seminar, one of the other students came up to introduce himself.

'I'm Kelechi,' he said, holding out his hand for me to shake. 'Did I hear you say your name is Eniola?'

I nodded.

'Ah, so you're Nigerian too?' said Kelechi. 'There are a lot of us here.'

'Yes,' I said. 'I was born in Lagos, but I grew up in Birmingham.'

Kelechi laughed. 'Oh, I can hear that from your accent,' he said. 'Have you been back much?'

I wrinkled my nose and shook my head. 'Not exactly,' I said.

I told Kelechi I'd been to Abuja to see my father get inaugurated as a senator. He raised his eyebrows. 'Ah, we'll need coffee for this,' he said.

For the next hour, I listened spellbound as Kelechi told me about his life in Nigeria. I didn't have any Nigerian friends in Birmingham that had spoken about the country with such enthusiasm, pride and love before. As he talked, it was as if he was tugging open a door I had blocked off six years before on the return flight from Abuja. Suddenly, I wanted to know everything there was to know about the country of my birth.

Kelechi had big plans for what he would achieve when he returned. After he graduated, he planned to sit the Nigerian bar exam, and encouraged me to do the same.

His father was a successful businessman, he said, doing business was easier there. Kelechi told me about the power of the Nigerian courts, about the judges battling to uphold the constitution that had been established the day my family had been pushed against the doors of the parliament building. The more he told me, the more Nigeria flowered in my mind as a place of endless opportunity.

Kelechi was warm, funny and interesting, and we connected right away. We were firm friends before the week was out. Wherever we went together, in lectures, at the student cafes, or the library, we seemed to meet other Nigerians or British-Nigerians. All of them were interesting, educated, dedicated, and had grown up in varying degrees of separation from Nigeria. Tobi, Melissa, Sam and Jokae are just a few of a long list of Nigerians I met at university who remain friends to this day. We would have cook-offs in halls, taking it in turns to cook tasty Nigerian cuisine for each other. We held bible study sessions, supporting and teaching each other through the faith and prayer all our parents had planted within us. God saw to it that I was put in St Margaret's halls, in a room opposite Jokae, a London-born British Nigerian girl who quickly became a close friend. The building was a stone's throw away from the athletics track used by future Olympian Mo Farah.

During this time, I built on the firm foundation of faith Mum had laid in me. When Jokae invited me along to Cornerstone, a small church in Shepherds Bush, I grasped the opportunity to gain my own experience of joining a congregation. There was so much joy in the church that I began going back every week. Through Cornerstone, I became part of an even wider West African community.

I had spent my whole life being the odd one out. Now I had connected with a whole network of people just like me. It was refreshing and stimulating to be among people who were curious and passionate about the same things as me. Through their stories, I began building a fuller picture of Nigeria that was vibrant, layered, complex and fun. I could feel my perspective shifting day by day, as if it were a physical change. As if a seed that had been planted long ago and kept in darkness was now sprouting roots in the sun.

This awakening wasn't always easy. There was often a competitive undercurrent to conversations with other members of the Nigerian diaspora. Until then, I had always been very British in my mind-set, the girl that played for England. Lots of people didn't understand why I was so late in connecting with my roots. But I never let it bother me, I resisted being put in a box. I knew already that having both identities only enriched me, made me more interesting.

My first year at university flew by in this way. I was blossoming, in awe of the people around me and the things I could learn from them. I often sat until the early hours of the morning in the communal kitchen with another halls neighbour, Golnar, who was of Iranian descent but raised in Denmark. Our long conversations, when we always put the world to rights, taught me a lot about global politics.

During the holidays, I did a work placement with the FA legal team. The FA took interest in my studies and word had got around that there was a law student on the women's senior England team. But apart from that, the two worlds rarely met. Student life provided a completely different outlet than football. It was refreshing to have friends outside of that bubble, and to have purpose and energy invested beyond winning trophies or tournaments. At the end of that season, when Charlton missed out on the title and the FA Cup, it didn't affect me so badly. I had another life to focus on; I could throw myself into my assignments, or going out with university friends.

The following year, the juggling act began again in earnest. The work load ramped up at university at the same time as England were battling to qualify for the 2007 World Cup in China. Every camp, every game, meant missing lectures and seminars that I had to scramble to catch up on when I got back. Weirdly enough, as the time pressure increased, I began to do better in my assignments. I found the less time I had, the more efficiently I studied.

I couldn't spend hours in the library reading a legal book back to front, so I had to cut through the material, bring it into sharp focus. I worked out a way of sifting through the stacks of reading to find out what our teachers really wanted us to learn, poring over past papers to figure out the patterns in the material the exams usually tested. As my grades improved, I was encouraged even more. When I ended my second year with a high 2:1, there was no more doubt in my mind: I belonged here, in law school, and I was bright enough to get a good grade. The degree became something I was doing for myself, something I wanted to do as well as possible.

This efficient way of working came into its own in the final year. I was able to boil everything down to the essentials. The same juggling act I'd been negotiating since GCSEs, through A levels, was now a well-practised routine. A large portion of my marks in my final year rested on my dissertation. I chose to write mine on legal regulation of oil firms in Nigeria, an idea that came from a conversation with Kelechi about oil spills and unrest in the Niger delta region. I went to Dad who, having left politics, was now director of political affairs at a multinational oil corporation. He was able to add a lot of valuable background information that impressed my tutors and made for an outstanding paper.

I got a first in my dissertation, which put me on track for a first-class grade in my overall degree before I even sat my final exams. Still, when I logged into the university results portal that summer, and saw it written there in black and white, it didn't quite feel real. I had a first-class qualifying law degree.

I stared at the computer screen for over an hour, reading and rereading the words until they were imprinted in my mind. First class. First class. First Class. This was a sign. I had done better, gone further, than I ever dreamed possible. Now I owed it to myself to take the next steps, to see this path through to the end. Another road, one of legal training contracts and bar exams, stretched out before me.

It had all paid off. All the years of prioritising learning, of juggling school and university with sporting commitments. I had pursued a career, without sacrificing my footballing dream. It hadn't been easy; more than once I had wanted to quit. But reading those words, first class, on the screen, made every commute, every late-night study session, every sacrifice worth it.

I chose education because Nelson Mandela was right when he said it is the most powerful weapon to change the world. It had changed me too. My education didn't just come in the form of lectures and seminars, it came from the people around me, through their perspectives on their own hyphenated identities. I had made friends from all over the world, some of them from places as far-flung as Brunei and Tahiti, places that at one time I would have I struggled to locate on a map. This diverse friendship group had taught me more about the world. They had made me colour-blind. Spending time in their company had made a nonsense of all the stereotypes society attaches to different races. Their friendship moulded and shaped my world view and encouraged me more than ever to appreciate the beauty in our differences. Later, I would draw on everything I had learned at Brunel through these friendships, conversations and perspectives to motivate me in my stand against racism.

And now, using education as my weapon, I had broken out of another of society's limiting moulds. I was now another example that black women could be lawyers as well as international footballers.

Inspiration comes from unexpected places sometimes. My role models, both fictional in the form of Atticus and real in the form of Fola, sent me down a different path when I was least expecting it. I hope my story does the same for others. I was lucky enough to be schooled and go to university in the UK, and I know there are many young people around the world for whom accessing education is much harder than that. But I want to appeal to all of you, whoever and wherever you are: choose education, whatever you can access, however hard that path might be to tread.

To all women, and to black women especially, I want to remind you that education will set you free. Whatever traditional roles others expect you to perform, education is your escape, your freedom. It will give you the tools to dream of a better future. Choose it and you will grasp the most powerful weapon to transform your world, and the world around you.

Class 4:

Find The Freedom Within

The imbalance stung. It wasn't fair; **it was time things** *changed*

I decided I would say something.

CHAPTER TEN

We qualified for our first World Cup in the rain, to the sound of 20,000 fans shouting for the other team. Three minutes before the break, the scoreboard was still blank, and the crowd was hungry for a goal. The clamour peaked as their forwards tested our defence. We were evenly matched; this was a psychological battle. We would need to dig deep.

The French team had the advantage of a home crowd. *Allez les bleus* rang around the stadium, so loud I couldn't hear my teammates on the pitch. I shut out the noise and focused on the ball. The autumn drizzle clung to my clothes and hair as I jogged down the wing, defenders in tow, ready to spin and sprint if a ball broke through.

The chant dropped, and a song drifted faintly down from the top of the stadium. I recognised the tune, strained my ears and picked out the words. *Shall We Sing a Song for You*. Warmth flooded my veins at the sound. A hundred England fans had come to Rennes to support us, among them Mum and Dad. If we qualified tonight, it was for them. If our fans weren't intimidated by this crowd, then neither was I.

The whistle blew for half-time and we filed into the dressing room. Hope was resolute as she reminded us what this match meant. She didn't need to. We all had our hearts set on qualifying for the 2007 World Cup in China, England's first since 1995. Now it was so close, we could almost touch it. We needed a draw; France needed a win. There was no faltering now.

We were confident we could do it. We had come this far unbeaten in our qualifying campaign. Qualifying would send a strong message we weren't the same team that had crashed out of the European Championships the previous summer. Hope had been a player the last time England had qualified for a World Cup, twelve years before. Aged seven, cheering on Manchester United in the 1995 FA Cup final, I hadn't a clue that England women were about to play a World Cup. Back then, very few people knew.

Hope took over as England's first ever full-time coach in 1998. As a player, she had experienced difficult conditions, and told us she once slept on a gym floor ahead of an international fixture. Hope's mission was clear: to push the women's game towards professionalisation. She had already taken great strides. National youth teams had brought through a generation of players with experience of international tournaments, me among them. More regular training had improved overall fitness levels, and all teams were now playing more fixtures. Getting Misia, England's first-ever psychologist, was Hope's latest triumph.

Standards were rising, but there was a long way to go. Even at the highest levels, women's football in the UK was semi-professional, with woeful finances to match. The game desperately needed investment. Qualifying for the World Cup would send the message, to the fans, to the FA, and to the TV executives, that women's football was worth investing in. Everything rested on this match. Hope had put the expectation on our shoulders, and we all felt the pressure. Personally, I had barely slept in a week.

The game had a long way to go, and so did I. As a player, I wasn't yet mature enough to shoulder that kind of pressure and convert it into results. Yet I was on the verge of a revelation. Events were about to be set in motion that would teach me one of the biggest lessons of my footballing career. I would learn how to perform under pressure, how to let go of expectation and crippling doubts, and how to conjure the sense of freedom I felt playing as a child. I would grow into the kind of striker who could turn games around, who could score, over and over, with a clear and free mind. I was good, but I wasn't there yet.

Adrenalin surged in my legs as I sought for chances back out on the pitch in France. Twenty minutes into the second half, forward Rachel Yankey won a free kick, and sent it sailing in towards the goal. Fara rose to meet it, a French player got there first, and the ball deflected into the net for an own goal. The pressure released. I ran to the corner flag with the others to pile on to Rachel. High above us, the England fans yelled and jumped. Clambering to my feet, I looked at Hope on the sideline. She motioned downwards with both hands: calm down. I nodded and jogged back into position. She was right, it was too early to celebrate.

The French came back hard. Veteran striker Marinette Pichon launched repeated attacks, but Anita, solid as ever, stayed cool and fought them off. We had our goal, the minutes ticked down, and I dared to hope for a win.

But it was too soon. France equalised in the final minute. I stood, stunned, staring at the celebrating French players. I couldn't believe it. We were back to square one. Now we had three minutes of stoppage time to play the whole game again. They needed a win; we needed a draw. They needed another goal; we had to deny them. We had everything to lose.

I sought frantically for space as, at the other end, our backline dug in. It felt risky to go too far forward and leave space for France to attack. Our nerves were frayed, and France were desperate. With less than a minute to go, I ran on to a promising through ball and the French keeper fluffed her footwork. I connected well, but my shot hit the post. Seconds later, the final whistle blew. I yelled in relief, and filled with sudden elation, ran to meet my teammates in the centre circle. We had our draw; we were going to China.

I spun around and bellowed up at our fans on the top stand. Tears pricked my eyes as I hugged my teammates. I ran to the bench, where Mum and Dad had come down from their seats six rows up to congratulate me. I hugged Mum tight as a photographer captured the moment, a photo that counts among the most emotional of my career.

'Well done,' said Mum, and grinned. 'China here we come.'

The relief, the release, was dizzying. Behind us, Hope beamed and shook hands with top FA officials. Her moment had come. We had broken through the ceiling of their expectations, proved ourselves good enough to face the world's best. Now we would be taken seriously.

I was on cloud nine. I didn't come down for days. I wandered around in a hazy high; throat sore from yelling, cheeks aching from grinning. I was wildly confident about our chances in the World Cup. There were another nine months to go until China. If we worked hard, we could really make an impact. There was no telling how far we could go. We might even surprise a few people.

A reality check came the next month in the form of a friendly against world champions Germany. They brought us crashing down to earth with a humbling 5–1 defeat, breaking our eighteen-month unbeaten run. It was a cruel shock, and we all had a hard time coming to terms with the loss. Hope said that from now on, there were no more friendlies. We would take every game as if it were the World Cup itself.

We met Germany again three months later, at the Four Nations tournament in China. The fixture was perfect practice for the big stage: a ten-day competition with games in quick succession against three of the world's best teams, China, Germany and USA. Playing in China would also give us a taste of the conditions we'd face in the World Cup later that year. In a word, conditions were terrible.

Our minuscule travel budget didn't help. We reached Guangzhou, a port city to the north of Hong Kong, a full twenty-six hours after leaving London. We checked into a grim hotel that backed on to the Guangzhou Olympic stadium. It was freezing, with poor hygiene. We were told to drink only bottled water and to slather our hands in antibacterial gel every five minutes. We had our temperature taken daily to detect infection and our breathing analysed to see how we were coping with the pollution.

By far the worst thing was the food. Everything was deep fried, or worse, unidentifiable and alien-looking. The hotel's attempts at Western food were, if anything, even more suspect. Breakfast was green eggs and cold leftovers from the night before. I stuck strictly to white rice most of the time. Once or twice, we even snuck out in the evening to a nearby McDonald's. That was all I saw of China on my first visit. There was no time to go sightseeing. We were there to play. And we played well. Despite the pollution, cold, and terrible food, we managed draws against both Germany and the USA, our best-ever results against the world's top players. We came home, more quietly confident than ever.

Still, I was relieved to leave China and get back to my student life in London. I threw myself into catching up on the second-year seminars I'd missed and juggling the usual back and forth to training. Charlton were having another decent run and we were battling Everton for second place. But there was no challenging Arsenal's dominance. They ended the season unbeaten, slaughtering us 9–2 along the way. They picked up the League Cup and became the first English club to win the European Cup, now the Champions League. Facing them in the FA Cup final in May, we were all that stood between them and an unprecedented quadruple.

We gave it our best shot and went one up in the first five minutes. But our lead was short-lived. Four minutes later, Arsenal striker Kelly Smith, at that time without doubt England's greatest player, curled a free kick in past our keeper Pauline Cope's outstretched hands from twenty-five yards. This side was unstoppable. We let in another four before the final whistle.

One positive could be salvaged from the day: the final drew a record crowd of 25,000 fans to Nottingham Forest, a 200 per cent increase over our win against Everton two years before. The fan base was swelling, and with it the argument to put the biggest game of the year on to a more fitting stage. Afterwards, both teams' managers called for the women's FA Cup final to be played in the grandeur of Wembley Stadium, like the men's event.

But for every step forward there was a lurch backwards. The night before our FA Cup final, Charlton's men's team lost a rollercoaster battle against relegation from the Premier League. If anyone saw the writing on the wall for the women's club right away, they didn't tell us. I was already home in Birmingham for the holidays in late June when I got a call from Keith.

He didn't mince his words. 'The club is shutting down our team.'

His voice sounded flat.

'But that makes no sense,' I blurted. 'They can't shut us down. We just played the FA Cup final.'

Keith sighed. 'I know,' he said. 'I'm devastated too. But it's the relegation. We can't get the funding to keep going.'

'But that's outrageous,' I said, panic rising in my chest. 'There has to be a way.'

'I'm sorry, Eni,' said Keith, sounding tired and resigned. 'The money isn't there. You'll be fine. Remember, we're family. Whatever you need, you let me know.'

Keith rang off and I was left reeling, gazing at my phone. The shock quickly turned to annoyance. All those years of dedication and commitment. All those weeks of busting a gut to get to training, of investing hard in the club's success, and the board hadn't even called a meeting to tell us the news to our faces. I felt bad for Keith, having to inform the players one by one, his grim last duty as manager. He had lost his job too, along with all his staff, right down to the youth academy coaches. It was all gone, the centre of excellence for the preteen players, the girls' academy, all of it. After seven years, one of England's most successful women's clubs had been abandoned, overnight, with no warning.

Our achievements meant little when things got tight for the club. Winning the FA Cup, reaching the final, and three League Cup finals, years of consistently challenging for the title. None of it mattered. It was the men that had failed, but their pay cheques would keep coming. The money wasn't there for the women, no matter what we did to raise the club's name. We were unnecessary extras, second thoughts, first in line to be cut. It felt miserable.

It also presented a practical problem. Suddenly, for the first time in six years, I was without a club. The new season was about to begin, and the World Cup was looming. It was a few days before a path opened up. I got a call from Chelsea manager Shaun Gore, saying he wanted to sign me.

Transferring to Chelsea seemed like a neat solution. Here was an ambitious, London-based club with a big name, and the commitment to the women's side seemed steady. Chelsea had finished that season, their second in the top flight, in eighth place, and they were clearly hungry to grow. I would be able to come in and make a difference straight away to their attack. There was a home there for good players. Shaun said he was also approaching my former Charlton captain and England teammate Casey Stoney. It didn't take me long to make my decision. Charlton folding had been a shock. I was glad to find a new home as soon as possible.

A month later, Charlton announced it had raised the money to save the women's club, but it was too little, too late. Trust and confidence in the club were at rock bottom. Almost all the senior players had left over the summer, and Keith was also gone for good. The women's team crashed out of the National Division at the end of that season. It was a sad end to what had been.

I tried to forget about Charlton and focus on the World Cup. Hope wanted us to be the fittest we had ever been, and had us on gruelling, twice-daily training sessions to increase our aerobic capacity, power and stamina. Back then, the whole team trained in the same way. It was only later that individually tailored training programmes came in. Speed, a focus for some players, wasn't an issue for me. I was a sprinter, a fast-twitch player, and I knew no amount of training was going to make me into a long-distance endurance runner. Still, this was the World Cup, and I gave it everything I had.

Hope said fitness would be the key to our success. Our unbeaten run during qualification had shown we could compete with the best, but skill alone wasn't enough. Skilful teams that weren't fit could still lose games in the last fifteen minutes of the match. But as our fitness levels peaked, a quiet confidence grew in the team. We were the underdogs, the dark horses that could surprise. Press interest was growing, and Hope reminded us to keep our heads. It was more attention than we were used to, and we all felt the pressure building. Here was a chance to raise the profile of our game in the UK, a chance to show how far we had come.

The squad was strong. Hope's intense fitness programme had got us in the best shape we had ever been. The team's big star, Kelly Smith, was on top form for her first World Cup. From Arsenal we had right back Alex Scott, as well as Kaz Carney and defender Anita. Another young striker, Lianne Sanderson, was celebrating her first England call-up and brought additional creative ability to our attack. Defender Mary Phillip, the only team member to have played in England's last World Cup, ensured we had solid experience on our side.

We flew out to Macau in mid-August, three weeks ahead of the tournament, to get used to the Chinese climate: a nightmare combination of heat, humidity and pollution. It took me a few days to adjust: at one training session I couldn't breathe; at another I got heatstroke. It was my own fault. I didn't hydrate properly, an oversight teammates still tease me about now.

Though the climactic conditions were tough, this trip was much easier than our last in China. Macau was particularly luxurious. The city, sometimes likened to a Chinese Vegas, oozed opulence and bling. We stayed in a five-star hotel with a golf range on the roof top. The Manchester United men's team had stayed in it the previous year, and we figured what was good enough for them was good enough for us. On one of our days off, I went with Lianne to a casino in our hotel complex. I'd never set foot in a casino before and Lianne had to teach me how to play roulette. From twenty dollars' worth of chips we won a jackpot of $250. Call it beginner's luck.

We moved to Shanghai ahead of our first group game. We were staying with several other teams in a hotel that backed on to the Hongkou stadium. This time, we were travelling with a team chef who took over the hotel kitchen. It was a crucial addition and meant we could all concentrate on delivering our best performance on the pitch.

All focus was on our first game against Japan. It was seeing my name on the starting eleven that really rammed home what was happening. I hadn't expected to start. Aged twenty, I already had twenty-six caps for England, but I hadn't yet considered myself a core player. I checked the list again and took a deep breath. I was about to play in a World Cup, in an England shirt, with a number 9 on my back. It was more than I'd ever dreamed possible.

My nerves were still jangling as I stepped out on to the pitch. On the halfway line, waiting for kick off, my shoulders felt heavy. I was a striker; it was my job to score. I thought of Hope, the coaching staff, the players on the pitch and on the bench. I thought of the fans who had come so far to be with us in the stadium. Among them Mum and Dad, who had flown all the way to China to watch me play. Every one of them was expecting me to deliver goals, to get it done for the team. There was a lot to live up to.

Kelly took the lead. She got her first shot fifteen minutes in, but it ran wide past the near post. My first chance came minutes later. Kelly broke away down the middle and, as she drew the defence, I ran on to her through ball. The defenders hesitated, but I fired my shot straight at the keeper's arms. I was mortified to hear a sigh of disappointment from the crowd. I told myself I wouldn't let it get to me. I would try again, get the next chance.

The opportunity came soon enough. A space opened suddenly on the right, and Kelly sent a lofted through ball. The keeper sprinted off her line, but I leapt over her, and the noise from the crowd swelled as I found myself in front of an open goal. Shocked to get such an easy chance, I fired a fraction too early. It was a tight angle and it went wide. I was unnerved, my composure was shot through. I couldn't fail again in front of all these people. I hung back, avoided the ball whenever Kelly and the others attacked. It wasn't a conscious decision, it was instinctive. If I wasn't in the position to score, I couldn't miss.

Japan's set-piece specialist Aya Miyama scored from a free kick ten minutes into the second half. I tried to pull myself together, told myself we hadn't lost yet, that it wasn't over. I knew we all had to try and turn things around, but I was still hanging back. When Alex Scott played a low ball across goal, I hesitated at the far post. By the time the ball reached me the angle was too tight. I got my shot away, but it deflected off a defender and looped over the bar. The disappointment descended again.

My self-belief was draining away, and Hope could tell. She took me off, and I watched from the bench as Kelly scored two goals in the last ten minutes to turn the game around. Kelly took off her shoe, kissed it and held it up to celebrate her first World Cup goal, an image that still resonates with players around the world. I stared at her in awe. She had turned the game upside down. I had some distance to go before I could do that under pressure.

Sadly, Japan had their own Kelly. With the last kick of the game, Miyama fired in another rocket free kick and ripped away our three points. We were gutted. The final score was 2–2, but we should have won, and part of that was on me. I often think back to my first World Cup appearance and wonder why I was unable to put those chances away. Perhaps, when the moment came, I just didn't have enough composure.

Hope kept me on the bench for the next game against Germany. The defending world champions had dispatched Argentina 11–0 in their opening match, but I watched with pride as Anita and our defence held them to a goalless draw. Germany went on to win the Cup without conceding once. We were the only team along the way to keep them out.

We flew to Chengdu for our final group game against Argentina. I was starting in place of Kaz. We took an early lead through an own goal, and the floodgates opened. But even as goal after goal flew in, none of my shots found the net. It didn't matter, we won 6–1 and made it out of the group on a high.

I kept my place for the quarter-final against USA. We knew our chances were slim; this team was second in the world only to Germany. Still, we could always dream. Sometimes one stray goal was all it took. It wasn't to be. As I struggled through the first half, so isolated from the midfield that I barely touched the ball, I realised just how good USA were. A tactical change saw me subbed off at half-time, and I watched as they crushed us with three goals in twelve minutes.

At the final whistle, Hope was philosophical. We had fought a brave campaign and held our own against the world's best teams. The World Cup was a wonderful experience, and another significant step in all our international careers. Reaching the quarter-final was respectable, and we were proud to have held Germany to a 0–0 draw.

Back in the UK, the pressure remained high. I was now in my final year at university, working hard towards what would become my greatest off-field achievement: my first class honours. Some of the other England players who weren't at university had it tougher. I didn't envy those who went straight from the World Cup back into juggling full-time jobs and looking after young children. The older players with mortgages had to take on extra work to fulfil their responsibilities.

The truth was we were all losing money playing for England. We were paid £400 per camp, or £800 for anything over ten days. It was a sporadic source of income; players who weren't called to camp got nothing at all and the FA gave us no contracts or per-match payments. For tournaments such as the World Cup, we got a reduced rate of forty pounds a day as we were together for longer. After five weeks' intensive work in China, we got a grand total of £1,400. Some players had to take unpaid leave to go to China, so they missed out on a month's salary. That was just the way it was. None of us dreamt of turning down the opportunity; representing England at a World Cup was a great honour. But everyone sacrificed something financially.

Fitness levels were down at the next England camp, and Hope was disappointed. A five-minute conversation with any of the players would have explained the reason why. Anyone would struggle to work overtime and look after a family while keeping up that kind of intense training schedule. England couldn't have it both ways. If they wanted us to maintain pro fitness, we needed pro salaries. The imbalance stung. It wasn't fair; it was time things changed. Something had to be done, especially now after we had been to a World Cup.

I decided I would say something. As a regular spokesperson for the team, I was often asked to do media interviews by the press officer, and I felt comfortable speaking on behalf of the team. Given the opportunity to speak to the BBC, I said that England players were losing money, that we felt undervalued and we needed more financial support. I made it clear we weren't demanding the kind of money paid out to the men in sponsorship deals.

We wanted a stipend, a central contract, like female players got in the USA. Otherwise, we would have to continue to work full-time to survive, and our fitness would suffer. Things needed to improve, I said. Pay us better, and standards would rise, it was a simple investment. Besides, players with one of the richest footballing bodies in the world shouldn't have to choose between full-time work and playing for England. We needed more certainty, more stability. We needed a wage.

The interview worked, everyone sat up and listened. My fellow players were grateful that finally I had said what we were all thinking. Many people were shocked at the low pay we were expected to get by on, and no one at the FA wanted any hint of embarrassment. It helped that I'd always been on good terms with the FA. That year, I had been made an ambassador in their 'Football for All' scheme. There was some push-back at first. The women's game was making progress, the argument went, but it wasn't lucrative enough yet to pay England players.

But ultimately, the FA wanted standards to rise, and, after a lot of lobbying on our behalf by Hope, among others, they eventually came around. In May 2009, almost exactly eighteen months to the day after my interview with the BBC, the FA announced it had signed contracts with seventeen England players worth £16,000 a year. In return, the players agreed to cut down other work to a part-time basis and to make themselves available for every game, training session or camp. It wasn't a huge amount of money, but at the time it was one of Europe's most generous deals for female players. We were all in no doubt. It was a massive step forward for the women's game in the UK.

CHAPTER ELEVEN

The call from America came out of the blue. Mum said it was sent from God, and I agreed. It made sense, we had both been praying for a way forward. The summer after the World Cup, I reached a crossroads. I graduated from Brunel and moved into an apartment in Isleworth, west London, that Mum had bought as an investment while I worked out my next step.

I knew what I wanted. The logical move was a training contract, a two-year practical placement at a law firm, but they were incredibly hard to come by. Competition for places was unbelievable. I must have sent out fifty applications in the last months of my final year. It's standard for law firms to send out automatic rejections by the sack load. They landed on the doormat every morning, regretting to inform me, and promising to keep my application on file for future reference. I didn't even see most of them. Mum didn't want me to get disheartened, so she kept them out of sight. This went on for a few months, until it got to the point where we began to discuss alternative options. It was looking like I would have to wait and apply again next year.

The timing was terrible. I was also facing what felt like a dead end in football. I wasn't happy at Chelsea. The set-up was mediocre, nobody was taking the women's team seriously, and I didn't like the blasé attitude of the coaching staff. After the World Cup, one Chelsea coach told a teammate of mine during a game that I would never make it as a professional footballer in another league. I wanted to prove him wrong, but there was nowhere left to go in semi-professional football, even if I put my career on hold. Football had lost its sparkle, and I was near ready to quit.

Then I got the call, and everything changed. It came one autumn evening, as I was driving up to Birmingham to see my family. I put the phone on speaker, and a deep, American voice boomed through the car stereo.

'My name is Jeff Cooper,' the voice announced in a slight southern twang. 'I'm the owner of a new professional women's soccer team in St Louis, Missouri.

'We're starting a new professional league here in the spring,' Jeff went on. 'We saw you play at the World Cup in China, and we love your profile. We want to draft you. Are you interested in playing with us?'

I drew breath and gripped the steering wheel. It was so unexpected. I thought for a second. Did I want to move to the States? Scenes of New York and Washington flitted through my head. I smiled.

'Yes,' I said. 'Of course, I'm interested.'

Jeff chuckled. 'Good. We'd need you over here early next year. Is there anything keeping you in England?'

I hesitated.

'Well,' I said. 'I recently graduated from law school. I've been looking for a training contract. If something comes through, I'll have to think again.'

Jeff didn't miss a beat.

'Oh, that's no problem,' he said. 'I'm a partner in a law firm. We have an affiliate in London, in the City. You can play in St Louis, and work in the firm during the off season.'

I caught my breath again. This one phone call had solved all my problems. This stranger was offering to pay me to play professional football, and in the down time, to give me solid practical experience in a law firm. It was almost too good to be true. Suddenly all the rejections from law firms made sense. I had been rejected because that wasn't my destined path at that time. Jeff's offer was a one-off, a unique opportunity to enter the parallel roads of football and law.

'That sounds perfect,' I said. 'Thank you.'

'Well, all right then,' he said. 'I'll be in touch with more details.'

Jeff rang off, and I called Mum right away. I was about to see her in less than an hour, but this couldn't wait. She had to know, now. I knew she was concerned about my next step, and here was the answer. I still couldn't believe my luck, pro football, combined with experience in a law firm. It was a dream combination. When I told Mum, I could hear the relief in her voice.

'Oh, what a blessing,' she said down the line. 'This is God's work. He has a plan for you in America.'

The US had a history of promoting professional women's football, and this was the second attempt at a fully professional women's league. The last, set up in 2000, had run three seasons before folding. Clubs blamed overspending, low match turnout and disappointing TV ratings. Yet many still believed the American sports system was able to offer professional women's football a home. And wealthy investors like Jeff were willing to give it another try.

The new league, Women's Professional Soccer, or WPS, would start with seven teams. Alongside St Louis, there would be clubs in Boston, the San Francisco Bay Area, Chicago, Los Angeles, New Jersey and Washington DC. The new clubs had scoured the globe for players and, with the offer of real money, had poached the world's best player, Marta, and half her Brazilian teammates. From England, they had lured me and four others: Kelly, Alex, Anita and Kaz.

The league would play a summer season, from April to August, with playoffs to decide the title. With another few months until I was needed in St Louis, I began working at Jeff's London affiliate, SC Andrew, a boutique litigation firm in Holborn. The partners there gave me an idea. While playing in St Louis, I could aim to qualify as a lawyer in the US. Once I was licensed in Britain too, I would be well placed to work in practices on both sides of the Atlantic. A new plan opened up before me. It was all fitting into place.

I got started right away, studying remotely for the New York bar exam. It was like starting from scratch. I had to know the US constitution and the New York state laws inside out. It was harder than studying law in England, where I had only needed to know common law, which applied to the rest of the country. In America, there were differences between law specific to New York and federal law applying to the rest of the United States. I was advised to attend a study group, but I decided it would be easier to fit my studies around my other work if I learned alone. The exam was a two-day ordeal at an assessment centre in Buffalo, New York. I took it in February, a day after my twenty-second birthday. It would turn out to be the hardest exam I've ever done.

I opened the exam paper and stared blankly at the questions. I had no idea how to answer any of them. I put my pen down, defeated, and sat out the rest of the exam, miserably trying to block out the scribbling of the other students. I told myself it was my own fault. It had been arrogant of me to insist on doing the course long distance and not to join a study group.

I was already in St Louis by the time I got my results in early May. I wasn't surprised to hear that I had failed. The pass rate was low, but that was no excuse. I hadn't approached the exam in the right way. I was determined to set things right, and I vowed to try again next year. Until then, I would put law to one side. For the next seven months I was to become a full-time footballer.

I moved to St Louis that spring, ahead of the new league's inaugural season. The city wasn't the most glamorous place. The downtown district sprawled along the Mississippi river, dominated by a gigantic gateway arch looming over the skyline. Beyond that, there wasn't a lot more to see. It didn't matter. I was just happy to be there to play.

For the first time in my life, I was getting paid to focus full-time on football, around $35,000 for the seven-month season. In the off season, I would receive a £20,000 salary from Jeff's firm SC Andrew. Then, on top of that, my then agent, Khaled, told me I would get an additional bonus from Nike for a boot sponsorship deal. I was almost embarrassed. At university I had lived off my Chelsea salary of £100 a week, plus £200 a month pocket money, which Mum sent regularly to avoid me having to rely on a student loan. It felt like a huge financial jump, commensurate to law school friends now on a £60,000 starting salary with magic circle law firms. It was a blessing, and my new reality.

However, my US contract meant I wasn't eligible for one of the new England central contracts, which were only for UK-based players. One downside was that my agreement was with the WPS league, not with St Louis. It's normal in American sports for a player's contract to be owned centrally by the league, and not the clubs. But it was completely alien to me. I had to get used to the possibility I could be traded between clubs without being given any choice. It was a terrifying prospect. I didn't want to get traded against my will, like a pawn. I'd have to make myself indispensable at St Louis. I'd have to hit the ground running.

Competition was stiff. St Louis Athletica had drafted some of the world's top footballers. From the US national

'Harper Lee's *To Kill a Mockingbird* was one of my set texts for English literature at school and I was drawn to the attorney at the centre of the story.

If I wanted to be a lawyer, like Atticus, I would need to knuckle down.'

FOR BEHAVING WELL

Awarded to

Eniola Aluko

For

~~proper behaviour~~ and a

~~brilliant~~ attitude in school.

At

Broadmeadow Junior

Signed

Mr. Storey

Date

3.3.97

**The girls on the estate weren't interested in what the boys were playing.
And I wasn't into whatever it was they were doing.**

I only wanted to play football, and that made me one of the lads.

It hadn't been easy; more than once I had wanted to quit. But reading those words, first class, made every commute, every late night study session, every sacrifice worth it.

I lifted my arms in victory and ran into the centre circle. My teammates piled into me, whooping and yelling. I couldn't believe it. We had won the Cup. I had scored the winner in the Cup final.

I still couldn't
believe my luck,
pro football,
combined with
experience in a
law firm. It was
a dream
combination.
When I told Mum,
I could hear the
relief in her voice.
'Oh, what a
blessing,' she said
down the line.
'This is God's work.
He has a plan for
you in America.'

I collected my first senior cap for England, at a friendly away to Holland. As hosts, England had qualified automatically for Euro 2005, but in the build-up to the tournament, the pressure was still on for me. At seventeen, I was one of the senior team's youngest-ever debutantes, and

I had a lot to prove if I was going to earn a place on the final squad.

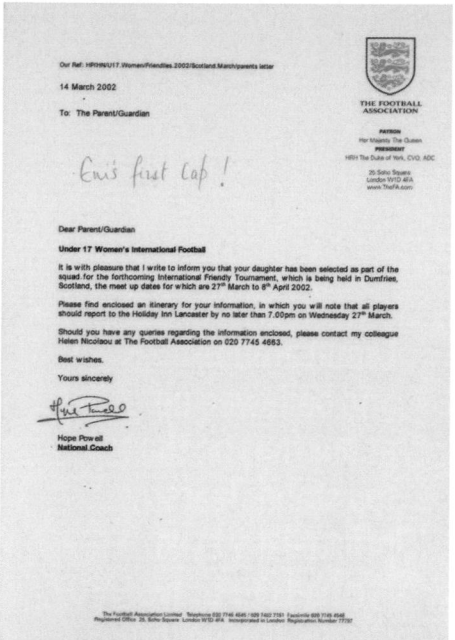

FRANCE
v
ENGLAND
30·09·2006

I spun around
and bellowed up
at our fans on the
top stand. Tears
pricked my eyes.
We had our draw.
We were going to
the World Cup.

team we had defender Tina Ellertson, midfielder Lori Chalupny, and Hope Solo, the world's number one goalkeeper. Athletica's biggest star was Brazilian midfielder Daniela. She had moved to St Louis together with her national team coach, Jorge Barcellos, considered one of the world's best. He had coached Marta and had taken his team to the World Cup final against Germany. I was excited to learn from them all.

Jorge was a serious man, with thick eyebrows and a forehead creased with frown lines. I could tell right away there would be no second chances, no excuses, no slack from Jorge. I would have to get it right first time. But there was a catch. Jorge's English was as non-existent as my Portuguese. In training, he spoke to us via an interpreter named Carlos who seemed frustratingly selective about what he translated. Minutes' worth of valuable advice and instruction from Jorge came out as only a few sentences in English. It left me constantly worried I'd missed something vital.

Our first game was at home against Kaz's new team, the Chicago Red Stars, in front of a sell-out crowd. Our temporary ground was on the campus of St Louis's Southern Illinois University Edwardsville. It was small; the club had added extra stands to extend capacity from three to five thousand. But this was my first match as a professional and it felt like a World Cup game. We went one down, and though I tried as hard as I could to create chances, the equaliser didn't come. We lost 1–0.

Next, we played Kelly and Alex Scott's new team, the Boston Breakers. I was subbed off at half-time, just before Kelly scored the first of two goals against us. We lost 2–0. Two games in, St Louis Athletica were stuck at the bottom of the table, the only club that hadn't scored. Jorge was stern and direct with us. He had high expectations, and we weren't delivering. I had a job to do, he said, I was a striker, I scored goals. It was frustrating: I was scoring in training and was confident going into games, but Jorge wanted me to do the same in matches. I couldn't understand what was going wrong. In the back of my mind, I started to worry that if I didn't score soon, I'd be traded to another club. This was pro football. It was sink or swim. With every game I felt I was having to swim harder against the tide.

We played Los Angeles Sol a fortnight later. This was Marta's team, but she was away playing for Brazil. Jorge told us this was our chance. We kept them from scoring, but we missed a penalty and were disappointed to only come away with a goalless draw. We still hadn't scored. A month into the season, we were rooted to the bottom of the table and people were beginning to write us off. We were a good team, there was no reason why we weren't winning games. The prospect of being traded in for a more prolific striker haunted me every day. It loomed over my head in training like a threatening rain cloud.

A few days after the LA game, at the end of a long, frustrating stint of shooting practice, Jorge beckoned to me. He stood, arms folded, on the sideline next to his interpreter, Carlos. My stomach clenched with nerves as I jogged over. Game after game had gone by, and I hadn't done my job. I hadn't scored. I had failed so soon. Jorge fixed me with his serious gaze and sighed.

'You don't look like you are enjoying yourself when you play,' Jorge said, via Carlos.

A lump formed in my throat. I stared at the ground, struggling to speak.

'No,' I said, still not meeting his eye. 'I'm not really.'

'So, what's the problem?' said Jorge. 'Why aren't you having a good time?'

The question surprised me. This was a job; I hadn't been expecting to enjoy it. Football hadn't been fun in a long time. I thought back through my near misses at the World Cup, through the games with Chelsea, back to Charlton folding. Maybe the last time I'd had fun playing football was winning the FA Cup final four years ago with Charlton. Or maybe even earlier, playing for Birmingham under Marcus. Something had been lost since then. Something was missing. That was it, I had put myself in a cage.

'I used to feel free when I played,' I said, looking at him. 'Now I feel like I'm stuck. Maybe I'm thinking too much.'

The interpreter translated this for Jorge, and his frown relaxed.

'Ah,' he said. 'Then, think back for me. When did you last feel truly free?'

I smiled. That was easy.

'When I was a kid, growing up on the estate,' I said. 'Playing with the local kids and my little brother.'

Jorge nodded.

'That's where you must get back to in your head,' he said. 'Put your mind back in that place when you are playing. Remember how free and easy it felt then. You believed it was easy, didn't you? You always believed you could score. You believed you were the best player on the pitch. You need to do that again.'

I stared at him. He made it sound so easy. Believe, and it would happen.

'OK,' I said. 'You're right. I need to go back to that carefree place. I'll try my best.'

I lay in bed that night, waiting for sleep to come, with Jorge's words rumbling around my head. To play good football, I had to feel free. To feel free, I had to conjure the joy I'd felt playing street football as a kid. If I could summon that feeling on the pitch, maybe I could shake off the paralysing fear of failure. Maybe then I could grow into the kind of player who could be relied on to turn games around. It was a strange paradox. I had to free myself in order to shoulder the responsibility; to deliver goals, I had to forget the pressure to score.

Our next game was away, against Washington Freedom. The irony of our opponent's name wasn't lost on me. Freedom was what I had been seeking, striving for, all week. Now we were going to take on the Freedom in their own backyard. This was my chance to put Jorge's guidance into practice. All I had to do was play free of expectation, for the joy of it, like a child. I told myself that even if I slipped up and made a mistake, I would keep seeking possession, and bravely take on defenders one-on-one, just like I used to as a kid. It worked like magic. Stepping out on to the pitch in the early summer rain, I told myself I wasn't in Washington, I was on a grassy slope off the Redditch Road in Birmingham. And I was about to fight, not because it was my job, but because I wanted to.

Daniela scored a solo goal seven minutes in. It electrified me, as if a spark had caught in the drizzle. St Louis Athletica had scored, we were free. Washington equalised, but Daniela regained our lead before half-time.

We came out slipping and sliding after the break. The rain turned the field to slush. I blinked and wiped the water out of my eyes. I was enjoying myself. Daniela and I began working fluidly, in tandem. I believed I would score; it was only a matter of time.

My chance came. A through ball unlocked the defence and sent me on a race to reach it before the centre back. I set off at a sprint, knowing I would get there first. I found the ball and, as the defender came sliding in from the right, I shot past the keeper and slammed the ball into the far corner. I screamed and clenched my fists. I ran to Jorge, grinning on the sideline, and gave him a hug. Relief washed over me; Jorge had been right. Nothing mattered apart from the ball, the rain-soaked grass, and the thrill of the game.

The goal shattered the barrier in my head. With one strike, I had smashed through the wall that was stopping me performing to the level I knew I could. In that moment, the wall of tension, over-thinking and self-sabotage came tumbling down. I was free, to let go and evolve, to step through to the other side and take my game to the next level. A weight rose from my shoulders. I had found it, the freedom within. I was having fun; I was playing with the kids on the estate. It was like Jorge had opened a window in my mind.

We drew with Washington 3–3, but not before Daniela was stretchered off with a season-ending knee injury. With her out of action, I had to take on a more prominent role, but I was careful not to get weighed down. During games, there was no duty. I banished all thoughts of responsibility from the pitch and we began to rise sharply up the league. We got our first win the following week against California's Gold Pride. Then, the week after that, we faced Chicago again, this time at their home ground. Nerves were high, we were missing our keeper, Hope Solo, who was away on national duty. Her stand in, Jillian Loyden, would have to stand firm against both Kaz and Brazilian striker Cristiane. We needn't have worried.

I surged forward twenty-five minutes in, hoping to force the keeper into a dangerous position. I sent the ball across the goalmouth and it deflected off a defender, looped over the keeper and into the net, an own goal. As I celebrated, I realised I hadn't thought or felt anything during the whole sequence. Instinct had taken over. Then, before the break, I ran on to a midfielder's cross and powered in a shot from ten metres out. I connected with the ball not doubting I would score. We won the game 2–0, and both goals had been down to me. I was buzzing.

After the game, Chicago manager Emma Hayes came up to congratulate me on my performance. She was

British, from London, and before moving to Chicago had been assistant coach at Arsenal during their historic quadruple-winning season. She had a warmth and comforting strength that I was drawn to straight away. I was impressed a manager would think to congratulate an opposing team's striker. After that, Emma and I always chatted whenever our paths crossed in the league. She would encourage me, and make sure I was getting on all right. I thought back to this trait years later, when Emma enticed me to play for her at Chelsea.

My game was growing by the day. Jorge said every player had a battle to fight, and now I knew mine was psychological. I had always relied on my natural gifts: my speed and dribbling skill. But this was pro football, and I was playing against the best defenders in the world. Now it was mental strength that made the difference. The more I released the pressure in my mind, the more I scored and enjoyed playing. In mid-June, we played the Boston Breakers again. I wasn't fazed, even against Kelly, and I scored the winning goal, my third in four games. The league named me player of the week, and the win shot us into second place.

We ended the season there, behind Marta's Los Angeles Sol. We had a spot in the final playoffs, but I had to miss them. The league's deciding games clashed with the 2009 European Championships in Finland, and Hope had picked me for the squad. I was now St Louis's top scorer, and Jorge was worrying what he would do without me. I'd become what the Americans call the Most Valuable Player, or MVP. It was a full transformation. Over the course of one season, I'd grown into a new skin and adopted a new mentality.

On the plane to Helsinki for the Euros, I could hardly sit still. I felt like a brand-new player. I was ready to put everything I'd learned at St Louis into practice. Jorge had helped me win a mental battle with myself, I was ready to be the striker England needed. I knew I could score, again and again. I was convinced anything was possible: I could win the Golden Boot, we could reach the final. I would help our England team get the recognition it deserved. I was bursting with positivity. Only five games stood between us and the final. All we had to do was take them one at a time.

Our optimism was dampened when we lost our first game against Italy, and a grim silence reigned on the team bus back to Helsinki. The loss piled on the pressure for our second match against Russia. Another loss would mean crashing out of the tournament at the bottom of the group, but somehow I didn't believe that was how it was going to play out. Staring out of the window, I relived the journey I'd taken at St Louis. I was ready to shoulder the responsibility for my team; I only needed the chance to show it.

Disaster loomed early in our clash with Russia. They put away a goal in the first two minutes, and a second twenty minutes later. I pushed the gloom away. No, this wasn't happening, we weren't going out now. I was a kid, playing free and easy on the estate. We would win this game, and I would score. I knew I could. When Kaz drilled home our first goal minutes later, it was the boost we all needed.

Then, Kaz sent me a ball into a space on the right of the box. It was a tight angle, but I timed my run perfectly. I shot the ball past the keeper and into the net. I clenched my fists and ran back to the centre circle. I had equalised, brought the team out of danger, and the familiar buzz filled my veins. There was still more work to do. Kelly hit the winner before the break, stopping the keeper's drop kick at the centre circle and belting a long-distance volley back into the net. Russia fought down to the wire, but we held on to our 3–2 lead. We had come from behind to deal the doubters a decisive blow.

We got the draw we needed against Sweden to make it out of the group. We had even avoided the defending champions Germany in the final eight. Our path to the final was clear. From here on in, every game would be the biggest of our lives. We faced hosts Finland in the quarter-final. Going into the match I felt good. I wouldn't let the home crowd sway me.

My break came fifteen minutes in. Space cleared ahead and Fara sent a ball into my path. I ran on to it, and let the weight fall away. To a striker facing a keeper one-on-one, time can be either a blessing, or a curse. Given too much time, and lacking the confidence to match, it's all too easy to make the wrong decision and miss the chance. But given both, time and self-belief, there can be only one outcome. This time, my mind was clear: I could score, I would score. The keeper ran off her line and I cheekily slotted the ball between her legs and into the far corner. I ran and yelled up at the outnumbered England fans. I had found my place in the game and reinforced my role in the team. This was how it should be. Fara doubled our lead after the break, and then, past the hour mark, Finland got one back. The crowd went mad, sensing a comeback, but I knew otherwise.

I hit back from the restart. I glanced up and traced a path to goal. The Finnish defenders lined up just like the kids had done on the estate. I would take them one at a time. The first challenge came from the left. I slalomed, cut a sharp right, and the defender skidded on to her knees. I dodged as another came in from the right and sprinted on. A third defender charged in for a last-ditch tackle and I dropped my shoulder and dribbled around her into the box. My mind was quiet as I struck the ball, willing it in. The keeper dived, and the ball flew in past her outstretched fingers into the top-right corner of the net.

The adrenalin surged, and the buzz rose in my chest. I spread my hands in celebration and shrugged as if to say, how did that happen? Kelly ran to me to join my celebration.

'Wow, Eni, what a goal,' she said, beaming wide.

I could hardly believe it myself. I had beaten three defenders and the keeper in a lone slalom run. It was the stuff of dreams. It was proof I was ready to play the way I was born to play. I spent the rest of the game in a hazy joy. Urged on by a deafening home crowd, Finland headed in another corner ten minutes before time. But we clung on. At the final whistle, I ran into the circle and flung my arms around my teammates, drinking in their praise. That second goal remains among the greatest of my career. It was no coincidence that it came at the end of the season where I had learned to find the freedom within me. On that run against Finland, I felt truly free at last, like I was flying.

We had knocked out the hosts, but now we were in unchartered waters. England had never made it past the quarter-finals of any major tournament. In the semis, we faced Holland. The side was known for digging in and stifling opponents and they put two defenders on Kelly. It took us an hour, but at last I picked her out in a crowded box, and she slotted it home. The Dutch equalised, and I was subbed off. On the bench I could hardly bear to watch as Jill Scott scored the winner in the second half of extra time. And there it was. We were going into our first ever final. A Germany–England final.

There was a lot of fighting talk on the bus back to Helsinki for the final. I believed we had a chance. After all, we were the only team to deny Germany a goal at the World Cup in China. But we all knew the Germans were a beast of a team. They were chasing their seventh major title and had won the last four Euros in a row. Striker Birgit Prinz was world class, second in the world only to Marta, with fellow forward Inka Grings not far behind. Deep down, we knew it would be a long shot.

Two nights before the final, Hope asked me to stay behind after the team meeting. She asked me how I would feel playing on the left-hand side rather than on the right, where I had played throughout the tournament. I looked at her in surprise; this was a big decision. The change would mean keeping veteran winger Sue Smith on the bench and playing me in her place. Her question indicated I was almost certainly going to start in a European final. For that, I wouldn't have minded her asking me to play in goal. I put aside any reservations about crossing with my weaker left foot. I had been performing well, and this was a strong vote of confidence from Hope. I left the meeting feeling buoyed. I was playing well enough to warrant a place on the starting eleven, even if it meant me playing out of my usual position.

I went into the final confident, but there's no denying it: we got absolutely spanked. In our defence, the final score of 6–2 didn't do our fight justice. The Germans had impressive power and technique that was beyond us, and we all knew it. Their goals were of the highest order. Looking back at Melanie Behringer's first half forty-yard strike there's no doubt it was worthy of some of the world's best male players, of Cristiano Ronaldo say, or Gareth Bale.

I can't say I wasn't disappointed with the result. All along, I had never let go of the slightly naive faith that we could win it. I was surprised to find losing didn't seem to hurt many of the other players too much. Still, we had made it to the final and enjoyed every second along the way. The disappointment was already fading as we stepped up to receive our silver medals. We beamed with pride as the silver medals were placed around our necks. This would send a message far and wide: The past was over; England had come a long way. And I had too.

CHAPTER TWELVE

I blinked away the tears and tightened my grip on the steering wheel. I took a deep breath and tried to focus on the highway. The road ran on into the distance, dead straight, shimmering in the heat. I had to pull it together; I had hundreds of miles to go across three state lines. It was already midday and I wanted to see my new home before it got dark. Tears pricked my eyes again; this would be easier if I wasn't alone.

I needed to get my head straight, so I pulled over at the next rest stop. I opened the car door and hot air hit me like a hairdryer. I walked around to the back of my jeep to check the trailer connection. I couldn't even remember hooking it up. There hadn't been much time, I had shoved my stuff into a trailer and left St Louis.

The shock hit me all over again: St Louis Athletica was gone. Like Charlton, another club had folded overnight. I climbed back into the car, a Jeep Wrangler Dad had helped me buy as my first car in America, and turned back on to the baking highway. The road stretched on, hard and long. I thought back over the last months. There had been no warnings.

I went to London after the Euros, to work for SC Andrew and study in the off-season. In February, I retook the New York bar exam, but the pass rate hadn't got any higher. When I heard I'd failed a second time, I said enough. I could qualify next winter, back in England, after another season at St Louis. I couldn't wait to get back to the US to build on last year's successful run, to see teammates who had become close friends, and to learn more from Jorge. The season started well, I scored a brace in our first game, and another three games later. Jorge was happy and so was I.

Six games into the season, Jeff called a meeting with the players, coaches, and staff. We knew it was serious, but not one of us saw it coming. We listened in shocked silence as Jeff announced the team was folding with immediate effect. The investors had pulled out without warning, Jeff said. He had done all he could, but the numbers didn't add up. Like that, with players on contracts, and matches set up for the next four months, St Louis Athletica went up in smoke. The news was devastating: all I wanted was to stay and build on last year's achievements. My plans had been blown apart.

Then I got a call from Fitz Johnson, owner of new team Atlanta Beat. He was after St Louis's best players. Fitz was a wealthy African American entrepreneur with big plans, and he was a born salesman. Atlanta were at the bottom of the table, but Fitz sold it like this was my big chance. I could be the star striker to take them to the top. I liked Fitz's positivity and drive, and I said yes. Fitz also signed four of my St Louis teammates and friends: keeper Hope, defender Tina, midfielder Lori, and Japanese midfielder Aya Miyama. The prospect of playing alongside great players and familiar faces made my decision even easier. Things went fast; after all, it was mid-season. Before I had fully registered what was happening, I was on the road to Atlanta, my possessions bumping along in a trailer behind.

Fitz had said he was wealthy, and he hadn't been exaggerating. He owned two huge properties in an affluent suburb of Atlanta, one across the road from the other. He lived in the first mansion with his family, and he offered to house me and the other former St Louis players in the other. That was Fitz's style, showy, glamorous, oozing wealth; I couldn't help but be impressed. After what had happened to St Louis, the money was reassuring, but it was also bizarre.

The day after I arrived, Fitz organised a surprise to welcome us new players to Atlanta. He told us he wanted to take us on a tour of the city and for us to be ready at a certain time. Tina and I assumed he meant he would show us around in his car. We couldn't have been more wrong. When he arrived to collect us, Fitz explained we would be seeing the sights of Atlanta from the air, in his personal helicopter to be piloted by his nineteen-year-old son. I stifled a laugh; it was too ridiculous. I'd never been in a helicopter before and I wasn't exactly desperate to try it out. But Fitz was deadly serious, and he had been very generous, so I couldn't exactly say no.

We piled into the car and drove a short way across town to the family's private helicopter pad. There, glinting in the sunshine, was a sleek, black machine. I settled into the seat in the back and put on a pair of headphones as Fitz's son climbed into the cockpit behind the controls. I caught my breath; this kid was actually going to fly. All along I had vaguely been expecting a pilot to appear from somewhere. My heart was thumping hard now, but it was too late to go back; the helicopter was already rising into the air. I sat frozen, petrified in my seat, staring at the fast-disappearing ground and wondering how I'd got here. Life had taken a glitzy, dizzying turn.

The next day, I was bewildered to be back on the pitch, reeling from the week's events. After a strong start to the season at St Louis, it took me a little while to find my feet in a new team. I missed Jorge's guidance, and with all the upheaval, an unsettled feeling crept in. Staff changes added to the uncertainty. My new coach at Atlanta seemed more interested in exploring the city's social life than in coaching the team. He was fired five games before the end of the season and replaced with Australian-Greek coach James Galanis. James was renowned as the personal coach of USA legend Carli Lloyd and owned a successful club team in New Jersey. I was excited by his credentials and keen to get back to training under a coach who would help me improve as a striker.

Atlanta were still rooted to the bottom of the table when James came in. His strategy was to play impressive football for the final five games, almost irrespective of results. James championed a tactic of possession and switching the point of attack, taking his cue from the success of the Barcelona men's team. We won just one of the five games we played under James and ended the season in last place. Still, I was sure that with time, his philosophy would bear fruit. I left the US in August 2010, fully expecting to return to Atlanta for a second season the following spring.

But in the American league, nothing was certain. That December, Fitz called to tell me I had been traded. He notified me matter-of-factly, like it wasn't much to do with me. I would move to New Jersey and play with the club Sky Blue. My heart sank; I had heard from other players that the club didn't cultivate the most professional environment. I was given no warning, nobody asked my opinion, I had no right to appeal. I asked my agent to push for the trade to be changed to Western New York Flash in Buffalo, upstate New York, where I sat my bar exam the previous year. It didn't work.

I didn't want to go to New Jersey. Life had become comfortable in Atlanta; I had made friends and I had started dating a guy. I had fallen hard for the city, which was home to many wealthy African American entertainers and millionaire businesspeople. It had been a daily inspiration to drive through upscale districts such as Buckhead and see black people out jogging through their neighbourhood lined with lavish mansions. I was fascinated by the city's history as the cradle of the civil rights movement and birthplace of Dr Martin Luther King. There was so much more yet to explore, but there was nothing I could do. My contract was very clear: I was the league's asset, and the clubs could do whatever they liked with me.

The idea of moving again was exhausting, but I knew I had to try. This was pro football and I wanted to make it work, at least for another season. Still, I struggled to see anything good about the move. New Jersey was dull, and the team, Sky Blue, didn't excite me at all. On top of that, conditions just weren't professional; I had to share a house with eight teammates and two smelly dogs. I'm not a fan of dogs, and I tried to avoid them, but they wouldn't leave me alone. The dogs weren't the only problem. Living with a lot of teammates at once is never ideal, it only breeds tension.

On the pitch, my performance suffered. All the instability was unnerving, and I lost the confidence I'd found with Jorge. Sky Blue had a wobbly start to the season, and I didn't score until our sixth game. It's no wonder; instability was in the air. The league wasn't drawing in the crowds it had promised, and investors were getting impatient and pulling out. Two more teams folded, including Kaz's Chicago Red Stars. The whole league had begun to look shaky.

Mid-season, I got a welcome break. The 2011 World Cup in Germany. This was our second World Cup, and Hope, the staff and the England players we were far more relaxed than in China. The team was confident, still on a high from reaching the European final two years before. I tried to get back there, to conjure the free and easy feeling I'd had at St Louis. I wanted to be professional, to shoulder responsibilities for my team.

The build-up to our first game was intense. Our success at the Euros had piqued the interest of the British press, and the pressure was higher than ever to make it out of the group. We were favourites for our first match, which was against Mexico in Wolfsburg. Stepping out in front of 26,000 fans, my stomach began to flutter. It had been a while since I'd played in front of such a large crowd and I had to battle to block out the noise.

The game kicked off fast in the warm evening. We were dominating, and it felt like only a matter of time before we scored. Twenty minutes in, Fara headed the ball in from Kaz's corner and we were away. Then, out of nowhere, Mexico's Monica Ocampo, my former strike partner at Atlanta, belted in an equaliser from thirty yards. The goal tore through the team's confidence, but the shock sent new energy firing into my legs. This was my moment.

Seconds later, I met a through ball at the edge of the area, and the noise from the crowd swelled. I fired the shot too early, and it went wide. A disappointed noise, like air rushing out of a punctured tyre, reverberated around the stadium. I lowered my head and jogged back towards the halfway line. I tried to take my mind off the fans; I felt the pressure, the expectation. I had to block out the crowd and believe in another chance. Next time, I would score.

Hope gave us a stern talking to at half-time: we were better than this, and we knew it. We tried to rally after the break, but our confidence was draining away by the minute. The burden to score settled on my shoulders; no matter how hard I wanted to break free, I couldn't shut out the crowd. I couldn't pretend I was playing with the kids on the estate. This wasn't a friendly kick-about on a summer evening. It was a World Cup game, and it wasn't fun.

The expectation followed me around the pitch like a shadow, dragged at my feet whenever I touched the ball. My legs grew heavy and the first twinges of cramp set into my right calf. Around the hour mark, the ball zigzagged into my path. Rachel crossed from the right and Kaz headed it back across goal from the far post. The cheers rose as I sprinted forward to meet it. I kicked the air, missing the ball by inches. A heavy sigh blew out from the spectators and rained down on to my head. That was a clear chance. I should have scored.

There was no stopping the demons now. A nasty voice piped up in my head, jeering, daring me to miss another shot. That was another easy chance you missed, the voice said, and at a World Cup, too. I told the voice to shut up, but it only grew louder, until it drowned out the crowd. You aren't good enough, it said, get off the pitch. The voice was insistent, and it took all my will power not to obey. Just leave, said the voice, forfeit your place to another player. I knew I couldn't mess up again, but it was all I could do to stay in the game. I was in no state to make the most of the next chance, minutes later. Kelly took the ball forward, the defenders closed in, and she cut back suddenly. I was in the right place, but I panicked, stabbed wildly, and shot wide. The rest of the game passed in a blur. We fought off a loss, but we knew we had been lucky to do so. We were all disappointed, but I was devastated. The nasty voice wouldn't leave me alone. Those chances had been mine, and I had missed them.

Back in my room, I slumped on to my bed. My phone started flashing and vibrating, so I picked it up. Twitter notifications. I hadn't been on the network long; it had exploded since our last tournament. For the first time there had been a significant buzz in the run-up to the World Cup, and I had enjoyed being part of it. But these messages weren't like the others. My eyes widened as I read the first tweet.

'Eni Aluko is a terrible footballer,' one user wrote, helpfully tagging me in so I could read it. 'She should be dropped.'

Who was this idiot? I tutted and clicked the next message.

'Eni Aluko is shit,' it simply said.

I gripped the handset and scrolled through the tweets. All of them had a similar message. I was a bad striker, they wrote, Hope should drop me. I stopped scrolling after about fifteen tweets and threw the phone on the bed. I was devastated; who the hell were these people? What gave them the right to pass judgement on me? What kind of person deliberately sends a player a tsunami of negativity, right in the middle of a World Cup? My thumbs hovered over the phone keyboard; this wasn't OK, I would let them know.

'How can you say that?' I replied to the first user. Then, to the second: 'This kind of negativity helps no one.'

I clicked send and sat stock still, silent, staring at the screen. A quarter of an hour must have passed before there was a knock at my door. I put down the phone and went to open it. I was surprised to see Kelly standing in the corridor. In all the years playing together, she had never once knocked on my door.

'Hi,' she said. 'Are you OK?'

'I don't know,' I said shakily and opened the door wider.

Kelly stepped into the room and stood in the hallway outside the bathroom.

'Listen, Eni,' she began. 'You can't let it get to you.'

I frowned. She must have seen the replies I'd sent.

'But I don't get it,' I said. 'Why can't these people get behind us?'

'I know it hurts,' she said. 'But you have to let it go. It doesn't matter what they think, unless you let it. They've probably never kicked a ball in their lives. Hope believes in you. I believe in you. Even the best strikers miss chances.'

I smiled at her. It had been good of her to come.

'Thanks a lot, Kelly,' I said.

Kelly nodded and stepped towards the door.

'Turn your phone off, yeah?' she said, and walked out of the room.

The conversation only lasted a minute or so, and Kelly has probably forgotten all about it, but I'll never forget it. Kelly's advice came at exactly the right moment and cut through the negative thoughts swirling around my brain.

I was overcome with gratitude. She was right, I shouldn't let it get to me. But how? It was easier said than done.

I sat in my room, thinking, for a long time after Kelly left. I needed practical solutions. How could I put myself back out there on the pitch, silence the booing crowd, the online critics, and the negative voices in my head? I thought of Jorge back in St Louis. He had been on to something when he said I had to let go of expectations, of pressure, and get back to feeling free. I would have to switch the negative voices off, and then drown them out with my own positivity. I made myself a promise: no matter what happened on the pitch, I would tell myself I was good enough. I couldn't control the outside voices, but the one in my own head was mine. I would have to change its tone.

Being a striker is a high stakes game. Only a handful of athletes are willing to put themselves in that glory position. Two goals in the next game, and I'd be an instant hero. But the limelight makes us vulnerable, too. Strikers thrive on the edge of the team, between shadow and light. You wait on the defender's shoulder for your moment to pounce, and when it comes, there can be no in between. Either you score, or you don't. Either you play, or you don't. Either you're on top form, or you don't make the team. Coaches love you, or they hate you, and that goes for the fans too. Strikers are divisive; everyone has an opinion.

Football hadn't changed, but technology had. Twitter invited people to air their kneejerk reactions. Mostly, the emotions were simple: I was a striker, they wanted goals, and I hadn't delivered, so they hated me. Sometimes, they hated me for other reasons; because I was a woman, because I was black. Faceless, anonymous on this forum, they were free to show their hate in public. This wasn't a sigh of disappointment from the crowd. These were spiteful messages, directed at me, about me. This was the new reality; I would have to learn to deal with it.

I picked up my phone, navigated to the settings, and switched off all notifications. I wasn't going to hide from what people were saying, but I needed to be able to control what I saw and when. Kelly was right: these people could say anything they liked, and it wouldn't matter. All that mattered was my teammates and my coach.

The negativity I'd seen online dogged me for the rest of the tournament. I started the next game, a win against New Zealand, but was subbed off at half-time. I didn't start again. We had flash of optimism when we won against Japan, who went on to win the tournament, and we came out top of our group. But our hopes were cruelly crushed by a penalty shoot-out against France in the quarter-finals. I watched the drama, dejected, from the bench. The tournament had knocked my confidence badly, and I left Germany under a dark cloud.

Back in New Jersey for the last six weeks of the season, I decided I'd had enough. I wasn't happy with my living situation or with the club. This was professional football, and I was being paid, but it wasn't enough to justify this discomfort, or instability. Getting traded might have been normal in American sports, but I couldn't get used to it. Everything I had learned about sports contracts was at odds with the practice. I was used to a player being free to choose which club they signed with. And, to my mind, if a player signed a three-year contract with a club, both sides were committed to seeing out the term. Legally, I felt, that was a fair bargaining position. But that's not the way it worked in America.

And besides, Britain was calling. The FA had launched a new Women's Super League, and London was to host the 2012 Olympic Games the following summer. Great Britain would play a women's football team for the first time, and I wanted in. I wanted to qualify as a lawyer. I wanted to move on. I wanted to go home.

Home was proving a little elusive. My family had by now all left Birmingham. Sone was playing for Aberdeen, and Mum had recently moved to Nigeria with my two younger sisters and my little brother. I visited my family in Lagos as soon as I left New Jersey. It was the first time I'd been to Nigeria since I was twelve. Since university, returning to Nigeria had been a top priority. Having my family there meant I could finally call Lagos home, too.

But I couldn't stay there with them; I needed to get back on track in the UK. I moved back into my London apartment and, that September, started an accelerated Legal Practice Course, or LPC, a concentrated year of vocational training in preparation for a training contract as a solicitor. It was hard work, but I was making progress with law again, and it felt good. I needed a distraction from football. In January 2012, the American WPS league announced it was folding, leaving Kelly and the others without clubs. The future of women's professional football was suddenly looking bleak.

The sacrifices didn't seem worth it any more. I'd won the FA Cup, played at two World Cups, two European Championships, had three seasons of pro football under my belt, and I was still struggling to find consistency in my career. Not only that, two clubs had folded on me, I'd been moved against my will, and forced to share a house with eight teammates and two smelly dogs. This wasn't the dream I'd had after visiting Fola in Manhattan, a decade before. I wasn't a kid any more, I was twenty-five, and I wanted more. I was closer to quitting than I'd ever been.

Then, another call came. My old club, Birmingham City, wanted to sign me for the 2012 summer season. Kaz was already back there, and I thought it couldn't hurt. One more season, while I was doing the LPC course.

Going back was a mistake, it felt like landing in another world, one I'd outgrown. It seemed like nothing had changed since I'd left eight years before. The facilities, the standard of play, it was all a far cry from full-time professional America. We trained only three evenings a week, on the AstroTurf at the University of Birmingham. It felt like a backwards step, and I hated it.

The club might not have moved on, but I had. My experiences in the US had changed me; I was mentally tougher and more focused. But some of the other players reacted badly to this change in me. They acted as if I was cramming the mentality of the big-time professional league into a smaller environment where it didn't fit. I felt a constant tension between the player I had become and the player I had been as a teenager.

Life was suddenly horribly familiar, right down to juggling evening training sessions and my full-time LPC course. My teenage commute to London was now reversed; I was studying and living in London, travelling to Birmingham and back three times a week to train. I prioritised my assignments and skipped training if I needed to, even if that didn't go down well with the team. I was sure now: law was my career; football was a dead end. Nothing could change my mind, not even when Birmingham won their first FA Cup that May. I watched most of the final from the bench, unusually unfazed not to be playing, marking time. I would hold out for a place on the Olympic team, then I would quit football for good.

Competing in an Olympic Games on home soil was a once-in-a-lifetime opportunity. Playing football for Great Britain was an even rarer chance. Team GB didn't normally enter an Olympic football team, male or female, in deference to the home nations' concern it might prevent them competing separately in other FIFA-governed tournaments. But as hosts, Great Britain had automatic qualification for all disciplines. As a one-off, for London 2012, the tradition was waived. As a British football player, this would likely be my one chance to become an Olympian.

Hope was appointed coach of the GB women's team, and she picked most of the core England team, including me. She picked two Scottish players, Kim Little and

Ifeoma Dieke, but no Welsh or Northern Irish. Looking back, it would have made sense to have a minimum quota to ensure fair representation. We were all excited, but none of us were prepared for what was about to happen. Football is self-absorbed a lot of the time, and players all believe the World Cup is the biggest and most important sporting event on the planet. We were wrong: it was the Olympics that changed everything, not only for me, but for all female footballers.

Maybe it was the timing that did it. Our first match opened the whole Games, two days ahead of the opening ceremony. We played New Zealand in Cardiff's Millennium Stadium, in front of 25,000 people; millions more watched us on TV. The whole country had tuned in for the start of the greatest show on earth. It could have been archery or any other sport, but when rising star Steph Houghton curled in her second-half free kick to put us in the lead, the whole country cheered as one. Millions sat up and took notice.

We also won our second match, against Cameroon. It was scheduled in Cardiff for the day after the opening ceremony, which meant we couldn't attend the big show. Instead, we watched it on TV in our hotel, all dressed in our official Olympic Stella McCartney tracksuits. They were red, white and blue, with a big, raised collar.

Some of the others didn't like them, but I thought they looked cool, if a bit Ali G. I recently had mine framed. As Danny Boyle's bombastic spectacle reached its climax on screen, it dawned on us we were part of something bigger than ever before. We pinched ourselves: we were the lucky few. We were Olympians now.

The real watershed moment was our third game, against Brazil at Wembley Stadium. None of us had ever played at Wembley before. To face Marta and the others in such an iconic ground was a dream come true for every one of us. As kids, all of us had imagined Wembley as the fantasy backdrop for our back garden five-a-side games. Now it was happening for real. Brazil–Great Britain at Wembley turned out to be a draw for the fans too, and just like that, 70,000 tickets were sold, smashing all records for women's football in the UK.

The noise was deafening as I stepped out on to the pitch under the lights. I gazed up at the packed stands stretching up to the roof. This was like nothing I'd seen before. This crowd was more than double the largest I'd ever played for in the past, and I couldn't help but feel a little daunted. I was grateful we were already safely in the quarter-finals. The pressure wasn't on the result, but on our performance. We were in the spotlight, on the biggest stage in British football. We had everyone's attention. We wanted to put on our best show.

Steph scored the only goal two minutes in and the crowd erupted as if we had just won the World Cup. At the final whistle we were walking on air. Coming off the pitch I was mobbed by TV cameras and journalists. Everyone wanted to know what it was like to beat Brazil at Wembley. It was a wonderful night for British football. The crowd, the result, the stadium: only five years earlier no one would have believed it possible. In a rush of passion, I remembered why I played football. For the thrill, for the joy of it.

The British papers were full of us the next day. It was a big story: 70,000 people had turned up to watch women play football. Millions more tuned in to watch online and on TV. These were figures broadcasters and clubs couldn't ignore. Women's football had been put in the shop window, and the public were responding. Given a stage, our game would become commercial, and here was the proof. The press and the public had seen us for what we really were: strong, beautiful, talented players, dedicated to the game we loved.

Our hopes of a medal were dashed, days later, when we lost to Canada in the quarter-finals. We were devastated to be knocked out. We saw how our Olympic run was revolutionising our game and we wanted to go as far as we could. We needn't have worried; not getting a medal didn't matter in the long run. The sea-change had happened, and there was no going back. Women had played at last under the arch at Wembley. Nothing would ever be the same.

We moved into the Olympic village; a utopian world made for athletes. The whole of London was Olympics obsessed, and we were showered with freebies and hailed as heroes wherever we went. It was a thrill to feel part of a wider sporting community, to see Mo Farah, and Jess Ennis, walking around in the same tracksuit I was wearing. I met Usain Bolt, and chatted to my childhood hero Ryan Giggs, who captained the men's GB team. In those days, in that place, a generation of British athletes came together. It was an experience none of us will ever forget.

But the impact of the Games was far broader than that. More than 600,000 people attended women's football matches during London 2012. That was proof of a fan base. It lent weight to the arguments of players demanding better pay or job security. No longer could the big clubs afford to resist investing in our game. The Games heralded a new era, not of astronomical riches, or lavish celebrity, but one in which female players could command the respect we deserved.

Celebrating in the Olympic village with my old friends, my teammates, all the sacrifices, the emotional, financial and personal struggles we had faced, suddenly felt worth it. Our game had taken a huge leap forward. Now a different future seemed possible. One in which little girls' dreams of playing Wembley could realistically one day come true, and in which all talented players could aspire to a professional football career. It had been a long arduous journey that stretched back generations before us. No doubt, there was a long way to go; but British female footballers were Olympians now, and no one could ever take that away.

I had also been through a momentous journey. The Olympics breathed new life into my passion for football and blasted away any thoughts I'd had of quitting. The women's game in Britain was teetering on the verge of revolution, and I wasn't about to miss out on whatever came next. Suddenly, the barrier I had been hitting up against my whole adult life was gone. And, after my time in America, I was a new player. I had found how to tap back into that inner freedom I had felt as a child. Women's football had been set free, I had been freed, to dream of bigger things.

Class 5:

Trust In The Hand Of God

There is always a lesson behind every failure.

If one thing is sure, there will be setbacks in life, and every one of them makes us stronger.

CHAPTER THIRTEEN

I wasn't meant to quit football; the Olympics had shown that God had a different plan for me. Football still had a lot to teach me, and a devastating failure was about to deliver one of the biggest lessons of my life. No one had taught me how to deal with failure, how to pick myself up, dust myself down, swallow my pride and put myself back into the position to win or lose again.

There was no way around failure, I had to go through it to find the success waiting on the other side. I had to learn that life isn't all plain sailing, and that when things go wrong, I had to trust in God's plan. I had to learn to make sense of the bad times, the failures, and look for the meaning, the lesson, behind every setback. They really don't teach this.

If I wasn't going to quit football, then something else would have to give. I applied for a central contract with England when I returned to the UK, and in May, just before the Olympics, the FA awarded me a six-month contract and told me to reapply for a full contract in December. Looking over the contract, it seemed like there was still a lot to improve. We needed a better wage, more in line with wages for women national teams across Europe, and improved terms that, for example, protected the players in case of injury.

I wanted to push for improvements, and so I contacted the Professional Footballers Association trade union, PFA. I met with PFA vice chief executive Bobby Barnes and Matthew Buck, who was in charge of player management. They were both open and receptive to the concerns of female players, and said they wanted to help us move things forward with the FA. That summer, we kick-started negotiations about improving central contracts. My legal background helped. It meant I could present our case, in a calm, diplomatic tone, as well as go back and explain all the legalese to the players.

It might take time, but I was confident we could get results if we presented a united front. Collective action meant no individual had to put her playing career before the interests of the team. Though we discussed it, we never got to the point of threatening not to play, as other teams such as Denmark would later do. Still, in our first collective action, that year all players refused to apply for central contracts until they were approved and negotiated by PFA.

Once the FA saw the team was united and ready to stand firm on the issue, their position began to budge. After several months of initial talks, at the end of 2012 the FA agreed to raise central contract salaries from £16,000 to £20,000. I was awarded a full-time contract early in the New Year. The pay rise was a colossal victory for us, the players, and our self-respect. But there was still more to do. We needed better contractual terms and our success made me wonder what else we could achieve.

Meanwhile, I was moving on in my club career. I wasn't happy at Birmingham, I felt stifled. I wanted something more fulfilling, I wanted to find my proper place within the game, and I was looking for a club I could call home. Chelsea was my first choice. The club had moved on since my dud season with them back in 2008. Former Chicago coach Emma Hayes was now at the helm. After being fired from Chicago, she had returned to England determined to build a team as successful as the formidable quadruple-winning Arsenal side she had once helped coach.

Emma had a vision. She wanted to seize the moment after the Olympics to push for investment and recruit top foreign and domestic players. She wanted to build a team that could fill Chelsea's empty trophy cabinet. I called Emma and told her I was desperate to leave Birmingham. She was interested, and when she offered me a transfer I didn't hesitate. It didn't matter to me that the Blues had finished last season in sixth place. The journey and Emma's vision appealed, and I wanted to be part of it.

Moving to Chelsea would be more convenient, too. Training was in Cobham, a town about an hour southwest of London. That meant it was possible to fit training around the next step in my law career. I had finished the LPC course and had landed a full-time training contract with a city entertainment law firm called Lee and Thompson. The firm represented musicians, film directors and authors, and had overseen a number of high-profile celebrity divorces.

Getting a training contract hadn't got any easier since the last time I had tried. Lee and Thompson didn't advertise for trainees, so I took an unconventional approach. I wrote to the head partner, Andrew Thompson, telling him how much I admired the firm's unique practice and how much I wanted to work for them. I told him I felt

I had a lot to bring to the table in terms of their sports practice.

We met and he agreed to make an exception and grant me a training contract. We also discussed an arrangement whereby I could fit football in around my work. I would leave the office early on the two nights a week I trained with Chelsea and I would also be able to take unpaid leave when I was called up for England. Lee and Thompson had offices on St Christopher's Place, a quiet, narrow street off Oxford Street in central London. It was tight, but if I left at five thirty, I could just about make it out to Cobham in time for training at seven. I was back to juggling.

My two-year training contract with Lee and Thompson involved moving through a number of seats, or departments, each specialising in a different area of law. Each department was like a self-contained firm headed by a different partner. I began in the litigation department around the time I signed for Chelsea. It was a wonderful place to start. In my first week, the department partner asked me to help work on a libel and defamation case between Scottish comedian Frankie Boyle and the *News of the World* newspaper. It was very exciting work that involved putting together court bundles for leading entertainment barristers representing Boyle and a lot of short trips back and forth from the office to the Royal Courts of Justice to file court papers.

Boyle was suing the *News of the World* for calling him a racist on their front page. The case turned on whether Boyle's jokes were factually racist, or whether they were, as he claimed, satirical and therefore anti-racist, designed to highlight and expose racial stereotyping. I was intrigued and, as I read the skeleton arguments, I could hardly believe this was my job.

After a month or so of preparation, I got to attend the hearing and help with note-taking. I loved the pace and the rhythm of the daily court sessions. I loved feeling the tension build in the room as the opposing side laid out their arguments. It was almost like football. The weeks of build-up and preparation were almost like training for a big game. Then, the hearing, facing the opposition, was like a match with a high court judge in place of a referee. When, after a week in court, Boyle won his case and was awarded damages, I got an extra thrill from being on the winning side.

Afterwards, I worked on the inquiry into systematic illegal hacking of celebrity's phones and emails by the *News of the World* to illicit private information. It was a dream job. Our department was at the cutting edge of changes in UK privacy law, and I got to be part of it every day. I was a little sad when, in spring, I was rotated out of the department and moved on to family law.

Chelsea, meanwhile, were supportive of my legal work. Emma knew how much I was juggling and was conscious the club couldn't compete financially with what I was getting at Lee and Thompson. The money wasn't there yet for American-style full-time contracts. Still, Emma was making great strides, and she had managed to secure some foreign stars, Brazilian midfielder Ester Romero and Swedish forward Sofia Jakobsson, to complement our home-grown team.

Our season got off to a shaky start, with only two wins in our first seven games. Yet this felt different from the bad spells I'd been through with other clubs. This time, I was invested in building something, however long it took. Playing for Emma was a breath of fresh air; she understood me as a player better than any coach ever had, and let me train as a sprinter rather than trying to make me into a long-distance runner. Emma got the best out of me by showing she believed in me. It was an effect she had on all the players. As a result, the team was closer and more dedicated to the club and to one another than any I'd ever played in.

I was reluctant to leave Chelsea when the league broke for the 2013 Euros in Sweden that June. Hope had picked a lot of familiar faces; we were an experienced side. At twenty-six, I was at the younger end of Hope's first choice eleven, which had an average age of twenty-eight. Seven of us had more than sixty caps – I was on seventy – and of those, four were on one hundred or more. Hope had me on the wing, supporting forward Ellen White with Kelly. Kaz was in midfield along with Jill Scott, Fara Williams, Anita and Rachel Yankey. Captain Casey Stoney, standing in for injured Faye White, led the defence with Steph Houghton, whose Olympic goals had cemented her place despite injury. Only a couple of new faces made the squad, among them Arsenal's attacking midfielder Jordan Nobbs, and a bright new forward, Toni Duggan, who was then with Everton. I clicked with Toni right away, she was sharp, with a wicked sense of humour.

Media interest in our campaign was higher than ever, and a whole cohort of British reporters had been sent out to Sweden to cover us. Expectations were high; everyone who had seen our core team beat Brazil at Wembley last summer had great hopes. We had won that year's Cyprus Cup, and reached the final of the Euros four years before. After the Olympics, we knew millions of new fans would be watching us. The pressure was on to make this tournament count.

We went one down in the first five minutes of our opening game, a five-goal rollercoaster against Spain. Minutes later, I raced a defender to meet Jill Scott's through ball. The keeper came off her line and I slotted the ball past her. But there was no time to celebrate; we had a fight on our hands. I came off in the second half and watched in agony as the game lurched from end to end in the final minutes. Spain scored five minutes from time, and all seemed lost until Kelly equalised with one minute to go. Then, in stoppage time, came the sucker punch. A Spanish striker beat our keeper Karen Bardsley to a cross and bundled in the winner.

The press ripped into us, and into Hope's leadership. She played it down; we had lost opening games before. Four years back, we had lost our first game and gone on to reach the final. We didn't feel any hint of danger going into our second game against Russia, the lowest ranked side in the tournament. We were favourites, and we were confident a win would restore faith in our chances. We needed to win. Hope needed a win.

We dominated in the first half, but it was Russia that went ahead before half-time. Our confidence slid away as the realisation hit that we were forty-five minutes from being sent home. I came off for Kelly and looked on glumly as we spent the last twenty minutes chasing possession. It was Toni who came to our rescue, coming off the bench to ram home a last-gasp equaliser. It was a close shave.

Toni was hailed as a heroine, while the papers drubbed the rest of us. England women were failing on a big stage and someone needed to take the blame. The criticism wasn't pleasant to read, but I tried to look on the bright side. The sports hacks were now ripping into us as if we were the men's team; at least we were getting attention. We had spent so long pushing for more media coverage. Now we had it, we had to be ready to take the bad press with the good. The most acerbic analysis was aimed at Hope. After fifteen years at the helm, they wrote, her style was out-of-touch and stagnant.

I didn't know what to make of it; Hope's leadership was certainly regimented. Still, I'd never known any different. I had spent almost half my life playing for her and I owed her a lot. She had believed in me and had given me my England senior debut when I was just seventeen. She had started me in England's first World Cup in twelve years and she had always been supportive of my education. She had done so much for the progression of women's football in England. I knew it was time for change, but at the same time I couldn't help feeling a little bad about it.

Our campaign was now on life support; only a win against tournament favourites France could save us. France scored early, and their defence closed up and strangled our attempts to reply. Around the hour mark they crushed any last hope with two further goals. At the final whistle I felt numb. Four years after reaching the finals, we had crashed out at the bottom of our group. Three consecutive summer tournaments – the World Cup, the Olympics and the Euros – had taken their toll. We were tired and injured. And we were out.

All eyes fixed on Hope. The voices calling for her to be sacked reached pain level. Hope had achieved great things, they said, but it was time for a new pair of hands. She was fired within the month, leaving assistant manager Brent Hills to take over as interim coach. I had mixed feelings: I felt loyalty to Hope, she had brought me in all those years ago, mentored me, believed in me. Others were happier to see her go. It had always been strictly Hope's way of doing things, and some had valid grievances. I watched and waited, anxious to see what would come next.

That summer, Mum moved back to the UK from Nigeria with my younger siblings. It was great to have them back, and they had moved slightly closer to London which meant I could see them much more regularly.

Meanwhile, I was glad to get back to Chelsea. Our bad luck continued for the rest of the season, despite new signings Ireland keeper Marie Hourihan and Japanese striker Yuki Ogimi. I scored a brace in our 4–0 defeat of bottom-of-the league Doncaster Belles; our only win in eleven games. A string of six straight losses saw us end the season on seventh place. Liverpool captured the title, toppling Arsenal's decade-long reign at the top. Emma was undeterred; the trophies would come, she said, it was only a matter of time, and I believed her.

Things had been complicated with Lee and Thompson. Towards the end of the season, my football-and-law juggling act started to wobble. I spent the summer in Lee and Thompson's music department getting a solid commercial grounding in rights, royalties and record deals. I enjoyed the work, but it had a downside. The department was fast moving and completed many deals with clients in America, so my bosses expected everyone to spend a lot of late nights in the office. While the partners and associates were themselves football fans, the game obviously took a back seat when it came to client matters. Me playing for Chelsea and England and needing to go off to training early was sometimes met with eye rolls and disapproval. The managing partner, Andrew Thompson, remained as supportive of my sporting commitments as he had been at the beginning, but I started to realise that this wasn't necessarily the case across all departments.

At law school they don't prepare you for how hierarchical law firms can be. There can be rigid power structures, no matter how casual the office dress code. Trainees are expected to do everything in their power to impress the associates and partners. I should never forget my place, no matter what I achieved for the firm in business leads or development. When I brought in a prominent Nigerian lawyer to help a multi-award-winning global artist out of his contract, I was taken out of the email chain. I was helping business development, but I was firmly reminded of my place in the pecking order.

All this made my special arrangement of leaving work early for training twice a week increasingly awkward. Every time I left, I'd sense the disapproval from the other trainees and junior staff, who routinely stayed long after hours. I understood their frustration; I'm sure they would have loved to leave work early now and then. But some didn't fully understand what it took to train hard after a full day at work and be up early the next morning to do it all again. Juggling work and training wasn't easy, yet I began to feel terrible about it, as if I were skipping off for a bit of fun.

Things got even trickier when I moved to the film department. For a start, film contract law wasn't as glamorous as I had imagined. It was less reading film scripts and liaising with directors and more overseeing long, tedious transactions with faceless joint venture companies. The work was purely financial: one party had bought the option for a book and a bank was set to transfer the money at this time. Worse, as with the music department, the business mostly operated on an entirely different time zone. Lots of our clients were in the US, which meant working late and sometimes, a clash with training. The head of film department could see my juggling act was becoming increasingly difficult to manage. The first few times I missed training to stay behind and work late, but it wasn't sustainable, I would have to choose.

A series of meetings followed. It became clear Lee and Thompson needed my undivided commitment, which I wasn't always able to give. I was torn in two. If I hadn't also been a footballer, it would have been an amazing experience, with fascinating legal work that was the envy of many of my friends from law school. But I had a commitment to Chelsea; the club was paying me a small salary, and it was clear the women's game was moving forward. I couldn't leave, not now.

It was a tough call. I had a prestigious training contract with Lee and Thompson, one that thousands of applicants would have died to get their hands on. Yet I wasn't prepared to abandon football. I rifled through my options, looking for a way out of the clash. I had gained solid experience and learned a lot during my four seats with the firm. That wouldn't be wasted if I left now. I got permission from the Solicitors Regulation Authority to move on to another firm to complete my training contract. I met with the partners at Lee and Thompson and, with a heavy heart, handed in my notice. The partners supported my decision, and I felt a weight lift from my shoulders. I was glad I would leave on a good note.

I wrote to the lead partner of a boutique sports and media firm called Onside Law and they gave me an offer. They were a leading firm in the industry and represented clients in football, tennis, cricket and rugby. They were keen to have someone with my football background on board. Crucially, the partners were happy to be flexible about my working hours. When, in the New Year, pre-season training began with Chelsea, I was glad I'd made the switch. In a big step forward, Emma had us training four times a week, twice in the day and twice in the evening. My bosses at Onside Law didn't blink; they said

I could work half days on the days I had training in the afternoons. I was very relieved. Things had clicked back into place.

Emma was full of drive and optimism ahead of the season. She was building an impressive side. She had secured fellow England players, including forward Rachel Williams, defender Laura Basset, and midfielder Katie Chapman, along with as-yet uncapped centre back Gilly Flaherty. Emma had also attracted international talent in midfield in the form of South Korean star Ji So-yun, Sweden's Emma Wilhelmsson, and Belgian Jackie Groenen. We had experience and skill and we were hungry to bring home Chelsea's first piece of silverware.

Debuting in the senior team this season was a young player called Atlanta Primus. Her father, Linvoy, was the former Portsmouth captain. I often ran into him around Cobham, and we became friends. We had a fair amount in common, especially our shared Christian faith. Linvoy was active in a charity called Faith and Football and became a kind of mentor to me. He understood the role faith could play in navigating the pressures of football. His faith, like mine, revolved around prayer, a constant, ongoing conversation with God that could happen anytime, anywhere.

As the season began, my prayers focused on the club, on Emma and on the team. I prayed that this season we would make an impact. I offered a financial contribution, a tithe, to my church, hoping to be blessed with a winning season. I believed that if I gave to God, if I sacrificed something for him, I would receive back tenfold in return and he would see to it that we won the title. Later I realised that this isn't how religious acts work. God operates on his own timetable.

At the time, however, my prayers seemed to be working. We had an impressive start with only one loss in the first four games. Excitement really began building through July, when a four-match winning streak sent us charging up the table. Along the way, we beat league newcomers Manchester City, the new home of my England teammates Toni and Jill Scott. In September, we reached the top of the table. It was a spectacular turnaround.

I could barely contain my excitement. For the first time, the title was in reach. No trophy, no award, compared to painstakingly climbing the table for months, game by game, and reaching the top. I was sick of coming second. It had happened so often – at Charlton, at St Louis, at Birmingham – that I had begun to accept it as the norm. Riding this wave with Chelsea, it felt like my time had come. I asked God to let it happen. I prayed to win,

I prayed for the title. I bargained with God, reminded Him how hard we had worked. I would believe and play my best, and God would let us win.

The title race came down to the wire. We woke up on the last day of the season two points ahead of nearest rival Birmingham and three ahead of Liverpool. A win against Man City would guarantee us the title and we were confident we could deliver. City had some good players, but they were fifth in the table and had no stake in the title race. They had other priorities and would play in the final of the Continental Cup for the first time later that week. For us, this game was everything. To them it was nothing.

There was a carnival mood on the bus on the way up to Manchester, and the party continued in the dressing room when we saw City's team sheet. They had played a weaker team, apparently resting players ahead of their upcoming cup final. No captain Steph Houghton, no keeper Karen Bardsley. We would need to watch Toni and Jill Scott, but the message was clear: go ahead, this game means nothing to us. I walked on to the pitch buzzing with expectation. The sun was shining, a good crowd was out, and TV cameras waited to record our league victory. The game felt almost like a formality before the celebrations could begin.

We went in strong. Ji and I weaved up front, pushing for an early goal. Seven minutes in, City's Krystle Johnston stepped up to take a free kick inside our half. The ball looped in towards goal and a cluster of players scrambled to meet it. Our keeper Marge charged out and rose, arms up, to catch it and collided with City's Georgia Brougham in mid-air. Marge somersaulted and landed on her right shoulder with a sickening thud. She stayed down, clutching her head in her goalie glove.

There was a horrified silence as the medics ran to see to Marge. Word ran around the pitch she had broken her collarbone and a shudder went through our side. The afternoon darkened and Marge was stretchered off the pitch. Emma stood grim-faced on the sideline; our options were limited. Our usual substitute keeper was also injured, and a semi-retired player, Clare Farrow, had been brought in as a last-minute replacement. Clare worked full-time as a policewoman and hadn't played a game at this level for years. I scanned the back line as she came on. Their faces said it all: set teeth, shocked eyes. One stomach-turning jolt, and our confidence had begun to slip.

My job hadn't changed. I ran down the wing, trying to shake off the shock. I found the ball on the left outside the area, flanked by three defenders. I swivelled, dipped with my shoulder and tucked the ball close behind me, leaving them behind. I reached the byline and chipped the ball to the far post, where Yuki met the ball with a flying header. The ball bounced tantalisingly in front of goal, but defender Abbie McManus was there to clear it off the line. The chance electrified me; we were by no means out of the game.

Yet City sensed our weakness in goal. All they had to do was wait for their chance. Midway through the half, Jill Scott fired in a weak shot from distance. Clare misjudged the bounce and dived under the ball. I stood staring in disbelief, unable to process what had just happened. A calamity goal, a second undeserved gut punch. This wasn't how it was meant to be. The dream was souring into a nightmare.

The mood had turned so quickly. We hadn't expected a difficult game and now we were frozen in the headlights, unable to avert the disaster playing out in front of our eyes. City didn't give us time to catch our breaths. Minutes later, Jill reached the byline and crossed to Toni, who controlled the ball on her chest, pivoted and volleyed, all in one smooth action. The ball sailed over Clare and slammed into the top of the net. It was a beautiful goal. Toni yelled, leapt into the air and slid on her knees as her teammates piled on top of her.

I watched stunned from the halfway line. Toni had celebrated as if she had won the title herself. This game should mean nothing to fifth-place City, but that celebration said otherwise. I understood at last: they wanted to deny us the trophy. City hadn't come along today to make up the numbers. Their motivation was to stop us winning on their patch. This was more than club rivalry. Toni was a close friend, she was fully aware of what the title meant to me, but there was no friendship on this pitch.

Our faith was draining away by the second. Ten minutes to half-time, we were two goals down. I looked at my fellow forwards Rachel and Yuki, hoping to find strength for the fight. They stared back at me in blank shock; there was no fire in their eyes. I was alone; it would be on me to turn this nightmare around. At the break we traipsed into the dressing room in numb silence. This had been our title to lose, and now our hopes were hanging by a thread. Elsewhere, Birmingham were losing, but as things stood, a goal for Liverpool would see them snatch our title on goal difference. I gazed at the dressing-room floor. This couldn't be happening.

'I don't know what you were all expecting,' said Emma, her voice trembling slightly, 'but we are currently forty-five minutes away from losing the title. We need to bring absolutely everything we've got.'

Emma looked around the team. No one spoke for over a minute. My throat tightened and I choked back tears of despair. Then our captain, Katie Chapman, stood up.

'We need to stop feeling sorry for ourselves,' she said, looking from player to player. 'We need to go out there and give our all in the second half.'

We plodded back out on to the pitch, still sunk in horrified silence. I wished this horrendous match were over. Fear electrified us in the second half, and we began to take control. Then, in the seventieth minute, we got our reward. Gilly Flaherty headed one home from a corner. Minutes later, City went down to ten players after defender Abbie McManus was sent off.

The goal shook me out of my shocked daze. The game was back on. If we could equalise, we could still win the league. Ji and I pushed harder than ever, dodging and weaving in front of goal, but City were resolute. They defended like their lives depended on it. I was stunned at their will to deny us. They couldn't bear the thought of watching us lift the trophy at their stadium. I wondered how they could hate us so much.

Ten minutes to go, I drew on the last of my energy reserves. We had nothing to lose and everything still to gain; I was desperate to claw it back. I dropped back into midfield and took on players alone, I did everything I could to kindle chances, create space, find a killer pass or weave in towards goal. All we needed was one moment, a flash of brilliance, an inch of space, a lapse in their concentration. The minutes slid away, and the backline closed down, solid and determined.

A last glimmer, a corner, came four minutes into stoppage time. I stood on the goal line, shoulder to shoulder with the keeper, staring at the corner flag. Time crawled to a stop. My focus shifted, and beyond, in the crowd, I caught sight of Mum. Desperation rose in my throat as my eyes filled with tears. This was on me; I had let everyone down: Mum, Emma, the team, the club, everyone. Mum's concerned face blurred through my tears. Here was our last chance, slipping away. The corner sailed in, we scrambled wildly, the keeper grabbed the ball. It was gone.

The whistle blew. One look at Emma told me the other results hadn't gone our way. The title had slipped from our grasp. I collapsed on to the field. I sat with my head sunk between my knees, sobbing out the devastation. Time passed, I don't know how long. I felt hands patting my shaking shoulders, heard voices coaxing, consoling. I batted them away, I couldn't make out the words. My heart was breaking. Everything was breaking. I felt like

I'd always been there, sobbing on the pitch, and I always would be. Arms slotted under my shoulders and tried to lift me off the floor. I sobbed louder. They could do what they wanted, nothing mattered now. A voice cut through the fog.

'Why are you crying?' said Toni.

I screwed my eyes shut at the sound of her voice and sank my face into my palms. Toni's celebration played out again on the back of my closed eyelids. Her voice came again, sharp and pitiless.

'Get your head up.'

I raised my head and opened my eyes. She stood in front of me, her face twisted into a weird, patronising smile.

'Don't cry,' said Toni. 'It's just football.'

I hung my head again and sobbed into the grass. For all I know, Toni meant well. Still, in that moment her consolation was hard to stomach. Toni had been overjoyed to prevent us winning the league. She had done her job, and I hadn't done mine.

Mum came on to the pitch and helped the others drag me to my feet. As I stumbled into the tunnel, my breath got short and raspy, and I began to hyperventilate. I was ripped apart: this wasn't only football, it was everything. All the years coming in second place and never reaching the top, all our hard-won achievements shredded on one brutal day. Liverpool had won the title by a difference of two goals. We had reached the Champions League for the first time, but in that moment it wasn't enough. The disappointment of the loss was too much to bear.

Still unable to speak, I went outside with Mum to her car and sat in silence in the passenger seat, tears rolling down my cheeks. Mum tried her best reassure me, but I shook my head and wiped the tears away.

'You don't understand,' I stammered. 'That was the only chance we'll get. We'll never make it that far again.'

I was crushed. Mum had to get back, and I had a date to eat dinner with the team. We had been so confident we would win the league that we had booked a big table at Rio Ferdinand's restaurant in Manchester. We had planned a celebration; we had thought we would be champions. Eating out was the last thing I wanted to do, but I couldn't leave the team, not now.

Grim silence reigned around our table that night. From my seat at one end, I looked down the row of shocked faces. Not one of us wanted to be there, drinking wine among mirrored walls and marble fittings. I stared down at the white tablecloth, wishing it would swallow me up. We ordered food, and I tried to pull it together. It was no use, my appetite had gone. I locked eyes with Emma at the other end of the table and saw that she was crying. My heart broke all over again. We had been humiliated and we had failed.

CHAPTER FOURTEEN

I opened my eyes and reached to turn off the alarm. For a brief, sweet moment, my mind was blank. Then I remembered: we had lost the title. I lay still, staring at the ceiling. There was no way I could go into work; only yesterday I had thought I would be in the office, entertaining colleagues with a blow-by-blow account of our resounding victory. I called in to Onside Law and told them we had lost the title. I was exhausted, emotionally and physically, and I needed a day to recover.

I dragged myself out of bed and on to the sofa. I sat there for the rest of the day, reliving the loss, crying and staring into space. I didn't feel like praying. The way I saw it, God had let me down. I thought we had made a deal, but He hadn't delivered on his promise. I felt I had kept my side of the deal: I had believed, worked harder than ever before, I had tithed, and yet the reward hadn't come. It was hard to take. Didn't the Bible say ask and you'll receive? I couldn't work out what had gone wrong. Our defeat had changed everything, my heart was broken and my relationship with God felt like it had been challenged. I felt betrayed and lost and left alone with an awful silence.

The following morning, I didn't feel any better, but I got an email from my boss:

'I understand you're disappointed, but you're being a little dramatic,' my boss wrote. 'People have suffered bereavements before and come into the office. This is not a bereavement. You need to come back into work.'

I read and reread the note. My boss was right, of course, though at the time I didn't think so. It was just football, only a game, but just then it didn't feel like that. The commute passed in a daze and at work I couldn't concentrate on much. I spent the following week like this, in a dull fog, as if my life was happening to someone else. I was absent, lost in my own struggle with disappointment and with God.

I was glad the season was over; I needed a break from football. I deleted Twitter from my phone for a while and tried to avoid games on TV and online. I found detoxing from football wasn't all that easy. It was only a few months after the men's World Cup in Brazil, and the game seemed to be everywhere I looked. Every screen, every advert, every shop window seemed to show footballers, scoring goals, celebrating and succeeding. I shrank away from the images. I couldn't bear the sight of other players enjoying the success that had been denied me.

I stopped praying completely, I no longer saw the point. It hadn't made any difference to my life when it counted. I had asked God for a that major win, and He had let me lose. I guessed He just hadn't been listening. It was a disturbing thought. The foundation of my faith cracked and shifted in my mind and I drifted further from God than I ever had before.

Work was a great distraction from these thoughts. Within a few months, at the beginning of 2015, I qualified from Onside Law. It was a huge milestone: after a decade of studying, cramming, juggling and commuting, I was now a qualified solicitor. It was a great relief to know that, whatever happened with football, I could always pivot into a second high-powered and fulfilling career. It gave me comfort as I geared up for another season. I was twenty-eight, with at least another five years left to play. There was still plenty of time for trophies.

I had mixed feelings about starting the new season. I missed training and playing, but a large part of me hadn't yet recovered from last season's failure. Still, there was a lot going on to distract me. There were big changes underway at the club. Emma had managed a miracle: Chelsea was going fully professional. I was offered an increase in my club salary, which meant I was able to take a break from law without too much financial pressure. The timing couldn't have been better; I had qualified, and now I could focus all my energy on playing. I felt positive for the first time in months.

Optimism was in the air as we began pre-season training. Emma had pushed through other changes on the back of last season's successful run. Our training sessions were no longer to be hidden away at night on AstroTurf. This season, we were training full-time, on grass, during daylight hours, and the club had also agreed to start providing us with lunch. These might seem like small achievements, but they were huge steps forward for all of us on the team. For the first time, we were fully integrated into the professional side of the club.

Emma was convinced this was our year, and her confidence was contagious. Many of the coaches and players now believed that this time around, we would not only take the title; we would also pick up the FA Cup along the way. The big news of the season was that for the first time, the FA Cup final would be played at

Wembley. Every side wanted to play in the first historic Wembley final and, though of course I did too, I have to admit the thought made me slightly queasy. I wasn't sure I could go through all that again, all the expectation and nerves, only to be ultimately disappointed.

Last season's wounds remained with me. I wasn't the only one on the team who felt that way. Emma understood that and focused a lot of time on building up the team's psychological strength. She saw what Jorge had seen back in St Louis, that sometimes the most important battle fought on the pitch is the one a key player has in their own mind with themselves. We needed strategies, mental safety nets, to catch us when everything went wrong. We needed to be able to stop the freefall into despair, focus, and turn the game around. As a striker, I had a special responsibility to do so.

'You're in control,' Emma told me. 'It's you in the pilot's seat. Imagine you are the pilot of a plane. If something went wrong when you were flying, you wouldn't give up and let the plane crash. You would fall back on your training, the procedures, the series of steps you had learned to go through in an emergency. It's the same on the pitch: you need to stop thinking about the final whistle before it has blown. You can affect the outcome now.'

Emma's strategies worked. We started the season with a four-win streak, and I scored the winner against Liverpool along the way, a small revenge for last year's title race. Ji and I gelled well with our new winger Gemma Davison up front. Two further new signings, Niamh Fahey and Millie Bright, found their place in our solid backline. With every goal, my confidence recovered further. In May I got a further boost when I was nominated for PFA Player of the Year. Later that month, Chelsea named me their Player of the Year, which motivated me even more to deliver for the club.

We were making great strides, topping the league and striding through rounds of the FA Cup. In early May, we faced Man City in the FA Cup semi-final, the first time we had met our rivals since the defeat the previous season. None of us could forget how delighted they had been to deny us the title. Man City were also desperate for trophies, and to play the first FA Cup final at Wembley. We smelt revenge. The game was goalless until the eighty-sixth minute, when our midfielder Drew Spence set up Ji, who belted it in from twenty yards out. Not very maturely, I celebrated the goal as if it had won us the Cup. Things were never really the same between me and Toni after that. True friends don't do that to one another.

Our victory over City secured our ticket to Wembley for the FA Cup final in August. We were also at the top of the table after not losing a game in seven. The team were hungrier than ever for both trophies, yet I couldn't help but worry we were setting ourselves up for another fall. In July we signed a new forward, Fran Kirby, to complete our killer front four with me, Gemma and Ji. Fran had been making waves at Reading in the Super League, two below our league. I had seen some of her goals and was in awe of her ability and goal-scoring prowess. She was already playing for England, and before she signed with Chelsea, I talked to her on a camp and told her how much I loved the club and what a good relationship I had with Emma. Forwards can often see other forwards as a threat, but I was desperate for Fran to sign with us. I knew she would complete our already terrifying forward line, which was the envy of the rest of the league.

Still, the summer wasn't all plain sailing. In mid-July we got a nasty shock. We faced Sunderland, an average team with a secret weapon in the form of the league's most prolific striker, Beth Mead. She scored a hat-trick to make up the bulk of our 4–0 defeat. The result brought us up short and knocked us off the top spot. Now came the real test of our new-found psychological strength. As fate would have it, our next league game was at home against Man City. Toni scored twelve minutes in, and the game was on. Ji, Gemma, Fran and I dodged and weaved together up front searching for an equaliser, but we were still one down at half-time. In the dressing room, Emma reminded us we were in the pilot's seat, and that we had forty-five minutes to turn the game around. Things were going wrong, but the final whistle hadn't come yet.

Walking back on to the pitch, I breathed deep and tried to put distance between myself and my fear. I was in control; I was in the cockpit. It was up to me. Three minutes in, space opened, I found the ball and drove forward. Keeper Karen Bardsley ran off her line and I pulled the trigger. I clenched my fists, threw my head back and yelled. We pushed for another, but four minutes from time, they curled in a free kick that deflected unfortunately off our left back Claire Rafferty and into the back of the net. It was our first defeat on home soil in two years, and City loved every minute.

The losses gave fuel to my worst fears. This was it, we were slipping. Our winning streak had been broken less than a week before we played in the first ever women's FA Cup final at Wembley. And the pressure was mounting, the build-up to the game had already begun. Thirty thousand tickets had been sold in advance and the match would be broadcast live on the BBC.

Pundits and journalists began saying we were a mentally weak team that, when it mattered, couldn't cope under pressure. It was tough to hear. I couldn't help it, I started to visualise us crumbling, losing the game and being hurt and humiliated in front of the whole country.

I spent the week in a state of nervous tension, visited regularly by fear. I declined all interview requests. Every night, I lay awake, sifting through the possible outcomes in my mind. One of my eyes became bloodshot with the stress. Our soft tissue therapist Eva Woods, who I relied on to treat my tight hamstrings and calves, suggested I go with her to do yoga for the first time to get me to relax. Nothing worked. I missed talking to God, but I had convinced myself there was no point in praying, it didn't change anything, so I stuck to the silent treatment. I reasoned that if I never asked God for anything, I couldn't be disappointed when I didn't get it. Still, lying awake night after night in the run-up to the final, my head was bursting with questions. I needed to talk to someone.

I decided to reach out to Linvoy; he had experience of both faith and football, he would know what to say. We met over coffee in Cobham and I told him I had stopped praying because I felt there was no point. I told him I couldn't take the disappointment when my prayers were ignored and that I didn't understand what had gone wrong. Didn't the Bible say my prayers would be answered? I had asked, but when it mattered, I had definitely not received.

Linvoy clasped his hands and looked at me.

'It doesn't work like that,' he said. 'There's a gap between asking and receiving. You wouldn't learn anything if you got everything you wanted right away. God is wiser than that: he won't give you what you want until it's the right time for you. He wants you to learn and grow, and sometimes that means you have to go through disappointment and failure. But God has a plan for you, all you have to do is have faith in it. Trust in Him. He has already written your story. The Bible says in Hebrews 11:1, "Faith is the substance of things hoped for, the evidence of things unseen."'

I stared at him, soaking up his words. Linvoy spoke as if he fully understood the place I was at in my relationship with God.

'We wouldn't need faith if every time we asked for something, we got it straight away,' he went on. 'Of course, your prayers will be answered. But that might not happen immediately, or in the way you expect. Sometimes we pray for things that aren't good for us, at least not at that time. God can see further than that.

It might not feel like it sometimes, but everything that happens is God's will, and He knows what's best for you.'

I thought about this for a moment and realised Linvoy was right. I needed to put more faith in God, and less in demonstrative religious acts. Faith was the invisible and unseen bond with God, the trust I had in my relationship with Him. Religion was something else, it was those actions on earth that could be seen and judged by others. When I tithed, I had expected to receive back from God straight away, I had expected we would win the title. But that isn't how God's relationship with me worked; it wasn't about giving to receive immediately. Tithing was never going to change the outcome God had already ordained. I had to trust He had another reward in store for me, maybe it was this year's trophy or maybe it was something altogether different. He had lessons for me to learn; I had to trust He knew when best to teach them. My life would unfold according to His timing, not mine. Then the terror rose again. What if I wasn't supposed to win this year either? I couldn't fail, not again.

'But what if God says the best thing for me is to lose again?' I said. 'I don't think I can take another public failure. I can't get it out of my head that we're going to fail.'

'OK, so let's tackle that head on,' Linvoy said. 'If you lose, what's the worst thing that would happen?'

I looked at him. 'Well, I'm going to be devastated again.'

'So, you'll be devastated,' he said. 'But are you going to die? Is someone in your family going to die? Worse things happen than losing a football match.'

'I guess so,' I said. 'But Linvoy, I really need this win. Part of me would rather be in a worse team and not have made it this far. I'm not sure I can go through losing it all again.'

Linvoy smiled and shook his head again.

'The way I see it, you have two options,' he said. 'Either you don't play because you're too scared you might lose. Or you play, give it everything you have, and afterwards, accept the result. Whatever happens, God has already allowed it to happen. You have nothing to lose, so enjoy the game, play for God, an audience of One. Put your faith in Him. That's all you can do.'

Linvoy had a way of making everything seem beautifully simple. Maybe it was that simple; maybe I only needed to relax, do my best and trust in God. It was a simple idea, but to my fear-addled brain, Linvoy's words were a stroke of genius and lifted a huge weight off my shoulders. Whatever happened, win or lose, it would be God's will. Even if it hurt, even if it was disappointing. God saw into my heart, he knew what was best for me, and what I could take. I thought back over the most unforeseen twists and turns of my life: joining Leafield Athletic, getting the call from St Louis, the Olympics and how it renewed my faith in the game. God had always had a hand in my life when I least expected it. I had to trust in it.

We went into the game as favourites. Notts County were rugged, dogged and determined. We knew they were going to make it difficult for us, not least their three young England forwards: Ellen White, Rachel Williams and Jess Clarke. We were under no illusions this time: we would have to work hard. If we won this time, it would be because we deserved to.

In the Wembley dressing room, surrounded by the echoes of hundreds of whispered pre-match prayers, I pulled on my number 9 shirt and raised my eyes to heaven. I knew exactly who this game was for. Walking out on to the pitch, I held Linvoy's words out in front of me like a shield. Whatever happens, God has already allowed it to happen. I had nothing to lose, I would play for God. I muttered a prayer: I will give you my best game, and I pray that you will let us win. If we don't, I will know it is part of your plan for me. Whatever the result, it will be your will.

The game started quietly as we felt out the other side. We dominated possession for the first fifteen minutes, and I had a shot on goal. I was feeling confident and, every time the ball came to me, I sensed I could outplay the Notts County right back. I went again, and the noise of the crowd swelled as I got the ball in midfield, dodged a defender and shot from eighteen yards out. Keeper Carly jumped and batted it away with both hands, but as I jogged down the wing, I felt positivity well up inside me. Something good was coming, I knew it. I was feeling free. Whatever happened now, God had already allowed to happen. Next chance, if it was His will, I would get it done.

The chances kept coming. Ji found the ball at the halfway line and passed forward. I ran on to the ball, defender in tow, left her behind me and hared down the wing. As she caught up on the edge of the box, I cut inside and chipped a deep cross over to the far post. Gemma found the ball but scuffed her volley wide back across goal. I lifted my hands to my forehead and sank to my knees; another chance gone. I rose, face screwed up in frustration. Please God, I prayed, I'm giving you my best.

Our breakthrough came just before half-time. Millie broke from the halfway line and as I sprinted down the wing, she found me wide in space on the left. I tacked in towards goal and, dodging a defender, played a disguised pass to Ji as she was tackled at once by both the keeper and a defender. Miraculously, the ball bounced out of the scrum and landed between Ji and an open goal. All that remained was for her to poke it in from six yards out. I spun around, raised a fist and ran to the corner where I slid on my knees next to Ji. I beamed and raised my hand to my ear; I wanted to hear the crowd.

Notts rallied around the hour mark. They got a corner and when it was cleared, Notts midfielder Desiree Scott was there to find it at the edge of the area. I felt the danger and charged her down with Katie and Gilly and forced her to rush her shot from twenty yards out. The ball deflected off Gilly and it flew inches wide of the left post. Another corner followed which Gemma cleared off the line. My whole body ached with the tension, I desperately wanted it to be over.

Linvoy's words rang in my head again. I had a choice: either give in to fear and don't play, or play, give it everything you have, and afterwards, accept the result. I had promised God my best game, and I was giving it to Him, I could do nothing more. Gemma found the ball on the wing and, pressed by a defender, passed to me in wide open space on the edge of the area. Faced with defender Alex Greenwood, I drove a long low shot past her. The keeper lunged and, with her outstretched fingertips parried the shot.

God kept his side of the agreement, and kept the chances rolling in. Ji took a corner. It sailed in and Katie rose to meet it, but a defender cleared it out of the box. Niamh found the loose ball and I ran back out to the edge of the box to meet her cross, swivelled and flicked it back towards goal. In the goalmouth, Gilly Flaherty tried to poke it in, but scooped it over the bar. We were ahead, all we needed to secure the win was a second goal, but despite our efforts, it just wasn't coming.

It was to be my last play of the game. Nine minutes before time, with us still clinging on to our slim lead, my right calf began to cramp, and Emma could see I needed to come off. As I walked towards the dugout, the Chelsea fans rose from their seats and gave me a standing ovation, a moment that will stay with me forever. I smiled and waved and my heart swelled with love and gratitude. I had given them my best game, there was nothing more I could do. I sat down on the bench to watch the final minutes of the game. I wanted it to be over. I just wanted to win.

And so began the longest five minutes of my life. An equaliser could come at any second and I didn't know how the team would react if we went to extra time with tired legs and tired minds. Three years of commitment to this team condensed into these final moments. We had run two marathons back to back, surely this time we would cross the finish line. Surely this time we would win.

Time slowed, and the noise from the stadium dimmed to a background hum. I clasped my hands and began to whisper my prayers. Please God, don't let them equalise. You wrote this before the ball was kicked; let this be your plan. Suddenly the players on the bench grinned and clapped me on the back as an announcement came through the loud speaker naming me player of the match. I looked up in time to see my face appear on the stadium's giant screens. I flashed a smile, but I barely registered the honour. It meant nothing compared to winning. I refocused on the pitch and my conversation with God.

The last minute arrived and we held our breaths. The final whistle blew, and the cord snapped, I leapt up and ran on to the pitch. Months of hard work and tension blew away like dust as I threw my arms around my teammates and we formed a circle and jumped for joy. I spun around to look up at the fans and the tears came. I put my hands together and whispered thanks to God. He had done what Linvoy said He would do, He had answered my prayers in his own time, and He had done so here at Wembley, on the biggest stage of all. Amid the pride and pure elation, I felt a rising tide of relief. The

oppressive fear that had covered me for so long like a blanket had lifted and I felt lighter than air. It was over. We had won.

The next moments were unforgettable. Walking up Wembley's iconic steps to the Royal Box, I finally understood the real genius of God's plan. Losing then had been necessary in order to win now. Without that loss, we wouldn't have found the strength to win here, to be the first women to climb these steps and raise this trophy in this place. God had known I would grow through defeat and He had wanted me to come back to the game humbled. He had wanted me to strive harder until I was truly deserving. At the top of the steps, as we lifted the shining silver, I praised His wisdom.

Our football rose to another level after that win. I found such joy in playing again, freed by the knowledge that we deserved to be champions. We won our last five league games and claimed the title. In our final game of the season, against Sunderland, we reversed our earlier defeat to beat them 4–0. Raising the league trophy at last, I was full of love for the players, coach, staff and the fans. We had been on a journey from the very bottom, we had been crushed once and made it to the top once again, wiser, older, better and stronger. Finally, we had something to show for it all. Now we had the double.

That season had taught me some of the most valuable lessons of my career. Never again would I walk on to a pitch taking a win for granted, and never again would I question God's wisdom. I saw now that there was a time for defeats, and a time for victories, and that both had a place in His plan.

Defeats were not only failures; they were invitations to grow. Football, like life, is a story of extremes, of highs and lows, defeats and victories. Of all the ups and downs of my career, it is that loss, and that win, that stand above all others. Those games taught me the biggest lesson of all: to trust in the hand of God.

For me, it is God's hand that dictates when I win, and when I lose. For those without God in their lives, it is still vital to know there is always a lesson behind every failure. If one thing is sure, there will be setbacks in life, and every one of them happens for a reason that might lead to success just around the corner. Looking back over the failures, and the successes, I understand now that one can't come without the other.

Knowing that helps me to no longer shy away from failure and remind myself that I may have to fail more than once to reach greatness. Remember that, and however hard it is, keep relentlessly putting yourself back in the position to fail. Take it from me. Only then can you win.

When You're Scoring, You're Safe

I always believed that in adversity, the best protection was to **perform.**

If I did my job well, I thought no one could hurt me.

CHAPTER FIFTEEN

Mark Sampson was still only a name to me on the day he was appointed England manager. I had seen him once or twice on the sidelines when Chelsea played his club, Bristol Academy, but we had never spoken. What follows is my memory of what happened from the day we met, right up until our last contact. This account is supported by documentary evidence submitted to three investigations and a parliamentary hearing.

This was a time in my life in which I learned a lot of lessons. The following experiences taught me how to react when, for whatever reason, you feel that your superiors don't want you to succeed. I learned how deal with isolation, how to self-validate, how to look in the mirror and tell myself I was good enough, how to go out and win even though those around me didn't always appear to want me to. And I learned that in those circumstances, the best answer to adversity is success. I came out of this time stronger because I figured out how to perform despite being miserable. I learned that no one can mess with you when you're succeeding and that, for the most part, when you're scoring, you're safe.

I had no opinion of Mark before we met, though his appointment as Hope's successor had raised some eyebrows in both footballing circles and the media. He was young, only thirty-one, and widely considered inexperienced for such a senior role, especially given he had never won any titles or trophies. Still, I reasoned, he had taken Bristol Academy to the Champions League, and he had to have impressed someone to get the job. Besides, a youthful coach was what the team needed after so many years under Hope's traditional approach. We were all excited for a fresh start.

Mark introduced himself to the squad at a camp in La Manga, Spain, in January 2014, ahead of a friendly against Norway. It was all change at England; he brought lots of new staff with him and a whole host of new players. Some, like forward Lianne Sanderson, had been brought back in after a spell of absence under Hope. Others came up from the youth system and still others got their first call up well into their twenties. He made Steph Houghton, who at twenty-five was among the younger players, his new captain in place of the vastly experienced Casey Stoney. For many of us, the message was clear: Mark was here to shake things up.

At his first team meeting, Mark came across as thoughtful and well spoken. He spoke about his fast, direct approach to football, which had brought him success at Bristol. He didn't believe in a strict football philosophy; his philosophy, if anything, was to adapt and win. He said we should learn to adapt to our opponents and have a number of different tactics up our sleeves. I was impressed; I had never heard a coach say that before. For years under Hope we had played the same style of football, often in the same formation. We had lost a fair few games because we hadn't adapted when we needed to.

Mark wrapped up the meeting saying he wanted to improve communication between staff and players. He wrote his mobile number on to a flipchart and said he wanted an open-door policy whereby players could contact him any time. Then he ended the meeting with a loud, playful clap. Most of the squad noted

Mark's number down after the meeting, but I held off. Somehow, it didn't seem appropriate to me to have my coach's private number. Maybe I was just stuck in the old ways. I had only ever used email with Hope and somehow that felt more professional. It didn't seem like a big deal; I knew I could get the number off one of the others if need be. All in all, Mark seemed like a decent guy, and it was clear he would bring a much-needed fresh approach.

At lunch, the conversation turned to Mark. All the other players were very positive.

'He speaks well, doesn't he?' one said to me.

'Yes,' I said. I was optimistic, but I wasn't about to get too excited. 'I guess we'll have to wait and see.'

I had seen enough coaches who, though they could talk a great game, when it came down to it lacked tactical depth to bring up players and the team. Like everyone, I was keen to get off on the right foot with the new coach, and I was slightly nervous going into our first one-on-one meeting. Still, I wasn't too worried, I was in good goal-scoring form, having scored four times in the first four games of our qualifying campaign for the 2015 World Cup.

The meeting went well, Mark and I had a constructive conversation about football. He said positive things about my speed, and how he wanted to use it better. His big aim for me was to work on scoring a variety of different goals, including those from outside the box. The only confusion came when he said he didn't know where to play me.

'I don't know what kind of striker you are,' said Mark. 'I don't know what kind of goals you score.'

I looked at him, confused. It was his job to know, I thought. I had been on the senior team for the past ten years, there was plenty of material to look back on.

'I feel I can score any type of goal,' I said and managed a nervous smile. 'Though maybe I don't score a lot of headers.'

Looking back, I think Mark had questions about how I fitted into his plans for the team and direct style of play even before I had kicked a ball in his first training session. At the time it didn't set any alarm bells ringing. After all, other players also said Mark told them they had things to work on in their game. It was a clean slate; we all understood we would have to show the new coach what we could do.

We played a friendly against Norway two days later. Mark started me on the left wing of a 4–3–3 formation, and I scored the very first goal of his England tenure, a shot that deflected in off a Norwegian defender. I was glad to have scored, even though it wasn't the kind of long-range shot Mark said he wanted to see more of from me. I left Spain certain I had nothing to worry about, confident I had done enough to be recalled for the next camp.

Still, Mark's line about not knowing what type of goals I scored stuck in my mind. It unsettled me. To me, the fact I was scoring goals was more important than what type of goal it was. I was an experienced footballer; I knew what kind of player I was. I was fast, with sharp feet in the box, and that meant most of my goals involved beating the defensive line, sprinting towards goal and slipping it to the right or left of the keeper. That had always been my strength, all the way back to playing as a kid on the estate in Birmingham. I had scored many goals that way, for club and country.

But now Mark had planted a seed of doubt in my mind. Maybe those goals weren't enough any more. He wanted me to score more long-range goals, he wanted more headers. I thought back over the past months. I had scored from thirty yards out against Turkey in our 4–0 win three months earlier. Had Mark seen that goal? Now I felt pressure to replicate it. I wasn't sure if Mark wanted me to pick apart my whole goal-scoring strategy. Should I prioritise changing the type of goals I scored?

Surely not at the expense of getting in the right position to score, regardless of what type of goal it was? I was confused.

The next England camp was at the Cyprus Cup in early March. It was Mark's first chance to see us play in a tournament setting and work out his best team before our qualifying campaign continued the following month. Having scored against Norway, I was hoping to start our first game against Italy. Instead, I started on the bench and came on in the second half to help the side win 2–0. I understood: Mark wanted to see the other forwards in action. He changed the whole starting eleven for our next game, which was against Finland, and I was back in to start. We had a good game: Anita scored half an hour in, Gemma Bonner headed a second in past the hour and I scored a third minutes later, securing our 3–0 win. I landed back on the bench for our win against Canada, which took us into the final against France.

Naturally, all the changes kept everyone on their toes. The morning of the final, Mark revealed his team sheet and I wasn't on it. It felt unsettling not to make the starting eleven, and I soon began to realise my starting place was less secure than it had been. I asked to see Mark to talk through what I could do to play more consistently for him. Others seemed to be striking up a rapport with him, and I wanted to do the same.

We met in the lobby of the team hotel. Talking in public, with players and staff milling around, was part of Mark's open door, open communication policy. I didn't mind, it felt easier and more relaxed that way.

'I'm trying to see the range of players,' Mark opened.

I nodded. 'Yes, I totally understand that,' I said. 'Still, I am scoring every time I start, so I want to understand better what it would take for me to be a consistent starter.'

Mark smiled and agreed with the goal-scoring part. Then he said something odd.

'At the moment, Eni,' he said, 'I want consistent players I can rely on to play for the group. But put it this way: if we went to war tomorrow, I'm not sure I would take you.'

I stared blankly back at Mark while my mind began to whirl with questions. Bit of a strange analogy, wasn't it? What did war have to do with football? Did he think I was selfish and didn't play for the team? Wasn't I a consistent player, after a decade on the team?

'What do you mean?' I said.

'I mean you seem to isolate yourself from the group,' he said. 'I saw you go for a walk on the beach earlier. I like that, but why did you go alone?'

So that was it. We didn't know each other too well yet. Maybe he was trying to figure me out, just like I was trying to figure him out. All I needed to do was explain I had always been comfortable in my own company. I'd holidayed alone, eaten out alone, and countless times gone on lone walks on England camps. There was nothing wrong with that. Right?

'I don't know,' I said. 'I guess I wanted to go alone. I'm quite independent.'

At this, Mark leaned back in triumph.

'I don't want individuals,' he said. 'I want a team that works as a collective.'

The meeting ended on this odd note. I stepped into the elevator and went back to my room, thoroughly confused. Mark had me all wrong; I had never been an outsider on any team. I was a people person, I got involved. That didn't mean I couldn't enjoy my own company now and then, did it? I thought quickly. What was really going on here? Could he have picked up on a petty argument I had had with Toni and Jill Scott? Perhaps he thought I was to blame.

That suspicion seemed to be confirmed soon enough. In our pre-match meeting before the final against France, Mark urged younger players not to be influenced by what he called the 'wrong crowd'. It was a strange enough thing to bring up hours before a cup final, but it was odd for another reason. Mark kept his comments vague enough that anyone in the room could plausibly have believed he was talking about them. I thought back to our confusing meeting in the lobby. Did Mark consider me the 'wrong crowd'? I certainly got on with younger players on the team, such as Toni and Alex Greenwood, both Liverpudlians with a wicked sense of humour. Could that be it? Could Mark have been referring to me as a bad influence in the team? It certainly all seemed to fit.

I left the camp feeling more confused than ever. I hadn't got a footballing answer about why I was now only starting two out of five games and I didn't know what the coach, or his staff, thought of me. It hadn't been a positive feeling on the camp in general. Several times during the tournament I had walked into a lift with the coaches only to be met with a sudden icy silence. Lifts are weird social spaces at the best of times, but there could be no doubt. This was properly awkward.

Back home one night, not long after the camp, I got to wondering again how I could improve. If Mark wanted different goals from me, I would have to work out how to deliver them. I logged on to our cloud-based replay analysis system, where whole games were uploaded for us to watch back and take notes on our own performances. I settled down to watch the Cyprus Cup Finland game, the one where I'd played the longest. As the game began, I noticed the microphone channel that the coaches used to communicate during games had been left on the recording. Under Hope, the replay videos had always been silent, but on this one I could hear staff members speaking back and forth on the microphone, commenting on the game. I didn't think much of it at first as I heard the new goalkeeper coach Lee Kendall chatting with the long-serving fitness coach Naomi Datson. Then, a few minutes into the game, I lost possession. Lee's voice came through the laptop speakers.

'Fuck off, Eni,' he said.

Bit strong, I thought, especially when I hadn't cost the team a goal or a chance. Still, this was football, I reasoned, people swore, I certainly did sometimes. But it struck me as weird, and as the game rolled on, I pricked up my ears. Lee wasn't speaking negatively about any of the other players, when they had possession he was encouraging and complimenting their efforts.

Then, when I was on the ball next, I heard Naomi's voice: 'Her fitness results are good,' she said.

'Yeah,' said Lee. 'But she is lazy as fuck.'

I gazed at the screen. What did he just say? I hit pause, scrolled back and played the clip again. There it was, loud and clear: 'Lazy as fuck.' I played it back, again and again. I couldn't believe it. Twenty-three other players had access to this video, who else had heard it? I was mortified. The criticism wasn't even fair; this had been a good game for me. I had kept possession well, I had scored, I had assisted. I skipped forward to the goal and the assist. Neither Lee nor Naomi said anything positive. This felt very wrong.

My heart was beating hard. I felt like I had just overheard a two-faced friend slagging me off behind my back. I knew staff must have said negative things about me in the past, but it was another thing to hear it with my own ears. Hope was smart. This must have been exactly why she had never left the sound on these replay analysis videos. She knew that players wouldn't like hearing staff members talking like this about them during a game. But there was more to it than that.

Alarm bells were ringing in my head, but I couldn't put my finger on why. I watched the clip again, and then it came to me. The swearing wasn't a problem, it was the word 'lazy'. Lee could have criticised my playing in any other way. He could have called me a bad defender, or said I should have tracked back. Instead, he chose to use the word 'lazy'. Some might say, and rightly so, that there are worse things to be called. But as a black footballer, something about the word in that moment didn't sit right with me. I wouldn't be the first black player to be called idle. It was a red flag.

To me, the word smacked of careless stereotyping and racist undertones stretching back to the time of slavery. Back then, in the United States, African American slaves were caricatured as lazy to justify withholding rights and having them perform dehumanising tasks. Slave masters would describe slaves as 'needing pushing', especially those who protested their captivity by slowing work or faking illness. After slavery ended, during the Jim Crow era of rigid segregation that lasted well into the mid-1960s, the same caricature was used to justify keeping black people in dead-end jobs. You don't have to take my word for it. Visitors to the Jim Crow Museum of Racist Memorabilia in Michigan can see the vivid caricatures for themselves: black men, lazy, idle and inarticulate, slumped against a tree.

Lee probably had no idea about any of this. If he did, he would not have dreamed for a second that calling me 'lazy as fuck' had any connotation with America's racist past. But in my experience, that's often how stereotypes work, they play out as a linguistic blind spot that comes out in a slip of the tongue. I felt Lee's choice of words was an echo, down the ages, that resonated in the modern day as an easily available critique of a black football player. Of course, anyone, me included, can be called lazy. But as a black person the experience feels very different. I thought back to studying *To Kill a Mockingbird* in school. The character Bo Radley had been a black man falsely accused of rape, a victim of the oversexualised stereotype. They had taught me the history and they had taught me the stereotypes. But they didn't teach me what to do when these stereotypes were applied to me.

I wondered what I should do. I had to talk to someone, so I called my Chelsea coach Emma and told her what I had heard. She couldn't believe how unprofessional the whole thing was. We agreed it would be best for her to call and speak to Mark about this, manager to manager. I sat, frozen to my sofa, waiting for her to call me back. I thought back over the Finland game and tried to work out if the criticism was justified. I had been used to Hope pushing my fitness and going on about how I should defend from the front, but nothing about this game warranted me being singled out like that. I reminded myself I had played well, I had scored, and assisted a second goal. It was pre-season, no one was at their peak fitness, but it wasn't as if my fitness levels stood out as bad. Even Naomi had said to Lee that my fitness levels were good.

Just then, Emma called back. She said Mark had asked Phil Worrall, the head of analysis, to watch the video and he had confirmed he had heard Lee's comments. Mark had promised Emma it would never happen again, and that the match recordings would be silent in future. But I was unsettled; Lee had spoken too confidently, too freely. It was only two months into Mark's tenure, but I suspected it wasn't the first time he had spoken about me this way. I couldn't grasp how the new staff could have such strong negative opinions of me so early on. I needed to speak to Mark.

I suspected Mark would be on the defensive. After all, Lee was Mark's friend, his hire. I felt I needed to be smart about it, so I asked Mark for a meeting to discuss what he wanted from me as a striker. A request for feedback on how I could improve felt less confrontational than demanding a meeting about the incident with Lee.

We met at Wembley Stadium a week later, where Mark took me into a glass-walled office to talk. On the way in, we walked past several coaches and FA executives sitting in the open-plan office. They were all pleasant, but a number threw me looks that said they were wondering what I was doing there. Mark seemed on edge; his head kept darting around as if he was painfully conscious that people could see us. I wasn't worried. There was nothing unusual about a player meeting a manager.

After some awkward small talk about my Tube ride to Wembley, I asked Mark for his views on my performances at the Cyprus Cup. He made positive points about my movement, my work rate, and my goals. He said he wanted to use me as a number 9 striker, and suggested that to improve my runs, I should study US striker Alex Morgan. He wanted me to copy her killer runs through the heart of the opposing defence and move away from my usual runs that often ended out wide. It was good, detailed advice which I took on board and later looked up Alex on YouTube.

We finished our review of the Cyprus Cup, and after about forty-five minutes, Mark began to wind up the meeting by asking whether I'd be getting a Tube home. He was polite, but I couldn't help but feel he was avoiding the huge elephant in the room. I hesitated. I had to say something.

'We need to talk about this other thing,' I said at last. 'About Lee.'

Mark avoided my eye.

'I apologise on his behalf,' he said. 'But Lee is a good guy. He's passionate, sometimes he uses bad language. It's nothing to take personally.'

'Well, we're all passionate people,' I said. 'Lee needs to figure out how to channel that passion. I wouldn't get away with talking about a member of staff like that and putting it down to being passionate.'

Mark looked up and met my eye. It was clear he hadn't ever dealt with a player like me before, someone who wasn't daunted by him, or afraid to articulate their feelings. I saw in his eyes that it annoyed him.

'Lee shouldn't have said that on the mikes,' said Mark. 'Still, you should know that I collaborate very closely with my coaches and that we share information about all players. Anything Lee is saying also reflects my view, and of the other staff: your fitness does need to improve.'

My eyes widened. Mark wasn't only being defensive; he was doubling down. Worse, he was hinting that the entire staff talked about me that way. Constructive criticism of an England player was one thing, but this didn't sound like constructive criticism. It sounded like irrational groupthink, and by the looks of things, Mark was the ringleader.

'I'll make sure Lee and Naomi speak to you and apologise at the next camp,' Mark said.

'OK, thanks Mark,' I said.

I stood up, still reeling slightly as he shepherded me out of the office suite, his head still flicking around nervously. I was glad to end it on a decent note. Emma had spoken to him; I had lodged my complaint in person, and I had been promised an apology. It would be best to leave it there. Thirty minutes later, on my way home, my phone buzzed with a notification from Twitter. Mark had posted about our meeting:

'Real good day today :) Great catch up with @EniAlu New @FA suit fitted & ready to wear plus a fun interview with @FIFAcom now #HomeTime'

I couldn't believe my eyes. This was a confidential meeting about what I considered to be a highly sensitive incident. If I wanted a catch up, I would have waited until the next camp. I didn't see why anyone on Twitter needed to know we had met. His tweet seemed calculated to skew perceptions of what had gone on in our meeting and twist it into a harmless catch up. It felt very much as if he were covering his arse in advance.

It was weird; I was entirely thrown. As much as Mark might have cared about making amends for a serious error, it was clear he cared equally about how it looked

ENIOLA ALUKO

100 CAPS
CONGRATULATIONS

TOGETHER FOR ENGLAND

VAUXHALL

Slumped on the pitch that day in 2014, I still had a lot to learn. That defeat shook me to my core. It shattered my love of football and even made me question my faith in God.
I felt humiliated.
I felt like a failure.
It was too much to bear.

We had been on a journey from the very bottom, we had been crushed once and made it to the top once again, wiser, older, better and stronger. Finally, we had something to show for it all. Now we had the double.

FA under pressure to explain payment after bullying claim

- England star paid £80,000 after complaint
- Coach accused of 'inappropriate' remark to a player

Eni Aluko claims England manager Mark Sampson once told her to make sure her Nigerian relatives did not bring Ebola to a match at Wembley

FA 'blackmail' shock

Sampson scandal Aluko's damning evidence leaves chiefs Clarke and Glenn fighting to save careers

Aluko in her own words: 'I'm shocked at how malicious this feels'

'I should have played a more active role to ensure they were handled more respectfully': Ex-England women's boss Mark Sampson apologises to Eniola Aluko and Drew Spence for racially discriminatory comments

Mark Sampson found guilty of racially abusing Eni Aluko and Drew Spence

The FA has lost the trust of the public, says chairman Greg Clarke

The chairman of England's football governing body says its "white hierarchy" failed to adequately handle race abuse claims

FA apologises to Eniola Aluko over Mark Sampson's racist remarks
England Women's striker accuses FA of blackmail during DCMS hearing

*Caro Juventus
tifosi, ho due
parole per voi...*

**Dear Juventus
fans, I have two
words for you...**

THANK YOU!!

to the outside world. Lots of people saw us go into that office and Mark would later claim he had tweeted to protect me and the team from any outside perception that something was up. I could understand playing our meeting down to people in the Wembley offices, but there was no reason to put anything out on Twitter. I didn't respond to the tweet, I ignored it. Though its tone was positive, it didn't sit well with me. My gut told me this was only the beginning.

I thought it best if I logged my meeting with Mark with someone higher up the food chain at Wembley. I wrote an email to the FA's then sporting director Adrian Bevington, with whom I had always had good exchanges whenever we crossed paths. I described the replay analysis incident, my meeting with Mark and the tweet, and explained I felt it necessary to log it in case anything else happened. It gives me goose bumps now to think I could see trouble coming for me, and potentially for others, down the line. I've learned to always trust my gut in these things.

I saw Mark again only a few days later, when the team met at England's national training centre in St George's Park ahead of a qualifier against Montenegro. Mark stopped me as soon as I entered our hotel lobby and pointed over to one corner, where Lee and Naomi were waiting to speak to me. I went over and sat down. Lee leaned forward in his seat.

'Listen, Eni,' Lee said. 'It wasn't my intention to offend you. I apologise for what you heard.'

I nodded.

'We want you to be better,' he went on. 'I'm very passionate about players improving.'

I nodded again, though I didn't buy it. That was just sugar-coating, underneath he was excusing his negativity by saying he didn't think I was good enough.

'I appreciate your passion, Lee,' I said. 'And I accept your apology. But everyone made mistakes in that game, and yet you didn't seem to speak that way about anyone else. I don't want to feel as if you are sat here apologising only because you got caught.'

I couldn't help but feel Lee was apologising only to diffuse the situation, not because he genuinely meant it. As a child I was taught that, no matter how right I felt I was, no matter how little I might mean it, I should apologise to anyone hurt by my actions. To refuse is prideful. It's my responsibility to diffuse the situation. At least Lee was doing that.

Lee left, leaving me with Naomi. We had always had a good relationship. She was a focused professional who had been promoted to the role of lead sports scientist after Hope's departure. I never had her down as the type to share opinions on players that weren't in line with the raw fitness data. I had learned a lot from her about how endurance fitness was a tougher ask for speed players like me with fast twitch fibres. Looking at her now, I could see in her eyes she was truly sorry.

'I'm just surprised, Nay, more than anything,' I said.

'Yes, I know,' she said. 'and I can only apologise. You've been working hard. As I said to Lee, your fitness results are good. Just keep doing what you're doing.'

I smiled; I couldn't be angry at Naomi. We hugged and went about our day. I tried to forget about the whole thing, but it wasn't easy watching Lee around the camp, laughing and joking with players and staff. I didn't trust him; I couldn't help wondering what he was saying about me when I wasn't around. My best reply, I decided, was to perform well on the pitch. Goals and assists were hard proof that whatever the coaches were saying about me was wrong. I fixed a smile and got on with our qualifying campaign. I contributed a goal to our 9–0 thrashing of Montenegro, a goal which, unusually for me, was a header. The following month we beat Ukraine 4–0 at home, and I scored a brace.

Ahead of the Ukraine game, the issue of central contracts came up once more. I was as committed as ever to improving standards after the watershed of the Olympics and a key sticking point had always been what happened to a contracted player if they got injured or went on maternity leave. The FA had wanted to reserve the right to cancel the contract without notice, but that wasn't going to fly. No employment law in the country would allow an employer to drop an employee if they were injured at work. I was sure of my ground; I knew the law. Together with Matthew Buck from the PFA, I was pushing to lengthen notice periods, and establish guarantees in case of injury.

All along, my contacts to the PFA and my legal background made me a natural default representative for the team. But now I was trying to improve terms, I wanted to make sure the whole team understood the collective benefits I wanted and were fully on board with them. I wanted to make things official. As negotiations ramped up again, I felt the team would be better represented by a small committee of elected reps.

At the camp before we played Ukraine, I went to the team and organised a ballot. I suggested we make a committee of four players, two younger and two senior players, and asked anyone interested to put themselves forward as representatives. Then I gave each player in the squad a vote sheet with all the candidates' names and asked them to complete them in private and bring them back to me the following day. The results returned me, Toni, Laura Bassett and captain Steph Houghton to the mini-committee. It was a big step in uniting the team to push for improved terms.

The negotiations ran on for several months, but the FA were receptive, and we stuck to our guns. In the end, we won another victory, and central contracts improved considerably. Annual salaries increased to £25,000 with £5,000 in maximum bonuses, and important contractual clauses were introduced that brought the contracts more in line with employment norms for women in other workplaces. It was a great achievement; one I remain very proud of to this day.

Meanwhile, our qualifying campaign went on. In mid-June, as the men's 2014 World Cup kicked off in Brazil, we set off on a ten-day trip to play Belarus and Ukraine. I scored the first goal in our 3–0 win against Belarus on the same day as England men lost their World Cup opener against Italy. Two nights later, I watched Argentina's opening game and made the mistake of tweeting about it at full-time at 12.45 a.m. With another four days until our next match, against Ukraine, I hadn't thought twice about staying up to watch Messi in action. Not everyone saw it that way.

The next morning, I walked into our team meeting to see a slide projected on to the wall with advisable sleeping hours for athletes. In ten years in the team I had never seen this presentation before. Mark was absolutely fuming; he rounded on the squad.

'Who was up late last night?' he said.

I was surprised. This was Mark's opening line? I looked around the team, no one moved. I had two choices: I could lie and pretend I hadn't been watching the game, or I could own up. I raised my hand, I had tweeted, I couldn't deny it. I looked around again; though I know for sure others watched the game, I was the only one with my hand up.

Mark gave me a meaningful look, and then launched into a lecture on professional standards. As before, he addressed the group, but I was left with the impression that it was me he was furious with. I fixed my eyes on the floor in embarrassment. He had prepared presentation slides for this. If he had wanted to tell me off, couldn't he have done it privately? Well, now he was well and truly on the offensive and I was the one caught on the back foot. I couldn't help wondering if he had been waiting for this, for me to slip up, so he could single me out.

By lunchtime, me staying up late had already become a running joke on the team. I laughed along with the others, but deep down I felt uneasy. It was becoming clear that under this manager I had to ensure that I didn't put a foot wrong. Later that week, when I scored again against Ukraine, there was none of the usual buzz. Instead, I felt vindicated, as if it were proof that staying up hadn't affected my game. It was a strange feeling, one I had never felt before when scoring for England.

Afterwards, Mark announced that all players were to have group meetings with him, the assistant coach Marieanne Spacey, and Lee. I went into mine, braced for a tirade about sleeping hours. It didn't come; all that stuff about late nights melted away like it had never happened. Without an audience, maybe, there was no point. Maybe none of it had been about sleeping hours in the first place, maybe it was about Mark showing he was boss in front of the team. The focus was back on football, and the three staff members gave their views on my performance.

Mark was complimentary. 'You're playing well,' he said. 'Your movement is good, you're staying on the back shoulders of defenders, and you're scoring goals. You're making it very difficult for me to drop you.'

My relief at hearing the praise soon drained away. That last bit was an odd thing to say to a player who was on form. He hadn't said I was cementing my place in the team; he had said I was making it hard for him to drop me. It was a slip of the tongue, perhaps, but it piled on the pressure. I was scoring, so why hadn't he said to keep doing what I was doing? Where did being dropped come into it?

I tried to reassure myself. Mark liked to rotate players, perhaps he was simply referring to healthy competition between us. Every player in a national team should feel their place is at risk, and talented players were coming up all the time. Still, the fact remained that right then I was England's most prolific striker. I scored goals every time I played for England and I was in the running for top scorer in our qualification group. My scoring streak in the league was helping Chelsea shoot up the table, so why was I suddenly feeling insecure about my spot on the starting eleven at England?

Again I asked myself, had Mark let slip that he wanted me to fail so he could drop me from the team? And, if I did make a mistake, he had shown he had no qualms about calling it out in front of the whole group. At the time, I didn't say anything. He knew my stats, what more was there to say? I left the meeting vowing to remain, at the very least, difficult to drop.

We qualified for the 2015 World Cup against Wales, at Mark's home ground in Cardiff, in late August. I scored a great goal in the first half. The ball bounced fortunately over the top of the defender's head, I chested it and volleyed it into the roof of the net. I felt good, I had continued my scoring run, and had helped the team seal qualification. I was enjoying being difficult to drop.

By then, others had begun to notice Mark's behaviour towards me. A few players could see he didn't like me. My close friends, such as Lianne, often asked why Mark was always so spiky with me. I could only shrug; I had no idea. I kept scoring for him, there was nothing else to do.

A new dynamic was entering the team. I was excited at first when our new team development coach, Adam Streeter, introduced a number of new team-building initiatives. Adam, who had replaced psychologist Misia after Hope left, worked for Lane 4, an outside consultancy hired by the FA to build performance within the England team. He was young, only twenty-five, and he was brimming with new ideas he wanted to try out.

I made an effort to get to know Adam and build a relationship, as I did with all staff. I was intrigued about his background and how he came into such a great role at such a young age. Adam and I got on well and exchanged stories and experiences. We had attended rival sports universities, Brunel and Loughborough, and both struggled with family issues. I listened to the story of how Adam had sadly lost his mother at a young age and I told him about my distant relationship with Dad. It was good to know there was someone around I could talk to on this level, a pressure valve in a high-pressure environment.

The rest of the team also responded well to Adam. He and Mark had the whole squad agree on a new code of conduct they called the 'Lioness Laws of the Jungle', or 'Lioness behaviour'. This was essentially a list of rules, including such gems of wisdom as 'make your teammate accountable', 'don't be an energy zapper' and 'speak to a teammate if you have a problem'. It was all well intentioned, but I found the advice to be pretty obvious and on the whole, slightly patronising.

In another move, Mark appointed a core leadership group of four players. The idea had been poached from the New Zealand All Blacks, a team that prides itself on its distinctive culture. In his 2013 book *Legacy,* best-selling author James Kerr explored the culture behind what is without doubt one of the most successful teams in the history of sport. Having read the book, I thought it was a great idea to try and replicate the All Blacks' success and cultivate our own culture, a Lioness culture. It sounded good on paper, but it was different in practice, mostly because we weren't the All Blacks. We were women, with different leaders and players, and we were playing a different sport.

Mark hand-picked the new leadership group from the squad. He chose four individuals: the captain and three other established players (who all happened to be white). The group's purpose was kept intentionally vague. When, in team discussions, I questioned openly what the purpose of the leadership group was, it didn't go down well with Mark, the staff, and some other players. Whenever I asked, I was told it was what the All Blacks do. Intentionally or not, in practice the group were elevated above the other players and given a say on tactics, direction and team culture as part of leadership meetings behind closed doors.

The leadership group, in particular, seemed counter-intuitive to me. It was difficult to creating a closeness and bond that would translate on to the pitch when some players were elevated to a position where they had a say over the others on the team. I felt things should be done differently. I was an experienced player, and I expected that to be respected, but I didn't like hierarchies, and I didn't need a captain's armband to feel validated.

Over time, I felt, the leadership group's role descended largely into finger-pointing and judging. I began to suspect the group picked out players who didn't fit: those who they believed refused to conform, those who were considered too individual.

I was made to feel like trouble, like I didn't fit, like it was me that had the problem. I was made to feel I was different, because I wasn't afraid to challenge a leadership set-up I felt was dangerous for the group dynamic. I wasn't alone in thinking that. I had plenty of conversations with teammates in hotel rooms, but when I said what many others were thinking, I found myself alone, out on a limb. For the first time in a decade, I began to feel isolated on the team. My ears felt like they were constantly burning.

Individuality unsettles a lot of people. Many are more comfortable when they are surrounded by others who are just like them. It takes strength to stand out from a crowd and stop needing validation from others. It's a lesson that can take time to learn. Mark was building a group of like-minded players who would eventually reinforce his team culture when I came to question it.

At this point I had a choice. Either I could march to the same beat as everyone else, or I could accept I was different and deal with the fallout, with being seen as an unsettling problem in the group. I would come to look back on navigating this time as a constant struggle between the little black girl inside who was desperate for acceptance, and the grown black woman, unapologetic for her differences and her individuality.

It wasn't pleasant, but my isolation taught me an important life lesson. I was learning to let go of the kid I had been back on the estate, the kid who wanted to be accepted by the boys, who wanted to fit in. Now, God had put me in a place of isolation, where I had no choice but to validate myself. Every day, I had to look in the mirror and tell myself it was OK to be different. And as I did so, I learned once more to stop looking for validation from others, from Mark or his leadership group. God forced me to look within, to control what I could, and to let go of everything else.

I sought advice from Adam, and he reinforced this. I told him I was feeling isolated from the group, and he told me to concentrate on what was within my control. Mark and his leadership group might not like me, but I could still be too good to drop. If I was scoring goals, I was safe. And that's how, in my isolation, scoring became a kind of safe haven for me – succeeding was the best answer.

For you, it might mean performing to the best of your ability at work despite your boss giving you a hard time.

Or it might mean exceeding the expectations of a teacher who doesn't believe you can get the top grades. If you work hard and succeed, you'll prove them wrong in the most powerful way.

But succeeding in these circumstances isn't easy. A lot of people struggle with this. What do you do when your boss has a problem with you? Most people can't quit or walk away. You need to find a way of sticking it out, of succeeding anyway. It's hard to remember who you are if you don't feel validated. If you are consumed with how bad others think you are, or how much they want you to fail, you forget your achievements and what you can do.

For me, the answer was to talk to myself in the mirror every day and tell myself I was good enough. Good enough to score; good enough to win. I would watch videos of my goals to remind myself of my achievements and the buzz I felt when I scored. It wasn't easy, there were a lot of setbacks along the way, but I was learning to let go of Mark and worrying all the time about why he didn't like me. I was learning to focus on myself, on my own self-belief, and no longer look to others to endorse me. That is self-validation.

And it worked, I kept scoring. In September, as the title race was heating up with Chelsea, we played our last qualifying game against Montenegro. We went in expecting to thrash them, having already beaten them 9–0 earlier that year. After that game, I remembered, Mark had lavished praise on Toni for scoring a hat-trick. Ahead of the game Mark took me aside.

'I want you to score five goals today,' he said. 'If you do that, you'll end the campaign as the highest scorer in our qualifying group.'

I nodded and smiled. I was encouraged. Here was a rare bit of personal positive management. Mark had challenged me to succeed, and he had told me he believed in me.

'OK, Mark,' I said. 'I'll do that.'

We won the match 10–0, and I scored a hat-trick, my first for England. I was ecstatic, it was a great release. Traditionally, players who score a hat-trick get to keep the match ball, and so I got everyone to sign it on the bus back to our hotel. I was buzzing, I had scored thirteen goals in ten games and ended the top scorer in our qualifying group. I was proud, I thanked God, and I felt safe.

Back at the hotel, we gathered for our post-match meeting. Mark took the signed match ball to present back to me in front of the group.

'Good result today,' said Mark, grinning. 'We could have been even more clinical, but we got the job done.'

Mark glanced at me.

'I'm sure she's not going to mind me saying,' he continued. 'We all know Eni is a pain in the arse, but she did well to score a hat-trick after I gave her the target of scoring five goals today.'

Mark held out the ball as all eyes turned to me. I stood up, smiled awkwardly, and stifled a nervous laugh as I took the ball off him and sat back down. I was annoyed now. What the hell was that? I had scored my first hat-trick for England, how about a simple well done? Any other player would have expected praise after scoring a hat-trick. Why did Mark have to deliver mine with a back-handed dig? My mind boggled. Did Mark have any idea at all about the principle of achievement and reward?

Back in my room after the meeting, my head was spinning. 'We all know Eni is a pain in the arse,' he had said. 'Pain in the arse' wasn't a term of endearment, not for a senior player. I didn't feel like a pain in the arse. I was engaged and was always involved in team activities. I shared opinions, sure, but only to the same amount as anyone else. And who had Mark meant by 'we' exactly? Everyone? My friends, my colleagues, my teammates of a decade? The players who came to me for advice with their problems? No one had ever told me I was being a pain in the arse, not Steph as captain, nor any of the others. All this collective 'we' business felt like Mark's behaviour was getting into the realms of workplace bullying. It would be if any boss in any workplace announced in a meeting that everyone thought a staff member was a pain in the arse.

It had been my most successful year in an England shirt, so I couldn't work out why I felt like my legs were always being cut from underneath me. It became a clear feeling that Mark wanted to undermine my achievements and no amount of goal-scoring would stop that. So, how safe was I really? I began to wonder if I should change tack. Maybe by scoring goals I had made myself even more of a target. Maybe I was caught in a vicious circle. The more I scored, the more I succeeded, the more isolated I became. In turn, the isolation drove me to my safe haven of goals, and the goals brought more isolation.

It was tempting to stop succeeding in order to feel less isolated. But that would have been wrong. I was proud of my success, but at first, I questioned the isolation that came with it. It took some time to realise I should be proud of the isolation, too, because it was a necessary part of succeeding. Great people stand out from the crowd, they break out of society's conditioning. I realised

I had to take my cue from the true greats. The ones who break the mould, are isolated, and succeed regardless.

It wasn't easy. Success can be lonely. Not everyone around you will rejoice in your accomplishments. Many, including your superiors, might try to belittle and undermine them. It may be that they are projecting their own insecurities on to you, or it may be outright jealousy. Or it may be that you are exceeding the expectations they set for you in their own minds. Your light may shine too brightly for some to cope with. But you can only really succeed if you understand that is their problem, not yours.

Back at Chelsea, I spoke to Emma. We agreed the only thing I could do was keep succeeding, keep scoring goals. I threw myself into our title race. The turmoil at England only made me determined to win the trophy. I was on top form, the whole team was, so I was expecting to win, and that only made it all the more devastating when our crushing defeat against City came a few weeks later and we lost the league. Seeing Mark after that was the last thing I wanted after such a cruel loss. I couldn't shake the thought that he and his leadership group must have been loving my failure.

Still, I would have to see them as there was one last England fixture left to play that year. And it was a big one:

a Germany friendly at Wembley, the first time England women had ever played in the stadium as England and not Team GB, as we had been at the Olympics. The hype during the run-up was as big as it gets, and tickets were selling fast. Not only was this another milestone for the women's game in the UK, it was also Mark's first chance to showcase his achievements with the team. We had been unbeaten in the qualifying campaign and expectations were sky high.

I was as excited as anyone when we moved into our hotel near Wembley. The whole squad was desperate to start in such an iconic game. When Mark set out his starting eleven in training, I was delighted to find he had me down to start up front. I guess I had scored too often that season for him to leave me out of such a high stakes game, but the way things had been going lately, I hadn't taken it as read that I would start.

There was a buzz in the air as the game approached. Every player could invite five guests to the game, and a couple to the after party, too. My family was coming; Dad and one of my uncles were flying in from Nigeria for the occasion. Everyone wanted to be there, and there was a lot of talk among the players about any unused ticket allocations in the last days before the game. Staff had set up a sign-up sheet outside the dining room of the hotel on which players could indicate how many people were coming and under which name. One night before the game, I stopped by the sign-up sheet on my way in to eat. Mark stepped up beside me. He seemed in a good mood and wanted to make small talk. I played along.

'Who have you got coming?' he said, nodding at the sheet.

'My family are coming from Nigeria,' I said.

'Oh, they're flying in for the game?' he said.

'Yeah,' I said.

'Well, make sure they don't come over with Ebola,' he said.

I laughed nervously and cut the exchange short. Reeling slightly, I went to grab my dinner from the buffet and sat down next to Lianne. I told her what Mark had said about my family.

Lianne's eyes widened. 'Again?' she said. 'He did another thing?'

I nodded.

'I know,' I said. 'It's actually getting ridiculous. But let's not make it into a big deal. I can't worry about it right now.'

Our conversation moved on. We were both starting in the game in a few days' time. We needed to focus on one of the biggest opportunities of our international career to date. It was only later that evening, back in my room, that the shock and hurt began to rise. What a thing to say about someone's family, to suggest offhand that they were carriers of a catastrophic disease.

There was no rational reason for Mark's behaviour towards me. So I hadn't taken down his number at the start. Big deal. So I sent an email about Lee to his superior and maybe he found out. So what? Was that enough for him to detest me? I had never fought back openly, even when he belittled me in front of the team. I had remained professional and continued to seek his advice on how I could improve as a player. I had worked hard for the team, I had played good football, I had scored, I had earned my place. So why the vitriol? Maybe he didn't like the way I looked, or the way I spoke? It had to be coming from somewhere.

Mark must have had the same little chat with others on the team. It was only small talk. Still, it was only when talking to me that he let slip a derogatory comment. He could have said anything else: 'Are they flying BA?' or 'What time do they fly in?' or 'Is it your parents coming?' or 'Oh, do they live in Nigeria?' Anything. Anything at all.

Gradually I began to understand. Here, at last, was a possible reason he kept singling me out. If Mark's only spontaneous association with Nigeria was a highly contagious, deadly haemorrhagic fever, was it possible he didn't like Africans? Was it possible he didn't like black women? Was it possible that, at the very least, my skin colour made him uncomfortable? Perhaps Mark lived in dread of saying the wrong thing? Perhaps he was so scared he would rather get me off the team so he could finally relax? It seemed possible.

I reasoned it out. I didn't want to jump to any conclusions. I'm a qualified solicitor, it's in my nature to analyse objectively. Ebola had been in the news a lot, maybe Mark was genuinely petrified and couldn't get it out of his head. Still, it didn't add up. If he had been following the story, he would have known the epicentre of the epidemic was in Guinea, about as far from Nigeria as Greenland is from Wales. He would have known Nigeria had seen only seven Ebola-related deaths and had been officially free of the virus for several weeks.

Mark hadn't spoken about the facts of the Ebola epidemic. He hadn't even shown concern. He had suggested, presumably in a dire attempt at humour, that my family were diseased, and that they might bring Ebola to Wembley. I wondered if he would have said that to a white player from Africa. I suspected he wouldn't have.

It was one of the few times in my life I felt someone was treating me badly because of my race. It had always been there as an option for why someone didn't like me, but I had never come to that firm conclusion in the past. Racism is a complex issue, but the subtleties are often overlooked. Racism is often much more complicated than simple name-calling; often that's the easy part to deal with. But racism can often be conditional and circumstantial and kicks in in certain situations. It's harder to deal with this kind of racism because it is hidden, insidious, and implied. To begin with, it's harder to call this kind of racism out. To do so, you first have to explain why it is the result of entrenched negative racial stereotypes. But this is where we are, so here goes.

It isn't as simple as saying Mark had a general issue with people of colour. He seemed to get on with other players of colour on the team. Demi Stokes, Alex Scott, and later, Nikita Parris all had much more positive relations with him. Looking back, I wonder whether, if I had been less sure of myself, if I had projected the insecure, apologetic black girl from Birmingham seeking Mark's approval, I might have had an easier ride. But I didn't do that. Instead, I stood out, I challenged stereotypes, and I bothered him in a different way.

The only comparable incident in my life had happened at school, when a careers adviser was sceptical about my chances to become a lawyer. I had excellent grades, so I can only think the image of a lawyer she had in her head didn't fit with the black girl sitting in front of her. Until that time, she had always been pleasant to me, but suddenly there was a stop sign in her mind. The entrenched stereotype she had bought into said black girls weren't lawyers. To her mind, black girls could go so far, and no further. Say I had said I wanted to be a nurse; that, presumably, would have been fine, because it was much more common to see African women working as nurses. To her, that's where black women belonged. There were no barriers to that.

Similar barriers are put up against black football players when they want to become managers. There's a reason why there have only ever been a handful of black managers in the Premier League. Black men aren't traditionally associated with leadership roles, so even if they are considered as candidates, they often aren't given the job. The black player might not experience racism until they ask to cross the barrier, break out of the stereotype, and become a leader. Then the entrenched racism kicks in, and the barrier comes down. That barrier doesn't exist for white players. The Frank Lampards and Steven Gerrards of this world easily transition into management, partly because they don't have to first defeat entrenched racial stereotypes to do so.

This is the way I make sense of Mark's behaviour towards me. He got on well with other players of colour, but they weren't lawyers, with a first-class law degree. They didn't have the kind of wealth associated with having a brother playing in the Premier League. They hadn't finished the top scorer in our qualifying group, and they hadn't dared questioned Mark or his staff. And, they weren't explicitly African, with an African-sounding name like Eniola Aluko. Anita Asante, another educated and outspoken British-African player, also struggled to find her way in Mark's team.

Mark had constantly jostled with my success. That he instantly associated Nigeria with disease showed me I had crossed a line in his head. I had challenged his negative stereotype, gone beyond his perception of what an African woman should be.

I love being a black woman, I wouldn't change it. It has always been a cause for celebration and empowerment, never a crutch or an excuse. Accusing someone of racism isn't something I would ever do lightly. It certainly hasn't been a pleasant experience. I'm willing to bet that no one ever cried racism for fun, or for power, and yet so many people of colour don't share their experiences because they would be shouted down, in the hideous phrase, for 'using the race card'.

So, I'll say it again. Until that night when I started asking those questions about Mark, I had hardly ever experienced overt racism. This time, it felt different, this time it felt like a confirmation. To my mind, that Ebola comment was explicitly racist even if it was intended as humour. It revealed an urge to put me back down, to instantaneously associate me with the dirty, diseased space my African heritage had predetermined in his mind. Suddenly it all made sense.

Walking on to the pitch at Wembley a few days later, I felt almost calm. I was still riled by Mark's comment and trying to make sense of it was the last thing I needed while trying to focus on beating German defenders. Still, at last I knew, in my own mind at least, why my coach was treating me with contempt. I felt he was putting up a barrier to my success because it didn't fit with his entrenched ideas about African women. Something clicked, and I knew it was his problem not mine. The knowledge gave me strength to offer my best response to adversity. To continue to perform, to battle on in an England shirt, for myself, for my career, and for my family. I had my best, and paradoxically, my most challenging, year behind me. I couldn't let anything, or anyone derail me now.

CHAPTER SIXTEEN

Mark's authority was growing by the day. He was more secure now in his position, and even our 3–0 loss to Germany at Wembley couldn't shake that. Mark was young, he was ambitious and hard-working, and he had earned power within the structures of the FA. Now, with a World Cup on the horizon, he wielded a different kind of power over us players. We were all desperate for a place on his squad, and he could make or break our dreams. He agonised over the selection for months in advance. Every game, every training session, counted. Any slip up could cost you.

Mark wasn't only establishing his own power; he was also overseeing a generational shift at England. I might have felt anxious on the team, but I was only twenty-eight, and I was on my best form, and I was feeling empowered. For some older players, though, it was time to move on. In February 2015, a few months after the Wembley game, Kelly announced she was retiring from England after twenty years on the squad. The whole squad bid farewell to the nation's top goal-scorer, the best England player of a generation. She had been our captain, our reference point, the best player many of us had ever played with, and I was sad to see her go.

The battle to get on to the World Cup squad was fierce, and Mark encouraged competition between us by chopping and changing his starting eleven whenever we played. Gradually, he began to phase me out, bringing me on as a second half sub in our first game of the year, a friendly against USA, which we lost 1–0. One night from that camp, I called Mum for a chat. I was just expecting a casual catch up, but the conversation soon morphed into a review of the whole situation with Mark.

Mum was good at making me look at my own actions and examine where I was at fault. I didn't want to fall into a victim role, and Mum helped me reflect on and hold me accountable for my own behaviour. It was a process we often went through during the time I was playing under Mark. Was I doing something to annoy him, to add to the problem somehow? What could I do to be less provocative? How could I improve the situation? I was grateful to have her take on things. She was always honest with me and didn't sugar coat the truth. It was exactly what I needed; I didn't want a pity party. I didn't want people who just felt sorry for me, I needed people who had solutions. I told Mum I wanted to learn how not to rise to the bait, and we both agreed the best answer was to focus on my reason for being there.

Then Mum said something that changed my whole approach to the England environment: 'We give power to others when we let their decisions dictate our emotions,' she said. 'Mark is the coach, he has the power to choose you, or not. You have to get to a place where you aren't affected by either decision. If he picks you, fine. If he doesn't pick you, that's also fine. You can't let your happiness be governed by whether you've been validated by someone else. Our validation comes from God. We have to wake up every day, look in the mirror, and validate ourselves. We have to know our destiny is far greater than anyone who is trying to block it. And your destiny is far greater than your immediate boss.'

Mum's wisdom was just what I needed. She reminded me, once again, not to focus on Mark; I needed to concentrate on my own happiness. Beyond playing the best football I could, I couldn't control whether Mark picked me or not, but I did have power to change how I felt about my own destiny. I realised I had fallen into the same trap as I had when I was a child and I let the other kids' parents tell me girls couldn't play football. I had to keep reminding myself not to go looking for validation in the wrong places, from others. Like Mum had said, true validation came from God, and it came from within. I vowed to tell myself every day that my destiny was bigger than anyone else's decisions. After Mum rang off, I looked at myself in the mirror, and said it out loud.

The lesson was tested soon enough. In early March, the Cyprus Cup came around again. I had come to dread going away with England. I spent every minute on edge, knowing that people around me weren't too keen on me succeeding. I withdrew into an edited version of myself. I'm usually an extrovert, but I became more reserved, avoiding doing anything to draw attention to myself. On the pitch, I put massive pressure on myself to score every chance I got, which often only meant more missed chances. It wasn't a happy time.

Mark used the friendly tournament to see as many players as possible, rotating the team at every game. He put me in to start in our first game against Finland, and I seized my chance. Lianne scored in the middle of the second half, and I got a second past the hour mark.

They got one back, and we scored a third before the end. Despite the comfortable win, Mark changed the whole starting eleven, bar two, for our second game, against Australia. I sat on the bench and watched forward Jodie Taylor score a hat-trick. I noted that afterwards Mark, quite rightly, celebrated Jodie's performance in the normal way.

Mark put me on to start our last group game, against the Netherlands. Before the game, I listened to a sermon by my favourite American preacher TD Jakes titled 'Opposition and Opportunity'. In the sermon, Jakes reminded me that all opposition was God's way of pushing me to evolve into something better. Opposition was a springboard. God meant for me to overcome this constant opposition to Mark and grow in the process. I thought back over the past year as I listened to the sermon. It made sense; I had finished the top scorer in qualification, despite the difficult environment. It had driven me on. There was opposition, I took my opportunity, I overcame, and I had grown. But if the opposition was still there, it meant I had further still to go.

Out on the pitch against the Netherlands, I was more determined than ever. When they went one up in the eighteenth minute, I told myself the equaliser would be mine. My chance came in the last minutes before the break. I got the ball midway in the Dutch half and set off on a diagonal run across the pitch, slaloming through four defenders before cutting on to my right foot and curling in past the keeper from ten yards out. I fell to the ground and lay before the goalmouth, my heart beating in my ears, only distantly aware I had scored one of the finest solo goals of my career. The pitch grew quiet and I saw myself from above, lying on the pitch surrounded by a sea of Dutch orange shirts. There was no buzz of celebration, no triumph, only relief.

The goal was all anyone could talk about after the game. A clip of it went viral on social media. Both Mark and I were interviewed about it on the sideline. Mark made all the right noises, said it was a great goal, said this is what he wanted to see from me. A clip of the goal was shared all over British press, and Gary Lineker added his voice to the praise, saying this was the level of goal he hoped to see from England.

I readied myself for Mark's response. Questions would surely be asked if he didn't play me in the final now, but Mark liked to plan his teams in advance of tournaments and now I had messed with the order of things by scoring a goal that went viral online. Mark asked to see me the next day.

We sat down together, and he smiled. 'Well done for the goal,' he said.

He sounded nervous. He cleared his throat.

'I want to keep you in a box, ready for the World Cup.'

I was confused. Here come the excuses, I thought. He was going to leave me on the bench for the final. I sat in silence, while, sure enough, Mark launched into a long spiel about how he wasn't going to play me, ostensibly because I was too precious. It felt like he was trying to flatter me into accepting the situation. It might have worked with another player; they might have felt proud their manager wanted to save them for the big moment. But I couldn't shake the suspicion that Mark wanted me to score, but not too much, and certainly not any extraordinary goals, while he eased me out of the team. And he wanted me to smile while he did it.

And smile I did. I left the meeting and conjured up my new knowledge. My destiny was bigger than his decisions. Whether I played in the final or not didn't matter, I had shown everyone what I could do in the face of the opposition I felt. That goal proved to everyone that all I needed was to believe in myself.

We met again in mid-April for a friendly against China. Mark called Anita, who hadn't reappeared since Hope left, back on to the squad. Neither of us started, and though I was brought on in the second half, Anita spent the whole game on the bench. Afterwards, we wondered why he had brought her back into the squad, presumably for her to try out for the World Cup, only to leave her on the bench.

Anita asked Mark for a meeting. During their chat, Mark told her she wouldn't make his World Cup squad. The decision was his prerogative, of course, but the timing was another matter. To tell a player she hadn't made it a month before the squad was announced wasn't the way things were normally done. Usually, we were all informed about World Cup squads on the same day. Anita was very upset. After seventy caps and many years' service, couldn't Mark have waited to tell her with everyone else? She felt hurt and singled out.

Mark announced his World Cup squad, to great fanfare, in mid-May. There were no huge surprises, the squad included the normal mix of youth and experience. Forwards were me, Lianne, Toni, Jodie Taylor, Ellen White, and my soon-to-be Chelsea teammate Fran Kirby. Four of the squad had a hundred caps or more: Kaz, Fara, Alex Scott and former captain Casey Stoney. Jill Scott and I were on ninety caps each and Katie Chapman on eighty-five. At the other end of the scale, half of the squad were relative newcomers, each with fewer than thirty caps.

We flew to Canada ahead of the tournament in early June. I was excited and confident, knowing that I had overcome Mark's opposition and grown. I felt stronger now I knew I could offer myself the validation I needed to succeed. I wanted to play as much as possible, but I was also ready not to play. I didn't believe for a second that Mark had been keeping me in a box for the World Cup. Instead, I felt I was becoming an inconvenience. It seemed almost inconvenient for me to score another world-class goal, on such a public stage. It was odd, because that would have benefitted the team, but I felt he would prefer to see top goals from another player. The better the goal, the bigger the outcry if he later tried to bump me off the team.

Ahead of our first game, Mark held a team meeting. He told us his approach to the tournament would be to take each game one at a time and switch tactics according to our opponent. That meant that for each game he would select the best team to fit the particular formation or tactic he had chosen. Even if a player scored a hat-trick in one game, he warned us, they might not play in the next, if they didn't fit the tactic. 'Horses for courses,' he called it. I didn't agree with it, I felt it went against the principles of performance and reward. But it was Mark's prerogative, of course, to play a World Cup whichever way he liked.

We were in a group with France, Mexico and Colombia. Our opening game against France was set to be the toughest of the lot. We were aware that finishing second in the group might potentially be better than finishing top in the group. Finishing second would certainly guarantee us an easier route forward. We could expect to beat Mexico and Colombia; and advance with six points with France finishing top. Mark never expressly said we should go out and lose to France, but we were all quietly aware of the benefits of doing so.

I've always hated this tactic. It goes completely against the basic principles of sportsmanship. Every team should always go out to win. I can't believe any team has gone into a group game wanting to lose and gone on to win the World Cup. It is always a psychological own goal that comes back to bite further down the line. Tactically, Mark showed his hand. He played me as a lone striker against France in a rigid defensive 4–5–1 formation. France were known for their lightning attacks, so it made sense from one point of view. The tactics were to sit off France, and not pressure their defence. But I also felt keeping me isolated up front displayed a lack of ambition to win the game.

We played the first nightmarish half in rain and high winds. I broke forward a few times, but there was no one there to support my run. I was isolated in the attack, running after long balls and trying to chase down two of the world's best defenders, Laura Georges and Wendy Renard. France began to dominate. Then, when they scored before the half hour, my frustration peaked. I had come to this opening game confident I could bring both goals and assists, but Mark's tactics had me playing with my hands tied behind my back. I was the lone attacking force, and without service, I was redundant.

Mark brought on Toni and Fran to support the attack and switched formation to 4–3–3. But France had tasted blood and shut us out of the game. We barely touched the ball for the final half hour. On the final whistle, overcome with frustration, I broke down in tears.

Later, I told the BBC I felt emotional because of the loss. But it wasn't the defeat that brought me to tears, it was our approach to the game. All the months of building frustration came flowing out on that final whistle. I just couldn't buy into this idea of being secretly happy to lose and come second in the group. To spend eighteen months fighting, to score, to prove the manager wrong, to qualify for the World Cup and make the squad, only to lose our opening game in that way. It was like none of the effort had been worth it.

I went into our next game, which was against Mexico, determined to play with the kind of freedom I didn't have against France. I knew I could score what would be my first World Cup goal. I knew I could help the team after our abysmal opening performance. I had a strong first half, once hitting the crossbar from a long range shot and linking up well with the midfielders. I was delighted when Fran Kirby came off the bench to score on her late mother's birthday and I knew then I was playing with a true star in the making. Kaz then fired in another to make it 2–0. We were all relieved. It was a comfortable win, and a respectable performance.

Mark wanted to meet with me after the game. After his comment about wanting to put me in a box, I felt sure he was disingenuous. I didn't feel he was a man of his word and I wasn't the only one who felt Mark didn't follow through on what he said in private. I wanted a witness, someone I trusted to uphold what had been said. I asked Adam, the development coach, to sit in on our meetings from here on in and take notes. Mark wasn't happy about it; I sensed he felt it was a challenge to his authority. Still, there wasn't much he could do to stop it.

In our meeting, Mark said he felt I had been missing 10 per cent of my usual energy against Mexico and that he was going to rest me for our next game, against Colombia. I nodded, normally there would be some rotation of players after two games on the bounce in a World Cup anyway. I spent the next game on the bench, watching Toni play in my place against Colombia. She didn't score, our goals came from Kaz and Fara, but she was attacking well. After the match, Mark wanted to see me again. He was emphatic about Toni's game.

'Toni was fantastic against Colombia,' he said. 'I'm going to start her against Norway.'

'OK,' I said. 'But I thought you said I was being rested. And anyway, I've been fantastic before and you didn't change your plans for me. I scored the goal of the season against the Netherlands in Cyprus and didn't play a minute in the final two days later. Back then you said that was about tactics, about horses for courses. So, I'm confused. Is selection about tactics or is it about performance?'

He wasn't listening.

'Fair points, Eni, but this is the World Cup,' he said. 'Toni is playing well. She's starting.'

I knew it was useless. It was Mark's choice, of course, to pick the best players. But when I was the best player, he didn't extend me the same flexibility. That was only for his favoured ones. This reinforced my concern that he was looking for a way to freeze me out.

I spent the rest of the World Cup glued to the bench. I didn't play a minute of our last sixteen game against Norway, or of the quarter-final when we knocked out hosts Canada. When one player is out, another player benefits, and both Toni and Jodie Taylor rightly benefitted from me and Lianne being on the bench. Jodie scored an outstanding goal against Canada in front of more than 50,000 fans. I knew then that this was her moment.

We reached the semi-finals, against Japan, and Mark kept me on the bench for the fourth game in a row. This was his moment too, and he was enjoying himself, strutting in front of the media, working his relationships with the FA big shots who had flown out for the World Cup. Watching him on the sidelines, I was conflicted. I wanted England to win. Still, a tiny part of me couldn't help but question whether Mark deserved to win. I struggled with myself, repressed it, and celebrated every goal, but the contempt Mark had shown me was difficult to forget.

As the World Cup rolled on without me, I sat on the bench, asking myself some hard questions. Could I have done anything more to play? By any objective measure

I had proved myself. I had finished the top scorer in qualifying, I had scored in all but one of our games. It felt like none of that mattered any more; I could score all I liked in this World Cup, but it still wouldn't be enough in this team.

We lost the semi-final after a heart-breaking own-goal from Laura Bassett in stoppage time. I played in the third-place play-offs against Germany, which we won 1–0, and I was proud to come home from Canada with a third-place bronze medal. I was disappointed at how little I had played, but glad to have been part of the first England team to reach the semi-final since 1991. I was relieved to be back at Chelsea, though with the FA Cup final approaching, the pressure remained at boiling point.

Going into the FA Cup final at Wembley, I was glad of Linvoy's words to me. God had everything planned out and could see much further ahead than I could. Trust in God, Linvoy said, offer Him your best game. The weight lifted, and I played the best game of my career. Walking up the iconic Wembley steps to collect my FA Cup medal, I understood. The failure last season, the difficulties with Mark, the isolation at England and now, the eventual triumph, they were all part of God's masterplan.

I got to the top of the stairs, champagne in my hair and bloodshot eyes, covered head to toe in celebration glitter. There was Mark, standing alongside his girlfriend and the other FA dignitaries, waiting to congratulate us and hand out our medals.

At the sight of him, a line from the Bible, Psalm 23:5, flashed through my head. 'You prepare a table before me in the presence of my enemies. You anoint my head with oil, my cup overflows.' Mark had been my adversary many times over the past eighteen months and here he was at Wembley stadium, handing me my medal. God had prepared the table, Wembley, and brought an adversary, Mark, and made my cup overflow with the blessing of winning the first-ever FA cup at Wembley. God was faithful to his word, just like Linvoy said he would be.

I went along the row, shaking hands, until I stood in front of Mark. I looked him firmly in the eye and smiled. Mark managed a wry smile in return. I can't say what he was thinking. But to me, the moment was filled with triumph. I had overcome adversity. I grasped his hand and heard a voice in my head, clear and calm as if I were speaking out loud. You will never stop me, it said.

CHAPTER SEVENTEEN

Mark continued to pick me for the squad. I had just won the FA Cup, I had been named player of the match, and I was on track to win the league. Dropping me, though it was Mark's prerogative to do so, might have raised too many eyebrows. We began our next qualifying campaign, for the 2017 Euros, in September with an 8–0 win against Estonia. Then, the following month as the season ended, we were invited to play in the inaugural YongChuan International Tournament in south-west China.

Weirdly, I found myself looking forward to it. I was feeling strong, my faith had been renewed, and I was still buzzing from winning the domestic double with Chelsea. I would go to China, I would play for God, I would score for Him, not for anyone else. It also helped that there would be a few familiar faces on the team. Mark had lost some of his core team to a clash with the League Cup final, so he gave four players their first call up. Three of them, Hannah Blundell, Laura Coombs and Drew Spence, were teammates of mine from Chelsea.

That year's title race had been bitterly fought, and the league rivalries followed us across the world. Tensions were high anyway; we had been given less than two days to recover from our twenty-four-hour journey before having to play. Before our first game, we split off into our different positions for unit meetings to discuss our respective individual and collective roles and watch video analysis. Strikers went first, then midfielders and, lastly, defenders. FATV were making a short documentary about the tournament and the individual meetings were all filmed by the FA's video assistant, Joe Bennett. After the meetings, we went into lunch. I sat on a table next to Lianne and Jill Scott.

'Did you hear what Mark said to Drew?' Jill said to me.

News travelled fast at England camp, especially when it was a cause of concern for players.

'No, what?' I said.

'Mark said something about Drew going to prison,' Lianne said.

Lianne hadn't been in the meeting, but as she was sharing rooms with Jill, it was safe to assume she had been filled in already.

'What?' I said. 'Seriously, are you sure?'

Lianne nodded. 'That's what I heard.'

Somehow, I wasn't surprised.

'I'll have to ask Drew what happened,' I said.

Along the table, a couple of other players chipped in. While they couldn't give details, they confirmed that Mark had made an awkward comment. After lunch, I went to Drew's room.

'Is everything all right?' I said when she opened the door. 'What happened in the meeting? Did Mark say something?'

Drew lowered her eyes.

'It was weird,' she began. 'Mark was there, and he was talking about pressing hard in midfield and how getting a caution was like getting a police caution. Then he turned to me and said: "Haven't you been arrested before then? Four times, isn't it?"'

My eyes widened. 'What?' I said.

'I know,' she said. 'It was awkward.'

I was gobsmacked. I wasn't surprised, exactly. A derogatory comment like that, directed at the only non-white player in the room, confirmed a level of ignorance

I'd always suspected in him and in Lee. The real shock was that a player on her first England camp should have to deal with that kind of prejudice from someone in his position. What kind of a welcome to the team is that? Mark was an England manager, representing the country around the world, and this was what he thought of a young mixed-race player, that she was a criminal? Drew didn't want a fuss, but it really bothered me. I had gone through the same thing as Drew, wondering how to react after my boss made a derogatory personal comment about me. I raised it again with her later that night on WhatsApp.

'Hey girl,' I wrote. 'I think I'm going to mention something to Mark later on about what he said. It's not the first time it's happened and it's just unacceptable. I know you don't feel offended but I think it's more so he knows never to make comments like that again in a group setting.'

'Eni, honestly, it's fine because I don't want him thinking I was offended when I really wasn't,' she wrote back. 'It's just really bad banter.'

I understood her position. Drew was young, she had her whole career ahead of her, she had been overjoyed to get her first call up for England. There was no way she could call Mark up on a prejudiced remark; we both knew it would likely guarantee the end of her international career before it had begun. I saw things differently: I had to make Mark know it wasn't acceptable to speak to people like that.

I had to make Drew see this was serious, that this wasn't just jokey banter. This was Mark picking Drew out of a meeting with seven other players who were all white. This was Mark choosing to demean Drew, rather than anyone else, by suggesting she was a criminal because that was a stereotype planted in his mind. I told Drew about what Mark had said about my family and Ebola before the Wembley game. Aside from Lianne, she was the only other England player I told about it. Drew agreed it had been a terrible thing to say. Still, she was adamant, she didn't want any fuss with Mark, so I left it at that and tried to put it out of my mind.

We played our first game, against China, the next day. It wasn't a good game. The changed team hadn't had time to gel, and Mark experimented at the last minute by changing the formation to a 4–4–2 with a diamond in midfield and me and Lianne up front. My goal wasn't enough to secure us the win we had expected against a side ranked ten places lower than us. In the post-match meeting, Mark demanded more of us forwards. He was right in some ways: though I had scored, it certainly hadn't been our best performance. Then he opened the meeting up and encouraged us to share where we felt we had gone wrong.

After a few players spoke, I volunteered my view. 'I think we need to communicate better on the pitch,' I said.

Mark looked at me, his face twisted in annoyance. 'You were the one not making the right movements,' he said with barely concealed contempt.

'OK,' I said. I was confused by what movement had to do with communication, but I couldn't be bothered to respond. Mark's message was clear: keep your mouth shut, Eni. Fine, I thought, I'll stay out of it, I'll speak when I'm spoken to. I wouldn't give him any more opportunities to shoot me down.

The loss was disappointing, and the atmosphere in our camp plummeted. Around this time, something started happening that I didn't think much of to begin with. It was to do with Lee Kendall, the keeper coach. Lee was a macho, Jack-the-Lad kind of a guy, with a big personality. He was close to the keepers and some other players but had always been tentative around me ever since he'd been caught calling me 'lazy as fuck' on the microphone. Since then, though, we always had friendly exchanges.

On this camp, Lee occasionally addressed me in a fake Caribbean accent. This wasn't an accent he used with anyone else. I don't think he intended it to be malicious, and I'm sure he's used it as a way to endear himself to other black people. Still, when he started doing it frequently, it began to get on my nerves. More so because it perpetuated the ignorance that I felt was underlying a lot of behaviour in the group. I'm not from the Caribbean. I was often tempted to speak to him in a Scottish accent, despite knowing he was Welsh just to make the point. I never did, and now I regret not making a point of holding up a mirror to his casual ignorance. But I was in survival mode, and I just got on with it.

It was another long four days until our second and final game against Australia. When Mark revealed his starting line-up, it was confirmed that Jill Scott was to get her one hundredth cap. It was a big occasion; Jill was only the ninth female England player to reach the milestone. In our pre-game meeting, the coaching staff projected a list on to the wall under the heading '100 caps club:' Kelly, Fara, Rachel Yankey, Rachel Unitt, Casey Stoney, Gillian Coultard, Alex Scott, Kaz, and now Jill. Assistant coach Marianne Spacey stood up to say a few words. She turned to Jill.

'When you made your debut, aged nineteen, against Holland, you became part of an international football family,' said Marianne. 'The England family. That family today are all extremely proud of everything you've done, everything you've achieved. We'll be locking arms at that anthem, and singing our hearts out, for your one hundredth cap.'

We all applauded, and Jill stood up gave a short speech thanking the staff and the team. Afterwards, Marianne played a video message from Jill's nephews back home. It was a touching moment. None of us realised that at the other end of the room, Lianne was cringing with embarrassment. This game wasn't only Jill's one hundredth cap, it was also Lianne's fiftieth, an achievement normally celebrated and recognised with the same sense of occasion. But Lianne had been forgotten. There was no speech, no special shirt, no video message for her.

Later, the staff would argue it had been a genuine mistake. Lianne was devastated; after the game we went for a walk together around the block and she was in floods of tears. We got a lot of stares. We must have been a funny sight for the locals; two dark-skinned girls, one sporting a yellow Mohawk, both wandering around in England tracksuits.

Lianne decided she would only get closure on the fiftieth cap omission if she spoke to Mark. She did so that evening, in a one-on-one meeting. Mark said she hadn't been forgotten on purpose and put it down to an administrative error. Lianne accepted this and begged him not to make a big deal out of it in front of the rest of the team. It was too late, she said, the damage had been done, the worst thing would be to rake it all back up in public. But Mark couldn't resist. The following day, our last before we left to go home, he stood up in our meeting.

'I'm a very honest guy,' Mark announced gravely. 'When I make mistakes, I own them.'

I glanced at Lianne. She sat stock still, horrified, staring at Mark.

'Yesterday, Lianne's fiftieth cap was forgotten,' he went on. 'But we have her shirt here now. So, Lianne, would you like to come up here and get it.'

Lianne stood up awkwardly and collected the shirt as the team gave a nervous patter of applause. She was mortified. Everyone was relieved to climb on to the plane home later that day. It had not been a good trip.

Lianne was never selected for England again. She was simply excluded from the squad for our friendly against Germany the following month. Then, in the new year, she was excluded from a team-building event at Center Parcs, to which the whole of the rest of the squad was invited. After two years as a solid fixture in the team, Lianne was out, and she was left to find out about it via

Instagram. For me, the way Lianne was treated says it all: the moment a player challenged Mark's authority, or picked up on his mistakes, they were gone.

To me, it looked like there was a definite pattern emerging. The players who were being treated badly, overlooked, insulted and summarily excluded had one thing in common: they were women of colour. Were we really all bad people? Me, Drew, Lianne, Anita, were we all bad eggs? Or was there something more sinister going on? I still couldn't give a definitive answer, and yet the question remains legitimate. Was this England set-up prejudiced against people of colour?

I wondered when it would be my turn. I was emotionally exhausted after two years of tension under Mark. Two years that, ironically, had been my most successful on the team and that had taught me a lot about myself, about other people, and about God. I was approaching one hundred caps myself, and though I was mentally drained, I couldn't throw it all away now. I was determined to stay on the team, determined to celebrate my hundredth cap.

At Center Parcs, I spoke to the development coach, Adam. I asked him about how best to convert the negative energy some of us were experiencing in the England environment into a more positive one. I wasn't the only player feeling anxious and constantly having to tread on eggshells; there were a few of us. We were the outsiders, and our position was in sharp contrast to the rest of the team who were always being endorsed by Mark.

'You need to break the cycle,' was Adam's advice. 'Don't mirror what Mark does. Treat him the way you want to be treated, give him what you want to receive.'

It sounded sensible enough, and I had nothing to lose. I needed to play the game, reach out to Mark, build a semblance of a rapport, or I would be off the team like Lianne, Drew and Anita. I tried one last time, gathered all my strength, and asked Mark to meet me for a coffee. I didn't want a repeat of our Wembley meeting, when he had turned a serious meeting into a PR opportunity, so I asked him to meet on non-footballing ground, at a cafe in Fulham called Local Hero.

The meeting went well. We led on football, and once again I asked him what I could do to make his starting eleven more consistently. The inaugural SheBelieves Cup was coming up in America, and, if possible, I wanted to avoid watching the whole tournament from the bench.

'There are other players ahead of you who are doing well,' said Mark. 'Still, you're not far off catching them.'

Fair enough, I thought. Mark was entitled to start whichever forwards he felt were on best form. There was another, quite delicate question I wanted to ask. I definitely didn't want him to think I was demanding to play. I took a deep breath.

'I'm on ninety-eight caps now,' I said. 'Is there a chance I'll achieve my one hundred caps in America? If so, I'd like to tell my family so they can be there too.'

Mark nodded.

'Yes,' he said. 'It's highly likely. We'll play three games, and I'd planned to rotate the squad so that everyone is going to play at least one and a half matches.'

I left the meeting in a good mood. I was close to getting my one hundred caps, and America, where I had honed my skills as a striker, seemed like a fitting place to celebrate that milestone.

I was so caught up in the idea, that when Mark officially announced the squad for the SheBelieves Cup, I posted on Instagram that I was on ninety-eight caps and counting.

Looking back, I shouldn't have revealed my excitement. It's become normal to share emotions, ambitions and plans on social media. But I've learned to be careful not to expose my hopes and dreams to those who may not wish me well and have the power to potentially sabotage them or view those ambitions as arrogant. We all have adversaries who would rather we fail. Sometimes it is better to dream quietly, and plan humbly.

The SheBelieves Cup was a high-powered line-up of the best sides in the world: Germany, France and the USA. Our first game was a 1–0 loss against USA. Mark brought me on for the last three minutes of the game, my ninety-ninth cap. Our next game, a 2–1 defeat to Germany, I sat out on the bench. Afterwards, Mark gathered the team together in the dressing room. He gave a short speech and presented Fara Williams with a special shirt to mark her one hundred and fiftieth cap. The whole team applauded and cheered. It was an amazing achievement.

There were now two days left to go before our final game, and still I was not sure whether I would achieve the one hundred cap milestone, especially as I hadn't seen the field in the previous game. I began to think maybe the staff had forgotten, like they had with Lianne. Mark had already told me I would probably make a hundred caps in America, so I asked for a meeting with Mark and Adam to discuss it with him again. The FA technical director, Dan Ashworth, was at the tournament too, and I asked him to sit in on our meeting, but Mark vetoed it. Adam would have to do as a witness for now. I went into the meeting confused and disappointed. Once again, I was being treated unfavourably.

'I feel like we're avoiding the topic of my one hundredth cap,' I said. 'I'm not demanding that you to play me. I was asking you in advance whether it's likely that I will make a hundred caps against France.'

'I can't tell you that,' he said simply.

I stared at him. I hadn't expected him to be so cold.

'What do you mean?' I said. 'It's standard for players to know when they're going to make a hundred caps so they can tell their families to come. Kaz and Jill both knew well in advance what the plans for their hundredth cap were. Kaz reached one hundred caps at Wembley and walked the team out as captain in front of her entire family. Jill started the game in China and the FA organised a surprise message from her family. Of course you could tell me if I'm going to play.'

Mark shrugged and shook his head. 'Both of those players were starters at the time,' he said. 'I don't tend to disclose my teams ahead of games.'

'That's a lie, Mark,' I protested. 'You've told me and other players many times before that we'll be playing days in advance of games.'

I couldn't believe it; this wasn't an administrative oversight, he was doing this on purpose. Mark had never been able to celebrate my achievements in a normal way. He just didn't seem to have it inside of him to see me as deserving as the rest of the veteran players who had made one hundred caps. Maybe there were barriers in his mind. I wondered whether he was resisting because I was the first British-African woman to make the milestone. Whatever the reason, he was acting as though I didn't deserve the same celebration given to every long-serving player. Jill, Kaz, Kelly or Fara could be celebrated, but not Eni. I wasn't asking for special treatment, I was asking to be treated the same as the others, but that seemed like I was asking too much of Mark. It was the last straw: Mark was trying to undermine the greatest achievement of my England career.

'Why do I feel like you're reluctant to acknowledge this, Mark?' I said, struggling to keep my voice steady. 'We discussed this in Fulham. It's no secret I'm on ninety-nine caps. I don't think I'm out of line to ask whether it's likely I'll play so that my family and friends could come and share this achievement with me. I don't care whether I play one minute, or ninety minutes. I was only asking you in advance to let me know.'

Mark wouldn't budge. His face was blank.

'You'll find out when I announce the team tomorrow morning,' he said.

'You're being ruthless and you are not ruthless with others,' I told him, and I walked out of the meeting.

At least Adam had been there, taking notes, I thought afterwards. I wanted everything to be recorded so that later nobody could claim I had been demanding to play. I knew there would be a later, and I knew he would try and spin this in his favour. Trust was at rock bottom.

The following morning, the day of the match, Mark revealed the team on a flip chart. I wasn't on it. I was gutted, tears pricked my eyes. My first thought was that I wasn't going to play at all. We had lost against America, and against Germany, there was no way we could win this tournament now. Players were tired after playing two games in four days and I had believed that gave me a better chance of playing than in any other game.

When the meeting broke up, Mark tapped me on the shoulder. 'As you know, I've taken the decision to not start you in the game,' he said. 'But you're definitely going to come on as a substitute to make your hundredth cap. I went with my strongest eleven for continuity. Casey told me I should check with you how you feel about that. So how do you feel?'

I couldn't speak; I burst into tears. Mark had the opportunity to say everything he was saying now several days ago. He knew full well it was too late for my family to join me. Instead he had decided to avoid the conversation entirely and let me get my hundred caps off the bench without my loved ones there to celebrate. I walked out of the doors of the hotel, crying uncontrollably. I didn't deserve this.

Adam followed me out and walked me around the block. I told him everything: that I felt Mark had a personal vendetta against me, that he couldn't bear to see me happy, or winning, that he was trying to get rid of me, that he was turning other players against me. Adam tried to comfort me, but I was inconsolable. Mark had intentionally undermined the celebration I had worked eleven years to achieve. This, surely, was his biggest power play yet.

Sitting on the bench waiting to be subbed on, I tried to focus on enjoying the moment and not allow anything to kill the joy I should have felt. When I came on early in the second half, Steph handed me the captain's armband. It was a grand gesture, and I'll always be grateful for it, but it was an afterthought in an incident that Mark had soured. We drew with France 0–0, our best result of the tournament.

After the game, in the dressing room, I was allowed to say a few words. I took a deep breath. It was important now to try and forget my deep frustration and make a meaningful speech. I managed a polite smile and thanked the players that had been with me throughout my eleven years on the team. I thanked the staff, and I thanked Mark for picking me, and I said how honoured I was to become England's tenth ever female centurion. I looked around a blank sea of faces. Everyone knew what had happened. All the joy of the moment had been soured. A lump rose in my throat and I struggled to hold back tears.

There was a limit to how much more of Mark's behaviour I could take. I wanted to talk to someone higher up. Before we left America, I approached Dan Ashworth in person to ask if we could discuss Mark's management of me since direct communication with Mark was becoming difficult. We agreed to meet back in London to talk it over in more detail. I focused on this meeting with Dan Ashworth as a ray of hope, convinced things would improve once he was aware what was going on.

The way I saw it my manager had singled me out to the point of wanting to voluntarily abandon an eleven-year England career. I had tried to stay safe through scoring and playing well but at this point I had experienced one negative incident too many. I compared myself to the rest of the happy camp of players on the squad. This wasn't about my performance. Sure, he had pushed standards higher on the team, but I had more than earned my place on it.

Many times, then and since then, I have wondered why, if Mark didn't like me, he hadn't put me out of my misery and dropped me from the squad. He hadn't stopped my other roles; I was still representing the team in negotiations about commercial rights with the FA and pushing for improvements in the central contracts. Perhaps I'll never know the answer, but I did know how I was being treated was wrong. This wasn't how the environment in a national team should be, this wasn't how any player should feel.

Mark picked me again the following month for a ten-day trip to play our next qualifiers against Belgium and Bosnia. This time Mark told me in advance of the Belgium game I wasn't going to start, but that he was going to sub me on. I was still hoping to turn things around, so I made sure to be on my best form and spoke to one of the coaches about my runs ahead of the game. Substitute or not, I prepared for every game just as seriously as if I was starting. I went through the same routine I would before any game: soft tissue massage with the physio, eating well and drinking lots of electrolytes, and soaking my legs in a magnesium bath the night before.

We were one down against Belgium when I came on with twenty minutes to go, and we equalised in the last five minutes of the game. I had played well, and afterwards, people said I had helped turn the game around. Suddenly, Mark was under pressure to change the team for our second game, against Bosnia.

Mark put me on to start. It was the first time I had started a game since China, and certainly the first I played a full ninety minutes for as long as I could remember. We won the Bosnia game 1–0 with a late goal from Kaz, and I came off the pitch beaming. Maybe this was a positive sign from Mark. I desperately hoped so. Given we had had a good game, we were all surprised at Mark's tone of voice at the post-match meeting.

'It's been a really difficult ten days,' he said, his voice trembling with fury. 'There are certain people in the team who have only thought about themselves. Certain people on the team who act one way when they're not starting and completely differently when they are.'

It was all very cryptic. I racked my brains as to what, or who, he could be talking about. Once again, Mark had spoken so vaguely that everybody in the room was wondering whether he was referring to them. I thought maybe he was talking about Toni. She had had a public argument with Mark earlier on in the week about her injury. I understood the situation to be that Manchester City did not want Toni to travel, but Mark insisted that she did. He had promised Toni could play, despite her injury, and then changed his mind by putting her on the bench for the Bosnia game. They had fallen out over it, in public. I decided that was probably it.

For once, I was sure Mark couldn't be picking on me. I thought back over my own behaviour. By now I was completely used to not starting. It had been six months now. At this point, I was happy if I got to play at all, let alone start. I had remembered what Mum had said about not letting Mark's decisions affect my happiness, and I had kept up a poker face around camp. No one could have said I was acting differently according to whether I was starting. No one had complained to me about my behaviour at the time.

I had spoken frequently to Adam about how I felt in the squad and trusted that these conversations were confidential. Anyway, Mark had not only started me against Bosnia, he had let me play ninety minutes. If I had done something so wrong, that wouldn't have happened. It felt like that was the kind of coach Mark had become: step out of line and you'd be on the bench or even out of the squad. Conversely, I was playing, so I was in the clear. I left the camp happy enough.

That was mid-April. Our next England game, another qualifier against Serbia, wasn't scheduled until early

June. I was waiting to hear from Dan Ashworth about our meeting, when, a few weeks later, I received an email from one of his assistants. Attached to the email was a letter, on official England-headed paper, and signed by Dan himself, inviting me to take part in a culture review for an FA initiative called 'The England DNA'. If I wanted, I could 'share my experiences' of 'what it means to play for England' in a conversation with an outside consultant.

'As an iconic England figure,' the letter stated, 'we firmly believe that your contribution would be valuable as we look to create a culture, identity and pride for all of our England players and develop winning England teams we can all be proud of for the future.'

I read the letter again. Our meeting hadn't materialised, but Dan knew I was unhappy. Here he was, offering me a chance to officially speak out about the environment and culture on the team. I trusted my answers would be treated in confidence and that I would be protected. I had no reason to believe otherwise. The FA had always treated me well; we had a good working relationship stretching back over a decade. All my grievances were with Mark, not with the FA. All I had to do was tell someone independent from the team what had been going on. Then, I hoped, they would become aware of his communication style and behaviour, talk to him, and we could all move on. How naive I was.

I replied to the email saying I would be happy to take part in the culture review. I was contacted by the consultant, Owen Eastwood, and we arranged a phone call for later that week. On the phone, Owen explained his brief was to explore English football's sense of identity. Then he went straight in with direct questions about what it was like to be a black player on the team. I took a deep breath. So, it was true, someone really was investigating the toxic culture on the team. Maybe Drew, or Lianne, or Anita had complained, and now they wanted my side of the story. It felt like a godsend.

I asked Owen to confirm my answers would be kept anonymous, and then I began giving him my answers. He asked about my experiences as a black player, but also for my views on the general culture of the England women's team. I was open and honest, and told him I did not believe any senior England international should feel as demoralised as I had done at times in the past two years, but that my faith, resilience and love for football had brought me through.

I told him about the groupthink culture of the team, and how those who didn't look the same, think the same, or who stood out too much as an individual were deliberately isolated. For me, I said, that just wasn't a team. A team had to bring every single player on board and ensure everyone felt confident and empowered. I told him lots of players only cared about their own place on the team. No one wanted to rock the boat on behalf of others.

As I spoke, I felt a weight lifting from my shoulders. Maybe this would help. Maybe this would change everything. I told Owen that on balance, my positive experiences throughout my eleven years on the team outweighed the bad. At the end of the call, which lasted about forty-five minutes, Owen complimented me on my career, and suggested I put my experiences and concerns into writing and submit them to Dan Ashworth.

Looking back, I see now that God was putting something into motion. It was better that I wasn't the instigator of what was to come. I wasn't supposed to quit voluntarily, instead, the FA would come to me, seeking my views. I didn't ask to be part of a culture review. They asked me. God set it up that way.

Twelve days after the phone call, I was training with Chelsea when I got a message from Mark: 'I'll be coming to Cobham tomorrow, can we meet?'

It must be about our next qualifier in Serbia, I thought, coming up at the beginning of June. He probably wanted to prepare me for sitting on the bench as a sub. It would be miserable, probably, but I was heartened by my conversation with Owen. I wasn't about to let Mark make me quit, not now I knew the FA were interested in investigating the culture on the team.

Mark seemed business-like when he arrived at Cobham the following day. We went into one of Emma's offices to talk after training. He didn't waste any time with small talk.

'I'm not calling you up for the next camp,' he said, 'due to your behaviour in previous camps.'

Panic rose in my chest.

'What behaviour?' I said immediately. 'What are you talking about?'

'Your behaviour no longer aligns with Lioness standards,' he said.

I looked at him blankly.

'I don't understand,' I said. 'What specifically are you saying I've done wrong?'

He thought about this for a few moments.

'You were withdrawn in meetings,' he said.

'And that's a crime?' I said. 'There are lots of players that are quiet in the group, have they been dropped too? And no wonder I've been withdrawn, Mark. You've been making me miserable for the past two years.'

Mark gazed past me; he had already stopped listening. I felt like he had punched me in the gut. This was utter nonsense. My manager was telling me I was being dropped from the team for breaching a non-binding code of conduct. A list of guidelines dreamed up voluntarily by the team to ensure everyone got on well. And then he couldn't even name an example of which rule I'd breached? I tried again.

'Being withdrawn isn't enough to drop me from the team,' I said. 'No one ever issued me any kind of warning about my behaviour. No one spoke to me at the last camp. Steph never said anything.'

Mark still didn't look at me. His manner was serious, but his eyes couldn't conceal his determination. He was on a mission and he had got his way; I was gone. My lawyer's instinct kicked in.

'Mark!' I said, trying to bring him back into the room. 'Give me specific examples of bad behaviour. I want times and dates.'

He looked up.

'The leadership group also feel you've behaved poorly,' he said. 'We feel you only think about yourself. You're miserable when you don't play, you only act professional if you make the team. We don't want players like that on the side.'

So that was his crutch, the leadership group. What was supposed to be a team-building strategy had, I felt, been warped and twisted by him into a control mechanism, and frankly, a device to isolate players whose faces didn't fit. Those favoured players got to sit in the room with a manager and judge my behaviour, but I didn't get to defend myself. I didn't get a right to appeal.

The knowledge came suddenly that I would never play under Mark again. I even saw how he would play it: he would present me as a bad team player. It was a farce, he didn't have a shred of evidence, but that's how he would spin it. I thought back to that first Cyprus camp; he had tried to paint me as an isolated bad apple from day one. A bad apple that the FA had described as 'an iconic England player' in their letter less than a fortnight ago. Now Mark was sitting here telling me my behaviour was so bad I had been dropped for the first time in eleven years. Nothing made sense.

Too late, I realised I should have been recording this meeting. I hadn't asked Adam to come along, I hadn't thought it would be necessary, I thought this would be a positive meeting. I reached into my pocket with the idea of trying to hit record on my phone, but I couldn't see the screen, and I knew it was too late anyway. I tried one last time.

'Mark,' I said. 'I've been on and off the bench for over a year. I have consistently sought your guidance on how I can improve on the pitch during meetings before games, regardless of whether I play or not. I'm not perfect, but I've been as professional as anyone else has been. You have nothing to use against me.'

His eyes glazed over again. It was useless, I fell silent. Mark left, and I remained sitting in the office, too stunned to move. Time slowed down as the suspicion began to rise. It had been only twelve days since I had poured my heart out to that consultant about my views on Mark's bullying and prejudiced behaviour, and now I had been dropped from the team. The timing was astounding at best. At worst, it suggested something had gone horribly wrong.

I wondered if I could have prevented all this. I always believed that in adversity, the best protection was to perform. If I did my job well, if I kept scoring, I thought nobody could hurt me. Too late, I understood there were people out there who would take against me for reasons I couldn't control, who would hate me no matter what I did. Too late, I realised that for all the times I had tried not to, I still ended up focusing too much on Mark. In doing so, I had given him more power, more strongholds, in my mind than he deserved.

Now he had won. He had isolated and manipulated me out of the team. Worst of all, he had made me doubt myself. But now that I was no longer his player, and he was no longer my manager, all that was about to change. Sitting in the office, I reminded myself I was stronger than he had ever imagined. I had logic on my side, I had evidence and I had my faith. And, if it came to it, I knew I had the truth.

Class 7:

Truth Doesn't Panic

It felt like much of my life had been leading up to this point, to a final confrontation with

GOLI

ATH.

CHAPTER EIGHTEEN

My head was full of questions. Why, after eleven years on the team, had I been dropped for being withdrawn in a meeting? And why had I been dropped less than two weeks after complaining about a culture of bullying and racial discrimination in the England team? Had Owen shared my feedback with Mark or with Dan Ashworth? Was this retaliation, or punishment, for speaking out about the culture under Mark? My gut told me this was no coincidence.

My heart was beating hard as I tried to push down a rising sense of panic. How to stay calm while the storm raged around me was a lesson life was about to teach in the hardest way possible. I wouldn't always get it right. At times, I would let the panic get the better of me; at times I would overreact, or react at the wrong time, in the wrong way. But ultimately, I would learn when to talk and when to stay silent, when to react and when to rise above the bait. I would learn to wait, to calm myself, to hold on to the truth, and wait for it to come out in its own time.

But I wasn't there yet. At this point, I needed answers. Dan Ashworth could straighten this out. He was the technical director, and Mark's line manager. He had commissioned the culture review, and he had known I was unhappy long before I was dropped. I began drafting an email to him as soon as I got home from Cobham. I explained I had complained about a toxic culture on the team and been dropped within days on flimsy grounds. Then I tackled my nightmare suspicion head on:

'I would like some reassurance,' I wrote to Dan, 'that my involvement in this culture review and my report will remain confidential and has not in any way directly or indirectly led to my non-selection in the forthcoming England squad.'

I stared at the words on the screen. It was a serious allegation; the natural defence would be to cry sour grapes. I clarified that it wasn't being left out of the squad that bothered me. Under normal circumstances I would never dream of questioning a manager's final authority over squad selection. This was different; this manager had a habit of treating me unfairly, and now he couldn't explain why I'd been dropped. And, well, the timing stank.

I offered to share my feedback in written form and attached the FA's original request, signed by Dan himself, for my views on the England culture. Maybe it was all a big misunderstanding. In case it wasn't, I added in the PFA players' union to my email. The lawyer in me said it couldn't hurt. I slept on it, and in the morning, hit send. That was 24 May 2016, the day after I was dropped.

Dan replied that evening. Squad selection had nothing to do with the culture review, he wrote, and claimed no one had yet seen Owen's report. He promised to get hold of the results and get back to me. Two days later, Dan wrote again. He had now seen Owen's report, he wrote, but it didn't include my name. 'Your involvement in this culture and identity review,' he wrote, 'has not led in anyway whatsoever to your non-selection in this England squad, nor will it affect any selection in future squads.' Then he invited me to repeat my feedback, either in a meeting, or in a written statement.

I didn't buy it. Mark had acted in our meeting as if my deselection was final, and yet he couldn't give me a proper reason for it. I felt that he had wanted me gone for the past two years. Why was he suddenly so confident he could drop me now? Could it be that Mark became aware of my involvement in the culture review in the six weeks leading up to that meeting, that he knew what was coming, and he had dropped me in retaliation.

I gave Dan the benefit of the doubt. After all, he was still in the dark, he didn't see the context of Mark's actions. I had wanted to speak to Dan about Mark for the past three months, since I approached him in America at the SheBelieves Cup. Now we were finally having that conversation. Dan had invited me to put my experiences in writing. I was sure that once Dan saw the gravity of what had been going on, once the FA leadership got wind of it, my questions and my grievances would be taken seriously.

I wrote it all down for Dan in a report, the whole miserable two years under Mark laid out in easy-to-digest bullet points, a list of incidents where I had been singled out for unfavourable treatment. I didn't include every incident, and I specified it was a non-exhaustive list. These episodes, I wrote, had the culminative effect of making me feel 'undermined, belittled and at times bullied' and showed Mark had a 'negative personal bias against me' that 'may be based on negative racial stereotypes'. Mark hadn't acted fairly or objectively towards me, I wrote. He had it in for me, maybe even because of my skin colour, and this report gave evidence to back up that claim.

I wasn't about to accuse somebody of racism unless I could prove it, so I was cautious. I went over what evidence I had, and where it would be my word against Mark's. As this was a confidential exercise, I was reluctant to involve other players at this stage. But I noted examples of when I felt I was deliberately undermined in a group setting. I had faith that, if it came to it, other players would remember the instances where I was repeatedly singled out.

I found and included my first email to Adrian Bevington back in January 2014. Looking at it, I was reminded this was a chain of events that began almost immediately into Mark's tenure. It had all begun straight away, as soon as he became manager. This was not a fresh complaint; this was a continuous pattern of behaviour.

I left out Mark's Ebola comment because I felt it would be tricky to prove without eyewitnesses. I had told Lianne and Mum, and another close friend, Jessica, what Mark had said, but I had nothing in writing. Or so I thought. Initially, I thought I had told Drew about the Ebola comment in person and had forgotten I had written a WhatsApp message to her about it in China, nearly a year after the initial event. I rediscovered these messages only months after I wrote the report to Dan. As things stood at the time, I felt I couldn't prove the Ebola remark, so I left it out.

There was another incident, one I felt I could prove without bothering witnesses. Mark had asked Drew how many times she had been arrested during the midfielders meeting in China. At the time, I believed there was hard evidence of that. I remembered that Joe Bennett, the cameraman from FATV, had been following us on that camp. The whole meeting would be on tape somewhere. Mark's question to Drew, the awkward silence, the giggles, Dan would be able to watch all of it on film and judge for himself. I wrote it in, describing it for what I felt it was, a 'racist statement' that proved Mark harboured negative racial stereotypes.

I didn't name Drew in the report. She hadn't wanted me to make a fuss at the time, and I felt it would be unfair to explicitly use her name without her permission. I referred to her only as 'the player', but I gave enough information for her to be identified if need be, should anyone need her to confirm the incident. I described her as a Chelsea player, of mixed-race descent, born and raised in south-east London, on her first international senior camp. It could only have been Drew.

I thought about Lee's treatment of me. I could prove he had called me 'lazy as fuck' at that first Cyprus Cup. He had said it on the microphone, on film, so I included it. Lee's comment was evidence that Mark and his staff had singled me out from the start.

I read and reread the report. I was aware that with eight examples, I was only scratching the surface. It wasn't easy to explain all the other, more subtle cues, the sharp looks, the body language, that had set me on edge and made me anxious. I wrote that I was aware of other players who had been through similar experiences. I was thinking not only of Drew, but also of Lianne and Anita, though I didn't name anyone. It was a week before I was finally happy with the report. On 2 June, I sent it to Dan.

Once again, on instinct, I copied in the PFA. I got a reply the same day from the PFA's assistant chief executive Nick Cusack, acknowledging the email and taking over handling of the case from Matthew, who felt conflicted because he personally represented other players on the team. Nick was to prove a godsend in what was to come. He never strayed from his role, which was to represent a player in a conflict with their employer independently and without conflicts of interest.

No response came from Dan that day or the next. That week, in a bizarre scheduling move, England played Serbia twice, at home and away, both times winning 7–0. Mark debuted two new forwards, City's Nikita Parris, and Rachel Daly, then playing in America. I wasn't the only one left off the squad. Katie Chapman and Toni Duggan had also been dropped from the team, though Toni was back within two months.

Looking back, I feel that if anything, Toni actually really did give Mark a reason to drop her. She fell out with him in Bosnia, but I never did anything close to that. Toni was soon forgiven for losing her temper, it was seen as out of character. But for me, if I were to have a public argument with Mark, I'm sure I would have found it harder to live down. I would have been dismissed as an angry black girl with an attitude.

It was an odd feeling at first, seeing the team play without me. I had been part of the England set-up for half of my life. There was nothing I could do, so I took my mind off it and threw myself into other work. As one door closed, another one was opening. My pundit career was taking off. Since my first appearance on *Match of the Day* two years before, I had been asked back a few times by the BBC, including as a guest editor of their flagship *Woman's Hour* programme. Now, ITV had invited me on as a pundit for their coverage of the men's 2016 Euros in France. I flew to Paris a few days after sending Dan my report.

It was a chance to look forward and not dwell on the abrupt end to my England career. I realised God had timed things perfectly. He had lifted me out of an environment that was draining so much of my energy and given me new exciting opportunities. It was a great honour. I was one of only a handful of British female players to have made it on as a pundit at a men's international tournament. I was excited to fly the flag for women's football and hoped to win over some fans of the men's game. I was also braced for a backlash; inevitably there would be fans who couldn't accept a female pundit. The pressure was on. If I slipped up, even in the tiniest way, I would be judged far more harshly than any man. Not only that, my sex would be identified as the cause of the problem.

I had already learned that the best defence was to perform. I researched every player inside out, watched their games, analysed their skills and tactics. I got to know the strikers, their finishes, the kinds of goals they scored. And I practised my delivery in the bathroom mirror, in the car, until my words flowed naturally. I aimed to give fresh opinions, a new perspective, not only as a female player but also as a current player. In the end, I was more prepared than some of my male counterparts. I knew my geeky approach to research would stand me in good stead when former Arsenal legend Emmanuel Petit rocked up ten minutes before we went live on air and asked which games we were covering. I loved every second of being a pundit. Even England's last sixteen loss to Iceland couldn't dampen my spirits for long.

Meanwhile, there was radio silence from the FA. The tournament ended in mid-July, and still nothing came from Dan. I guessed he had been busy with the Euros, so I gave him another fortnight. On 28 July, I decided I had waited long enough. Two months was plenty of time to respond to serious allegations. I emailed Dan asking if he had received my report. Dan wrote back claiming my email had never arrived.

I sent it again. Alarm bells were now ringing loud and clear. The PFA had received my email right away, it seemed extraordinary for Dan to say he hadn't got it as I had not got a 'failed delivery' message. By this point, Nick from the PFA was unsettled by the whole thing too. I had raised very serious complaints that had now been overlooked for two months. Concerned the FA were trying to sweep my grievances under the rug, Nick suggested a meeting with Dan to discuss them in person.

We met Dan at Wembley on 18 August. The FA's director of Human Resources, Rachel Brace, was also there. Dan and Rachel went in very strong, flatly denying any wrongdoing by either them or Mark. I was shocked by their tone. Though I had been expecting denials, I had also expected some conciliatory concern, not a solid brick wall. Nick and I protested: these were grave allegations of bullying and racial bias and they deserved a serious response. The arrest comment, at the very least, warranted further scrutiny. At this, Rachel and Dan relented, and agreed to launch an internal investigation.

Now we were getting somewhere. An investigation meant witnesses could now be involved. I suggested Rachel and Dan speak to Lianne and Anita about their similar experiences of being isolated, we believed, on grounds of race. Drew's name wasn't mentioned, but I had given them enough information to identify her and ask her what had happened. I reminded them that FATV should have Mark's arrest comment on video. Nick jumped in at this point and emphasised it was up to the FA to decide how to conduct an internal inquiry into allegations of racial discrimination.

I went away reasonably happy. I still wanted to give Dan the benefit of the doubt; it had been a busy summer. Maybe he really hadn't seen my email. He and Rachel had been defensive, but I believed they were now taking things seriously. I trusted Dan and Rachel to get to the bottom of Mark's behaviour. Maybe it could all still be straightened out.

I left the next day for a weekend in Spain. I planned to visit a friend and watch the Barcelona men's team play their first game of the season. I was having a wonderful weekend until, when we were walking to Camp Nou, my phone buzzed with an email from Dan. Still walking, I opened it up and scanned it. Dan had forwarded me an email from Rachel to Nick asking permission to contact Mark and the other players I had suggested they speak to. Then, in the final paragraph, I read a sentence that stopped me dead in my tracks.

Rachel then dropped a bombshell and mentioned I was being investigated by the FA Integrity Unit relating to a part-time consultancy job I had with a sports agency called Platinum One. She claimed she had no further information, but that 'it was an entirely separate and unrelated issue'. Unrelated issue. I read the words over and over, my heart thumping loudly in my ears.

I stood stock still on the path, underneath a huge billboard plastered with Messi's face. I was gobsmacked. The timing was as sinister as could be. This was the first I had ever heard about any investigation into my legal work. This was an advisory role I'd been doing with various clients for years. I had never kept it a secret. Why would the FA inform me now, in the same email about an investigation into my allegations of racism in the England management? Did they want to intimidate me? Make me withdraw my complaint? If so, this was victimisation, pure and simple. There was a reason why there were laws to safeguard whistle-blowers against exactly this kind of treatment.

All the pleasantness, the cooperation, was gone. This felt like a naked threat, like they were trying to get at me. Hands shaking, I punched a reply to Dan and Rachel into my phone. When and why had the FA begun this investigation? Was this normal procedure when a player raised a grievance? Had Mark Sampson and all the players also been investigated? I clarified I hadn't broken any rules, I was a legal consultant, not an agent or intermediary for players. I copied the PFA back in and hit send.

Rachel replied several hours later. 'Please be reassured,' she wrote, 'it is entirely coincidental.' I wasn't reassured it was anything of the sort. The investigation had begun on 9 August, around a week after I re-sent Dan my report. And they were telling me it was unrelated? Rachel herself had seen how it looked, and she herself had conflated the two matters by bringing it up at the end of that email. This didn't feel like coincidence, it felt like intimidation, the equivalent of 'we know where you live'.

I couldn't relax. The FA were trying to ruin me, and even watching Messi score twice against Real Betis couldn't take my mind off it. Rachel's email had wrecked everything, I couldn't concentrate on the game. Afterwards, back at my friend's place, I booked an early flight home. There was no way I could be around anyone when my head was all over the place. I had already lost my England career, and now they were after my job. I had to talk to Nick at the PFA, I had to get home.

Nick said I shouldn't write to Rachel and Dan again. On my behalf, he gave permission to approach Mark and provided Lianne and Anita's contact details. That same week, the FA Integrity Unit contacted the agency to ask about my role. I was still in shock. The FA had always supported my legal work, I had even done a week-long placement with their legal team in my first year at university. How many times had they pushed me forward in front of the cameras? Eni Aluko, our England player and lawyer? Now all that was gone, an eleven-year working relationship up in smoke. Why? Because I said the England manager had said something racist? Would this have happened if I had told Owen I didn't like the England kit?

I was in limbo. There was nothing to do but to hear if I could keep my job. As usual, Chelsea was a welcome distraction, and I was having a great season. By early September, I was the top scorer in the league. Then, with England's next qualifier on the horizon, Mark said publicly the door remained open to me to return to the squad. I'm convinced this was a decoy, he had no intention to choose me for any future squads. Still, on 6 September, I sent Mark an email, the first and only time I tried to contact him after our final meeting in Cobham. I pointed out I was on track to win the Golden Boot and asked him politely for a more detailed explanation of why he wasn't picking me. I never got a reply. To this day, I have never been given any performance-related, statistical or tactical reasons for being dropped.

The FA were about to double down on Mark's nonsense. Rachel and Dan wrote to Nick to say they had completed their investigation and called us in for a meeting on 13 October to present their findings. Nick tried to get a written summary of their results ahead of time, but none came. It didn't bode well, but it wasn't until Rachel opened the meeting by repeating Mark's reasons for dropping me that I was sure the investigation had been a stitch up.

'We've spoken to Mark,' said Rachel. 'He feels he was justified in dropping you because of your behaviour.'

My eyes widened. I shook my head.

'But Mark hasn't specified what he means by bad behaviour,' I said. 'Nobody has. I deserve better explanation than that. I'm the top scorer in the league and I'm still not getting picked. I emailed Mark and he won't respond. None of this is normal, and yet you claim this has nothing to do with the complaint I raised?'

Nick leaned forward to interrupt. 'And what about that complaint?' he said. 'What about the grievances Eni raised in her report?'

Rachel nodded. 'We found no wrongdoing or misconduct by Mark,' she said slowly. 'We spoke to a number of players and they all said they had never experienced any racism in the England team. They weren't able to confirm or deny whether any comment about arrests was made to any player.'

I gawped at her.

'What?' I said, trying to keep the frustration out of my voice. 'Who did you talk to? Did you ask Lianne and Anita? Did you ask any people of colour?'

Rachel shook her head. 'No, we haven't spoken to them yet.'

I shook my head again. This was madness.

'How can you conclude your investigation if you haven't spoken to the key witnesses?' I said.

At this, Nick leaned back in his chair, visibly disgusted. 'This isn't acceptable,' he said. 'Do you have an itemised list of Eni's grievances, together with your evidence, and the reasons why you have dismissed them?'

Rachel looked blank. I tried again.

'Didn't you watch the video of the midfielders meeting in China?' I said. 'The arrest comment should be on there.'

Dan turned to Rachel. 'I guess we should have watched that,' he said quietly.

I was staggered. They hadn't even made a basic attempt to investigate my complaints. They hadn't watched the video. They hadn't spoken to Anita or Lianne. This whole exercise hadn't been to find the truth. They had only wanted to clear Mark of wrongdoing.

'This is a complete farce,' said Nick, fuming now. 'You haven't taken this seriously at all. We left you to it, we didn't tell you how to conduct your own investigation. But how can you possibly have reached a conclusion of no wrongdoing without looking at the evidence or speaking to witnesses?'

Rachel and Dan looked uncomfortable. They promised to speak to Lianne and Anita. Still, it seemed a pretty empty gesture. They had already completed their investigation, what was the point? I left the meeting more distraught than ever. The FA had closed ranks against me to protect Mark. Mark, Dan's recruit, the golden boy who won England bronze at the World Cup. Everything had to be done to keep him in place. This was a race issue; they knew full well how serious it was. But that only heightened their impulse to protect their guy, to shroud, to bury. The point of this so-called investigation had been to make it all go away. To make me go away.

I wasn't going anywhere. If the FA had hoped to fob me off with a pretend investigation they were in for a disappointment. I knew my rights as a contracted player inside out. I had evidence, I had a case, and if the FA couldn't deal with this internally, I was fully prepared to take it to an independent employment tribunal. The PFA contacted Nick Randall QC, a barrister who had worked many high-profile discrimination cases in football, including Lucy Ward's at Leeds United. He agreed to represent me, and we met for the first time with Nick Cusack at a coffee shop in Notting Hill.

Nick Randall was warm and intelligent, and I quickly realised he was a legal mastermind. Throughout the process, as things got more serious, he always reassured me I was doing the right thing. He advised me to sue for loss of future earnings. If we could show I was good enough to play for England, but that the timing of my dismissal from the team was linked to my discrimination complaint, I could argue I was entitled to earnings for the time period Mark was manager. I began gathering more evidence, which is when I found the WhatsApp exchange with Drew in China. The messages would turn out to be crucial. They had us discussing the detail of both the Ebola and arrest comments six months before I was dropped or had raised a full complaint.

The season ended, and I won the Golden Boot. Now I knew for sure my England career was over, at least under Mark. If he wouldn't pick me when I was the top scorer, he would never pick me again. It was unusual to exclude the league's top scorer from the international team, but however much it looked like a personal vendetta against me, I let it go. After eleven years, more than one hundred caps, three European Championships, and three World Cups, it was over. Looking back, letting go only gave me more power. The FA no longer had anything I wanted.

On 25 November, Nick Randall and the PFA sent a stunning letter to the FA laying out all the ways in which they had failed to respond properly to my grievances. It slammed the FA's internal inquiry as a 'sham not designed to establish the truth but intended to protect Mark Sampson'. We notified the FA we had new evidence Mark had made the arrest comment. We also detailed new allegations, the Ebola comment, and the fact that Lee Kendall had occasionally addressed me in a Caribbean accent, for the first time. The letter demanded a response within seven days or we would proceed to a tribunal. It was incredibly powerful.

We sent the letter via the PFA to Rachel and Dan, copying in FA chief executives Martin Glenn and FA chairman Greg Clarke. The FA's only response came from Greg Clarke: a short, dismissive, and disrespectful note of only fourteen words: 'I have no idea why you are sending me this,' he wrote. 'Perhaps you could enlighten me?' Thankfully, I was saved seeing it until much later.

The FA were silent for another two weeks. Then, on 9 December, they sent us a letter. There was no mention of the new allegations, the Ebola comment, or Lee's fake accent. Instead, they announced a new investigation, to be overseen by a barrister, Katherine Newton. I looked her up online and my heart sank. She was a black woman and, I was stunned to discover, she wasn't a QC, she was a junior barrister. She also appeared, from what I could see, to have a track record of defending big firms against whistle-blowers, which did not entirely fill me with confidence. Why had the FA hired a junior lawyer to investigate alleged racism in the national team?

Trust had hit rock bottom. I had completely lost faith in the FA or anyone hired by them. For over eight months now, the FA had done nothing but deflect, deny and ignore me. In their letter, they asked if I would talk to Katherine for her investigation. Instinct said not to. Nick Randall was sceptical, too, and advised against it. We would hold out for a legally binding tribunal.

Early in the new year, I had to quit my consultancy job. The FA involved Chelsea in their integrity investigation, and in the end, I was forced to choose between playing for my club and working at the football agency. It was a no-brainer, of course. I chose Chelsea, but I was miserable about it. All I had done was tell the truth, and now I had lost my England career and a job I had worked extremely hard for. It felt like the FA had won.

The FA probably thought that too. On 9 March, I received a fifteen-page letter from Katherine summarising the results of her investigation. I wasn't allowed to see her full confidential fifty-seven-page report. I read the summary in disbelief. Katherine went through my grievances and dismissed them one by one. There had been no bullying, she wrote, and no discrimination.

Katherine based her conclusions on interviews with Mark, and a group of players put forward by the FA, who said they had never witnessed any bullying or racism in the team. She hadn't spoken to Drew.

It was a repeat of the previous farce. The arrest comment, Katherine found, had probably never happened. She had watched the China video but claimed not to have heard Mark say it. She hadn't asked to see our new evidence or felt the need to speak to Drew. Later, the FA would claim this was because I hadn't identified Drew in my report, but many people didn't buy that. Katherine had my description, she had watched the video, there could be no doubt she knew exactly who I meant by 'the player', and yet she never even approached Drew to ask if she wanted to talk. I could not understand how she could conduct an independent external investigation without speaking to a key witness. She would later claim this was 'in accordance with good employment practice', as I had asked that Drew should not be involved in the investigation, but this is not the case. I had not named her because I did not have her permission to do so, but I had not said she was off limits.

If anything, Katherine's report made me even more determined. I wasn't about to sit there and let the FA insinuate I was lying about Mark's behaviour. I wanted a rigorous investigation, not this rubbish. I was building a strong case to the tribunal and I had proof of both race discrimination and victimisation. The FA were refusing to hand over the China video so we could check it, but it didn't matter. We had the WhatsApp messages, and, on 18 March, Drew emailed me a statement confirming the arrest comment. What was the FA going to do? Say we were both lying?

In April, we lodged my claim with the tribunal. In the end, I decided to settle with the FA. I was ready to take it all the way to a public hearing, but that would mean dragging everything out into the public eye, which was the last thing I wanted. I had done everything I could to keep these matters confidential to this point. The FA were also keen to avoid bad publicity, and we entered negotiations. We reached an agreement in early June. Later this caused many misunderstandings. So, let's set the record straight.

We settled on a pay-out of £67,000; the equivalent of two years' wages. This was the sum I would have very likely been awarded at a tribunal. I paid national insurance and tax on it because it amounted to loss of earnings. After tax, I would get a total of £45,000, paid over two instalments. Our agreement also included a confidentiality clause, a standard feature of most out-of-court settlements, specifying what both parties could do if the settlement became public. I would be permitted to speak, provided I didn't bring the FA into disrepute.

It was a clause I would come to regret agreeing to. It didn't make much sense. I never set out to speak badly of the FA. Quite the contrary: I was happy to co-operate. But what did it even mean to bring the FA into disrepute anyway? There was only either the whole truth of the matter, or there were lies. Later, confusion over what I could and couldn't say would cost me a lot of time. But in the end, that time was just what I needed to learn a big lesson. I learned that those with the truth on their side don't need to rush, and that sometimes, it is better to stay silent than to panic.

At the time, I was relieved to have come to an agreement. At last I could put a stressful year behind me. Besides, things were looking up. The 2017 Euros were around the corner, and Channel 4 had invited me to the Netherlands as a pundit. I wasn't sure at first. I hadn't done anything wrong, there was no reason to hide. Still, I didn't want anyone's pity, or scorn, as the girl who got dropped. Then I thought again: here was a wonderful opportunity, not only to build on my media experience, but to show the world I had moved on. I could be objective about England in a different role, off the pitch.

The more I thought about it, the more I warmed to the idea. My adversaries had tried to ignore me, intimidate me, and fob me off with two questionable investigations. But I had held my nerve, built a solid case, and had my grievances vindicated with a settlement. Now they probably expected me to withdraw, to spend the Euros trembling somewhere in a dark corner. But that wasn't my style. Instead, I would send a powerful statement. I would stand proud on camera on the sideline; a gracious, well-prepared professional.

CHAPTER NINETEEN

The Euros went well, aside from a couple of minor awkward moments. The very fact of me talking on the sidelines metres away from where my former team were playing placed a glaring question mark over my head. Why, if I was the top scorer in the league, wasn't I on the pitch? Channel 4 were keen to side-step any tension on air, and we discussed beforehand how best to navigate the issue.

A lot of effort was made to avoid Mark and me meeting on screen. I made it clear to the producers I didn't want to be involved in conversations with him, though I didn't explain why. I suspect the FA also intervened to make sure we were kept apart. Once or twice, when Mark was due to be interviewed pitchside, I saw FA staff reminding

Channel 4 producers that I shouldn't be in shot. It was awkward, but to be expected.

It was odd being around the team but not with them. Some of my former teammates waved from a distance and gave me the thumbs-up, others resolutely ignored me. That the feeling was largely cold I felt said a lot about the perception of me within the team. I wasn't particularly surprised, though of course they knew no details, I knew they were being fed some nasty lines about me being a troublemaker. Some were encouraged to believe my dismissal was all my fault, that I had a bitter, calculated agenda to distract from their European championship campaign. Others knew who I was and knew the truth.

I knew the FA had gone to some extraordinary lengths to portray me as a bad egg. At some point over the past year, a black actress had even been brought in to act out a role-play scenario in front of the team about a selfish player who was jealous of her teammates. The feeling from some in the group was that the actor was meant to represent me. It seemed a pretty desperate attempt to manipulate perceptions and justify the decision to drop me from the team.

I knew that if I was going to get through this, I had to find ways of rising above it all. Practically, that meant pushing the individual people out of my mind and concentrating instead on their game. I had a job to do, I was going to do it well. Now I could demonstrate to myself and everyone else that I had moved on. It helped that England were smashing it so that I could strike a positive note with my punditry. England topped their group, having thrashed Scotland 6–0 in their first game, dispatched Spain 2–0 in their second, and Portugal 2–1 in their third. As the games rolled on, and I praised individual players and Mark's tactics, any suggestion I was resentful or bitter melted away.

By the time England faced France in the quarter-finals, I was well into my stride. The FA's head of communications even emailed my agent Jo, praising my positive punditry and the way I was handling the situation. The email sounded surprised. I think some people within the FA thought I would go on air and tell the world about the awful year I had gone through dealing with complaints of discrimination in the England team. It struck me as odd, and I was disappointed. After eleven years in the England set-up, it was like the FA didn't know me at all. It was as if they didn't know I would rise above it and act like a professional.

Besides, it wasn't difficult to get enthusiastic about the football, it was an electric tournament. The same night England knocked out France, Denmark ended Germany's twenty-two-year reign as European champions. With the eternal victors gone, it was shaping up to be one of the most exciting tournaments in decades. All eyes were fixed on England's semi-final, when I got a message from Jo saying she needed to talk to me urgently. I called her back from my hotel room.

'I got a call from the *Daily Mail*,' Jo began. 'They've had sight of the report you sent to Dan Ashworth last year and they want to run the story.'

She paused as her words sank in. I gripped the phone tighter.

'But that report was confidential,' I said. 'What do you mean, they've had sight of it?'

'Somebody must have leaked it,' said Jo. 'They want to run a story about allegations of racism in the England team.'

Nightmarish scenes flashed through my head. The story couldn't come out now with England heading for the semi-finals, and me on air. Not only would it be utterly mortifying, it would certainly spell the end of my blossoming media career. The FA might claim I had leaked the report myself to distract from the Euros and the team's success. The timing couldn't have been worse.

'I can't deal with this coming out now,' I said.

'I'll see what I can do,' said Jo, and rang off.

I stood rooted to the spot, phone still in hand, staring blankly out of the hotel window as my mind whirled with questions. Who had leaked my report, and why had they done it now? Only a few people had access to that document. Was it someone who wished me harm, or wanted to embarrass me on air? Or was it someone on my side? Another whistle-blower, perhaps, who wanted to expose what was really going on behind closed doors at England? Or maybe it was simply someone wanting to explain why I was on the sidelines, and not on the pitch? I'll never know.

Jo wrote back later that day. Together, she and the FA had persuaded the *Mail* to hold the story until the tournament was over. It was a merciful delay, enough for me to keep smiling through another week on air. I put the story out of my mind entirely and concentrated on watching and analysing some excellent football.

England's hopes were decisively dashed by the Netherlands in a 3–0 semi-final, while Denmark took out Austria on penalties. The final, in which hosts Netherlands hammered Denmark 4–2, contained some of the best play I had ever seen. Everyone was swept up in the fairy tale of the Netherlands winning on home soil, not least their mad troop of orange-clad fans. It was a wonderful end to a thrilling tournament, and I was delighted to be part of it.

The next morning, 7 August, I caught the first flight back to London in time for afternoon training with Chelsea. The women's league was switching back to a winter format and pre-season training was set to begin right away. On the plane I was happy, still buzzing from the euphoric final, and I was pleased with myself; I had wrapped up an amazing experience and kept my cool in challenging circumstances. I was looking forward to the new season, and to the next chapter.

I landed at Heathrow at around nine. As the plane taxied towards the terminal, I pulled out my phone and switched off airplane mode. The phone began buzzing and didn't stop. Within seconds, I had received around thirty messages, and a flood of Twitter notifications. I opened the first message from my agent, Jo. It simply said: 'Call me when you land.' That didn't sound good. I opened Twitter. The first post linked me to a *Daily Mail* story. I read the headline with a growing sense of dread.

'FA pays £40,000 to striker bullied out of the England women's squad: Star claims she quit the national team because players were "undermined and belittled" by coaching staff.'

So here it was. They had run the story within hours of the final whistle. I clicked on the link, scrolled down the article and gripped the phone in panic. My eyes widened. There, among extracts from my confidential report, was a naked picture of me. The *Mail* had lifted it from a charity shoot I had done back in 2015 for *Sport* magazine. The original shoot had been tasteful, a celebration of the athletic body designed to promote healthier body image among young women. Splashed across a tabloid, it made me look like a page 3 model. I've never been so mortified in my life.

I glanced up as the plane rolled to a stop on the tarmac and the other passengers undid their belts and jumped up. I sat rooted in my seat, heart thumping, waiting for the doors to open. I forced myself back to the article. It was all wrong, lots of facts had been left out, the story twisted beyond recognition. I had quit England, the *Mail* wrote, and afterwards claimed I had been bullied off the team. Then, despite an FA inquiry and independent investigation finding no wrongdoing, the FA had given me a new contract and 'an extra £40,000' in what the article called a 'confidentiality agreement'. It didn't even make sense.

The FA's fingerprints were all over the story. I now believe they had a week's head start, after they were first approached by the paper, to spin it to their advantage and take the sting out of it. The FA were quoted saying they had paid me in a 'mutual resolution', aimed to 'avoid disruption to the [2017 European Championship] tournament', not to 'prevent disclosure'. The FA went on to say I was free to speak about the facts of my complaint. Yet as there was nothing in the article about my tribunal claim, or our out-of-court settlement, the article made it look like I had taken hush money to keep quiet.

It got worse. There was no mention of race. If the paper had my report, they knew I had complained about more than just bullying. Yet the article only reported Lee Kendall's 'lazy as fuck' comment and left out everything else. Nothing about the arrest comment, no hint of racial discrimination. If anyone had been hushed up, it was the *Mail*. Hands shaking, I scrolled back to the top and stopped at the naked photo. Was that their sick way of saying I'd do anything for money? The FA had got to have their say; I hadn't. I was naked, exposed, linked to a bundle of half-truths cobbled together to paint me as a greedy, oversensitive liar. I felt numb.

I looked up. Down the aisle, passengers were filing out of the plane. I got to my feet, gathered my things and stumbled into the terminal, my phone still buzzing with notifications. I called my agent and we had a garbled conversation as I went through passport control. I couldn't think straight. Jo said she was trying to get the article taken down, but I knew it was too late, the damage had been done. The only way to set things straight was for me to speak, but Jo wasn't sure what I was legally allowed to say. I had to talk to the PFA, and to my QC.

I called Nick Cusack at the PFA. He insisted I keep quiet while we checked the settlement agreement with my QC. I was impatient and I was annoyed that I had agreed to a clause that made me look like I had been gagged, but I agreed to stay quiet. We decided we would work on a statement based on what I could say. Until then, Nick told me to sit tight and turn off my phone. It was deeply frustrating; all I wanted to do was to clarify the situation. I wanted to explain I had been dropped after complaining about racism and I wanted to say I had evidence, explain about the settlement, explain the payment wasn't hush money.

I made it home in a daze. From the backseat of a cab, I waded through the messages from friends, family and acquaintances. My skin crawled with embarrassment as I read them. Everyone had swallowed the article whole.

Nobody asked whether there was more to the story. I was choked with panic and I felt like screaming the truth into my phone.

I dragged myself into training that afternoon. I was still in shock but staying home alone wasn't going to be any easier. I tried to turn off my churning thoughts, but it was without doubt the worst training session of my life. Though my teammates and Emma had clearly read the story, nobody said a word. Their silence said it all. It hurt a lot, but I get it. They had nothing to say. People avoided me, or worse, whispered in small groups and threw me wide-eyed glances. The article hung heavy, unspoken, over the afternoon.

The nightmare enveloped me that evening. Sitting alone at home, I felt alien, like an intruder in my own life. I didn't speak to Mum, not yet. I couldn't stomach hearing the heartbreak in her voice. Mum is a very private person. It was too much to bear. I had moved on, risen above all this nastiness. I didn't deserve for everything to be dragged out now, in someone else's words, skewed without background, context or explanation, for the world to judge.

I tried to focus on practical steps. I had to respond to the article. The following morning, 8 August, I called Nick again at the PFA and we agreed a statement for me to put out on social media. There was so much I wanted to say. I wanted to tell the world this was serious, this was about race, and that the FA's investigations had both been shams. The PFA and my QC held me back; we needed to clarify my legal situation before I could speak about what led to the settlement. They were right, I wasn't about to end this sorry story with me being sued for breach of contract. Our caution meant the statement ended up bland, vague and generic:

'In response to the *Daily Mail* article yesterday 7 August 2017, I can confirm that I raised a grievance against the FA as a result of treatment that I and others previously suffered. As the FA have confirmed, a financial settlement was reached, but this still remains confidential. Contrary to the article, I have not and did not quit the England team and remain a centrally contracted England player.'

I ended the statement with an expression of support for England, and my wish to move on. Once it had been posted, I took a deep breath, and called Mum. As I had feared, she was upset. Despite its tasteful intentions, Mum hadn't been happy about that photo shoot at the time. To see it in an article, then, wasn't what she would have wanted.

I rang off. I was deeply hurt too, of course. I had dared to stand up to a bully, and then I had stood my ground when the FA tried to ignore me, intimidate me, fob me off and bury me. I had been prepared to take my case to a tribunal, and, as the settlement showed, I would likely have won. I tried to shut out all the noise, the reaction, and focus on my next move. I had said all I could for now. I would have to ride it out.

Things went eerily quiet for a few days as behind the scenes, questions were being asked. There was clearly more to this story. Why had there been a pay-out if there had been no wrongdoing? It didn't add up. Meanwhile, Kick it Out – English football's equality and inclusion organisation – called for my allegations and the findings of both investigations to be made public. Daniel Taylor, chief football writer at the *Guardian*, was intrigued. He got hold of my report, and, seeing the allegations of racial discrimination, took them back to the FA. He contacted my agent too, but as we still didn't know what we could say, there was nothing to do but stay patient, and not panic.

Everything exploded again on 17 August, when the *Guardian* ran Daniel's piece on their front page. His article led with my allegation that Mark had made a comment with 'racial and prejudicial connotations' to another player. Quoting from my report, the piece described the arrest comment and the full description of Drew, without naming her. The FA issued a statement in which they named Katherine Newton and said she hadn't held up any of my complaints, but emphasised I was free to speak.

This put me in even more of a quandary. I came to regret that stupid clause in the settlement agreement. The FA said I could speak, but how could I tell my story without bringing the FA into disrepute? The story was about what the FA had done wrong. I desperately wanted to set things straight, but I didn't want to breach an agreement. What did they expect me to do? Tell the story in a way that was favourable to the FA? I didn't know another way to tell it than to speak honestly and freely. I was stuck.

Everyone had seen the FA say I was free to speak, and so I was bombarded with messages from journalists. It was overwhelming; this was everything I had wanted to avoid. It was deeply frustrating; I couldn't wait to correct all this nonsense about hush money and refute all these solemn referrals to what had in fact been sham investigations. But the longer I kept silent, the more people believed I had been gagged. I contacted my QC Nick Randall and asked him to inform the FA that I would talk. I wanted it in writing, so there could be no backtracking later.

The FA were scrambling now the racial element was out. Everyone saw there was a lot more to this story than first reported. A few hours after the *Guardian* article was published, the FA press department put out a statement on its website together with a link to the summary of Katherine Newton's investigation. It was astonishing behaviour; I was given no warning that this was going to happen. This was a confidential document, addressed to me personally, that the FA had now posted on their site for everyone to download and pore over. It was a desperate and adversarial move.

The FA didn't seem to have a strategy beyond covering their own backsides. Still, they taught me an important lesson in what not do. It had been little over a week since I had posted my statement, and though it felt more like a year, I realised I would be better off waiting until the right moment to speak rather than rushing into anything in a panic. The truth was on my side, there was no rush, I could wait to tell it properly. That night, at the end of a whirlwind day, I tweeted a message to the world: 'The truth doesn't panic.'

The next day, 18 August, the FA acknowledged and accepted that I would talk. I could see they were in a bind; they didn't want me to tell the whole truth, yet they wanted to show I was free and that I hadn't been gagged. They wanted me to say something, but they didn't want me to say anything critical.

Jo and I agreed on two interviews. One with the *Guardian*, and one with the BBC. I chose Daniel Taylor, Danny, because he seemed interested in finding the truth, rather than covering for the FA, or judging me without knowing the facts. I met him and a photographer in a hotel in London on 19 August, two days after his front-page splash. I could tell right away he was sharp; he had already worked out the burning questions on his own. I answered his questions slowly and deliberately. There was no rush. This wasn't the FA's reaction, fighting fires, this was the truth.

A huge weight lifted as I spoke. I had waited the longest eleven days of my life to set the record straight. I told Danny everything. I told him about the Ebola comment, about Lee's Caribbean accent, about how I was dropped and lost my job when I complained, about the flawed investigations and the settlement. I told him I felt sorry for Katherine Newton and that I believed she had been deliberately chosen as a black woman, behaviour which in itself wouldn't be legal. We talked about Lianne, Anita and Drew. Danny had worked out

Drew's identity from my description but agreed to keep her name out of print. Danny got it, all of it. I knew I could trust him to get my story straight.

Later that day, I sat down for a second interview with BBC sports editor Dan Roan. This interview, conducted on camera this time, was less sympathetic. Dan pushed back hard on several points. He questioned whether Mark's Ebola comment was racist, and whether what I had experienced was bullying. It was tough, exacting, and just what I needed. I'm thankful to the BBC for pushing me to explain myself under pressure, to show the strength of my convictions. I didn't want a pity party; I wanted people to know the truth.

There was a long way to go yet. Even as I waited for the interviews to come out, lies and half-truths continued to swirl, mixed with thinly veiled opinions passed off as news. Journalists judging me, calling me a snowflake. A whole lot of white men, explaining what racism was, what bullying was. On the morning of 20 August, the day after my interviews, but before they came out, I got a warning message from Jo: 'Sky Sports doing segment on you and the FA for Sunday Supplement,' it said. 'Don't tweet.'

I watched it live, skin crawling, toes curling, wondering which producer thought it would be OK to put four white men around a table to discuss how sensitive I was about race. I couldn't believe my ears. How on earth would any of them even know? All four seemed convinced I had made it all up. After all, they said, two investigations had found no wrongdoing. Footballers were so soft these days, they said, Mark Sampson was a great guy. I switched it off in disgust. Not long now, I told myself. Stay calm, wait. The truth was coming.

At 6p.m. on 21 August, the *Guardian* published two of Danny's articles online. One laid out our whole interview in Q and A form, and another summarised my allegations of misconduct under the headline 'Eni Aluko accuses England manager Mark Sampson of "racist" Ebola remark.' An eight-and-a-half-minute cut of my BBC interview aired that evening. It was a great relief: at last, the truth was out.

People are fickle. They believe what they are told. After I spoke out, there was a collective 'ahh' as everyone realised the seriousness of my complaints. Now the pressure was back on the FA. Why had they bungled two investigations? Why hadn't they spoken to key witnesses? Why hadn't they looked into the Ebola comment? The PFA, Kick it Out, and shadow sports minister, Rosena Allin-Khan, called for a fresh investigation. The FA PR machine went into overdrive in response, but they had only one defence: blame me. It was my fault, they said, because I hadn't named Drew in my report, and I hadn't spoken to Katherine Newton. They didn't care if it made sense, they were frantic.

It was too late for the FA. The story was already bigger than me and other former England players were coming out against Mark. Over the next week, Anita and Lianne spoke to Danny, backing me and describing how they had been frozen out by Mark. I was very grateful to them both. Lianne, who was recovering from injury in the States, had wanted to speak out about Mark for a while. I had said I didn't want trouble, and she had always been kind enough to respect my wishes. Now it was all out, she wanted to share her story too.

On 23 August, two days after my interviews came out, I went to Austria with Chelsea for a pre-season tour in the Alps. The timing was perfect, and I was grateful to leave London for some mountain air. We were training in the most stunning scenery, amid alpine forests and alongside wide babbling rivers. I spent a lot of time alone on that trip. Most of the other players, even close friends, didn't want to get involved. Some because they played for England, others because they just didn't know what to say. I'm grateful to Fran and Kaz, both Chelsea and England players, who never took sides.

Things between me and the team were awkward for another reason: Drew. All along, since China, I had only wanted to protect her. Still, she had confided in me, and now what she had told me was plastered all over the papers. She had helped me where she could, and I had endeavoured to keep her name out of the public eye. Neither of us could have known it would all come out. Neither of us dreamed her anonymous role in all of this would degenerate into a guessing game to amuse the press. I was mortified, and she was understandably a little distant.

I prayed for it all to blow over. Surely the press would lose interest soon, I thought, but I was wrong. It seemed the story had a momentum of its own, and ran on, day after excruciating day. Before long, tempers began to fray, including my own. Two days into our Austria camp, on 25 August, Mark's brother tweeted that Lianne and I were both bad eggs. Lianne wrote back calling him a bully and tagged me in. I lost it. I called him disgusting and desperate and pointed out that clearly the apple hadn't fallen far from the tree. It was a mistake: rising to the bait only reignited interest in the story. Not for the first time in this whole episode I came very close to deleting Twitter from my phone to remove the temptation to react.

But there was still more to come. That night, the *Mail* named Drew, describing her as 'the player at the centre of Eni Aluko's original racism claims against Mark Sampson'. I felt terrible, and it only worsened the atmosphere in the camp. It was all right for me; I had a QC to go to for advice. Drew had none of that, no counsel. Her name was put out there and she couldn't confirm or deny it. Chelsea stepped in to act as her advisors.

Drew's name was even more fuel to the flame. When I got back from Austria, commentators were still lining up to give their two cents. On 30 August, *The Times* columnist Matthew Syed wrote a piece with the headline 'Twitter hysteria threatens to ruin Mark Sampson's career' in which he said the whole affair risked 'trivialising racism'. The Ebola comment was 'innocuous', he wrote, and could have been a 'misjudged joke'. Citing the Katherine Newton investigation, he wrote there was no evidence against Mark, and that he was the victim of a 'synthetic scandal'. There was no mention of any flaws in the FA's response.

I was livid. How dare he tell other people what they were supposed to take as a joke? I knew I shouldn't, but I couldn't leave it out there unchallenged. He was a journalist, he should know better, I had to respond publicly. I wrote a sarcastic tweet suggesting I probably should have found the Ebola comment about my family 'really funny', adding that he had been poorly briefed and wasn't in a position to comment on evidence without seeing it. Danny jumped in to defend me, patiently explaining to Matthew the flaws in Katherine Newton's investigation.

Looking back, my tweets only fanned the flames. I was also responsible for rising to the bait, but it was a highly emotional time. Those days were a sharp learning curve; it wasn't easy to know when to speak or how to act. One of the most important lessons I learned was to take a step back and stop pandering to lies. It wasn't an easy lesson to learn, I got it wrong, over and over, until it hit home at last that reacting only made things worse. In those moments I told myself I needed to learn to hold on, take a deep breath, and try to see ahead. The truth was on my side, so I could afford to be selective about when I spoke, to take control of how and when information was released. Fighting fires on Twitter made me look no better than the FA.

I came to realise this was no time for emotion. This was a crisis, the biggest of my life, and I had to focus on solutions. It reminded me of what Emma always said about how to react during a game when we went a goal down. I remembered her analogy about the pilot remembering his training, his routine, in times of emergency or crisis. Stay calm, she would say, stay conscious, stay deliberate. In a crisis, step back, wait for your emotions to quieten until you find the best way forward. On the pitch, that meant finding a new route to goal. Now, that meant taking advice from my team, from my lawyer, my agent, my union, from the people whose job it was to find a way out of this mess.

Still, as the crisis entered its fifth week, exhaustion began to set in. On 31 August, the deadline for the second tranche of my settlement money came and went without any payment arriving. My lawyer contacted the FA about the hold up. I wondered what had gone wrong.

Meanwhile, in the newspapers, the story rumbled on. Pressure was mounting on Mark to break his silence. On 5 September, he gave an interview at Wembley to two handpicked media outlets in which he claimed he had a 'clear conscience' and point-blank denied any wrongdoing. He told an open press conference the same thing at St George's Park a week later, on 12 September. Mark said he was 'disappointed' by my allegations and insinuated that they were entirely false.

I ignored him. This time, I knew better than to react. The whole truth wasn't out yet, and Mark's press conference at the England headquarters was only a distraction. It was what was happening behind closed doors that counted. At that very moment, back in London, conversations were taking place that were about to turn this whole story on its head.

CHAPTER TWENTY

Two things happened within forty-eight hours of each other to change the course of this story, and I had no hand in either of them. I didn't instigate the end of this crisis, just as I didn't initiate its beginning. It was God's will that I was asked for my views on the England culture, and it was His orchestration that brought things to a close.

On 12 September, as Mark was speaking to press in St George's Park, Drew was sitting at the Chelsea training ground, talking to the FA. She had come forward of her own accord to say that Mark really had asked her how many times she had been arrested. She gave them a written statement and printouts of our messages from that day in China. I'm sure the FA representatives in that meeting, Rachel Brace and the FA's director of legal and governance, Polly Handford, were spooked. Here was written proof and a second witness. What were they going to do? Call Drew a liar too?

The second development also came out of nowhere. On 11 September, the day before Drew came forward, I was contacted by Conservative MP Damian Collins, chair of the Digital, Culture, Media and Sport Select Committee of the House of Commons. Damian was appalled at how the FA had handled my grievances and invited me and Lianne to give evidence at a hearing set for 18 October. FA chief executive Martin Glenn and FA chairman Greg Clarke would also appear, alongside Dan Ashworth and Rachel Brace. I felt a flicker of hope: someone high up was interested in the truth.

Things were moving fast now. The FA asked if Drew would talk to Katherine Newton if she reopened her investigation. She agreed, and on 19 September, a fresh inquiry was launched into my complaints. I was ambivalent about the news. It felt like a small victory, but I didn't trust the FA to stop playing games with the truth. It seemed odd to use Katherine again after I felt her initial investigation to be so unsatisfactory. Still, I knew Katherine's name and reputation were on the line, and I hoped things might be different now she had Drew's testimony and our messages. So, when Katherine asked to speak to me, I said yes. Our meeting was scheduled for early October.

That night, a few hours after the new investigation was announced, England played Russia in a qualifier at Prenton Park. I didn't watch the game; I went shopping instead. I was on my way home when my phone began buzzing frantically. I parked outside my house and, still sitting in the driving seat, checked to see what was happening. It was Twitter. Lots of people had tagged me into a video clip posted by the BBC with the caption:

'Nikita Parris scored England Women's opener and sent out a message with her celebration.'

I clicked on the clip. Nikita fired home, then sprinted to Mark on the sideline and flung her arms around his neck. She turned and beckoned, and the rest of the team flocked to their manager and formed a tight group hug around him. One of the comments underneath the post said: 'says everything you need to know'.

I burst into tears. I know how these things work. No matter what anyone claimed later, that wasn't a spontaneous outpouring of joy; that celebration was choreographed, discussed and agreed in advance. If we score, we're going to run to Mark. We're going to close ranks around him; the tight, favoured, inner circle. And we're going to shut out those on the outside, all those whose faces don't fit: Eni, Lianne, Anita and Drew.

I never expected the team to defend me in public. I understood better than most the risk going against the FA would pose to their international careers. But such a public show of support for a manager who was being investigated for alleged racism was a slap in the face. Many others also viewed it as such.

Most of the players on that team played along, they bought into a culture that isolated others. They just didn't care: as long as it benefitted them, they were protected, they were on the inside. Here was a team that liked to laud itself as one of most together in the world. Yet when it came down to the well-being of others, they were willing to turn a blind eye. That's not a team. Later, I came to understand that not everyone can take a vocal stand against wrongdoing. Not everyone has the character or the wherewithal. I understand now that it isn't easy, at times I didn't think I had it in me.

Still, as I watched the team lock their arms around Mark, it hurt. I had played with some of these women for over a decade, battled together through three Euros and three World Cups. I had stuck my neck out for them when they needed me. These players had elected me their representative, their spokeswoman, and were now on central contracts I had helped secure. These were players who had sought my help when they wanted to get out of their club contracts. I had been happy to do it for my teammates, because that is what teammates do. I wasn't perfect, I had my moments on the team when I was miserable and frustrated under Mark. But one thing I prided myself on was always being there for my teammates. And yet, throughout this whole nightmare, not one of them reached out to me, Anita, Lianne, or Drew in private to find out the other side of the truth.

I couldn't understand it. These players knew a lot of what had gone on. They knew about the arrest comment, the Ebola comment, it was all out there. Some of them had been in the room with Drew at the time. None of that mattered. It seemed they had swallowed the narrative that was being fed to them. They believed I was bitter and planned to sabotage the team's success. Daring to speak out had turned me into a troublemaker, a black sheep, a rogue element to be rooted out and expelled. Enemy number one: Eniola Aluko.

My thumbs hovered over the phone keyboard.

'For the most together team in the world,' I typed. 'Tonight's "message" only shows a level of disrespect that represents division and selfish action.'

'The same players who unanimously voted me as their representative to discuss the team's central contracts with the FA,' I added. 'A benefit for all.'

I put my emotions on display again and it only stoked the fire. Lianne saw my tweets and wrote to me, so I called her back. We talked for close to an hour on the phone, as I tried to hold back tears of shock. Lianne was appalled at the team's gesture, as were many others. I was grateful to have good friends in that moment who were strong, solid and courageous, and who made me feel less alone.

I woke the next morning, on 20 September, to a message from my agent: 'I just had word that Mark Sampson is going to be sacked.'

I did a double take. Sacked? How could Mark be sacked? I hadn't seen that coming at all. England had only last night thrashed Russia 6–0 in a World Cup qualifier, and the players had run to their manager as if he were a saint. Firing Mark now didn't make sense. I felt no release or cause for celebration. Maybe if Mark had been humble enough to tell the truth from the beginning, perhaps he would have kept his position. Still, that wasn't my affair; I never asked for Mark to lose his job. All I ever wanted was for him to treat me fairly as my coach. This was between the FA and Mark.

Later that day, Martin Glenn announced Mark's dismissal. He said the FA's decision was based on a two-year-old investigation into an 'inappropriate relationship' Mark had during his previous job as manager of Bristol City. I had heard rumours before, never anything conclusive. Mark had been investigated, and cleared, by the FA's Safeguarding Unit back in 2015. The FA's credibility took a nosedive. They struggled to explain why, if Mark's previous conduct had been known to the FA when he was appointed, it was suddenly now bad enough for him to lose his job.

I suspect that in truth, Mark had become too much of a liability for the FA. Drew's testimony was the nail in the coffin. The FA had tried to discredit me as a liar; that was trickier now there were two of us. A fresh investigation, if conducted properly, was going to find that Mark really had said those things. Then, at the very least, the FA leadership would face awkward questions about why they had so vehemently defended him. He had to go before the truth came out.

If the FA had only taken my grievances seriously from the start, rather than covering for Mark in a blind panic, this whole crisis would never have threatened to engulf the leadership. It was too late now. Their response had been so catastrophic that the accusation of institutional racism had now entered the room.

I kept silent about Mark's sacking. I had other issues to deal with. It had now been more than three weeks since the deadline for the second tranche of the settlement payment. It was clear there was some hold up from the FA side. The PFA and my QC Nick Randall arranged a meeting with the FA to discuss the situation.

We met Martin Glenn and Polly Handford at the PFA headquarters on 22 September, less than forty-eight hours after Mark was sacked. It was quite something to be in a meeting with the FA chief executive himself. I had met Martin briefly once or twice before, but had never spoken with him properly. I went into the meeting expecting an explanation for why the FA were withholding a payment they had legally agreed to. I was disappointed.

The FA's tone was extremely aggressive. They opened by accusing me of breaching the terms of our settlement agreement. I had brought the FA into disrepute, they said, while speaking publicly about their handling of my complaint. Because of this, the FA board, which Martin headed, was withholding the second instalment of my pay-out. Martin even appeared to blame me for the FA board agreeing to the settlement in the first place. He projected all his anger on to me.

My first reaction was bafflement. We had specifically agreed in writing that I would talk. When I pointed this out, Martin flew into a temper and he threatened me with legal action. If I said another word, he said, the FA would take me to court.

'If you continue speaking and defaming the FA,' he said, 'we're withholding the money.'

I was deeply shocked at the venom in Martin's voice. I thought we had come here to resolve things, to agree on a way forward. The FA had repeatedly told journalists that I was free to speak but now it appeared that was all for show. Too late, I realised the FA's motive for signing the settlement agreement really had been to keep me quiet. They wanted me to speak because my silence was making them look bad. Yet they didn't want me to speak the truth. When I did, they resorted once again to trying to punish me.

'You can't withhold money you've agreed to pay,' I said. 'We've signed a legally binding agreement.'

'We agreed on the basis that you wouldn't defame the FA,' said Martin.

That stupid clause in the settlement agreement again. It had been drafted so vaguely, once again I regretted ever agreeing to it. I should have known it would play out this way, that the FA would hold me out in front of them like a shield. Free to speak, but not to tell the whole truth. I tried reasoning with Martin.

'Well, I'm not too sure what defaming the FA means,' I said. 'The FA have defamed themselves. You haven't acted properly. This case has been handled terribly from beginning to end. What do you want me to say? The FA are brilliant? What else is there to say other than the truth?'

At this point, Martin clasped his hands together and leaned across the table.

'There is one way we can try and resolve this,' he said. 'Perhaps if you issue a public statement apologising for your previous comments and stating you do not believe the FA is institutionally racist. Then we'll think about releasing the second payment.'

I looked at him in shock. What he was suggesting was bordering on blackmail. This was money the FA were contractually obliged to pay me. This was compensation I would have got at an employment tribunal. This was my lost earnings, money I had wanted to earn by scoring goals for England and could not, money I would have earned as wages if I hadn't been unfairly mistreated. We had been over all of this, and the FA had agreed a settlement with me.

And now the FA were trying to impose an extra condition. Who was I to judge whether there was institutional racism within the FA? All I had done was raise a legitimate complaint, one that deserved to be taken seriously. And now I was being asked to judge the whole organisation? How ridiculous would it make me look to absolve the FA of wrongdoing?

I had had enough. In my mind, in that moment, I let go of the money. They could keep it. They had already taken my England career, my legal job. Why not take the money I was legally entitled to? This nonsense had gone far enough; I had nothing left to lose. I took a deep breath, and felt a new power rising in my chest. Then I told Martin, in the most diplomatic way possible, that he could shove his offer.

'I'm not doing that,' I said. 'We're about to go into a parliamentary hearing. Do you honestly want me to tell the committee I haven't been paid on the basis that I spoke out? That looks very bad.'

And that was that. The battle lines were drawn, once and for all. I stumbled out of the meeting, exhausted. Some part of me had still been expecting a resolution, some remorse even, an apology or explanation from the FA's top official. Instead, the situation had escalated drastically. This was no longer Eni versus Mark Sampson. It wasn't even Eni versus the England team. Now, this was Eni versus the full might of the FA. At this point,

Chief Executive Martin Glenn was personally furious with me. I had no idea how it had got this far.

This was war now, and I was scared. The committee hearing was still four weeks away. Until then, I would have to be careful. I already knew the FA could get at me. Now they had tried something verging on blackmail and threatened me with court action. What else might they try to shut me up? I was thankful I wasn't hiding any dark secrets they could use against me. It started to get to me, I wasn't sleeping or eating much. I prayed for protection, kept my head down, and waited for the hearing.

I was relieved the story had largely moved on from me. Now Mark was gone, the FA itself was under fire, with Dan Ashworth facing questions about everything from Mark's appointment to mishandling my complaint. The other main focus was the new investigation. Katherine Newton's integrity was now openly being questioned, probably the worst fate a lawyer can face. Things got even worse for her when Martin Glenn let slip to the *Guardian* she had deliberately been chosen as a black woman. He later went back on that, because, well, that's illegal.

The FA had begun to look ridiculous. Once again, they had displayed an almost comic ignorance of discrimination law. In that moment, when hiring a lawyer to investigate accusations of racism, they had only seen my skin colour, and hers. I knew Katherine Newton had been used. On any other issue, a lawyer would be hired for their expertise. Imagine, hypothetically, someone from Manchester claimed to have been physically abused. Would the FA pick someone from Manchester to defend the case? It would have been laughable had it not been so sinister.

When, at last, I met Katherine at the PFA headquarters on 5 October, I felt nothing but sorrow. To sit facing her and her assistant, another black lady, across a large table, filled me with a deep sadness. It was a disturbing picture. Here we were, Katherine and I, two black women from the legal profession, used by the FA to fight it out among ourselves. We had both worked hard to break out of the moulds that society had set for us based on the colour of our skin. Like so many other women of colour out there we had given our all to break down the barriers and here we were, two calm, professional, highly educated black women. And yet we had somehow been pitted against each other. It felt very wrong on many levels.

I answered Katherine's questions as calmly and slowly as I could. We went through the Ebola comment and the arrest comment, but she didn't ask about any incidents of bullying, or about the circumstances in which I was dropped from the team. Towards the end of the meeting, Katherine opened up a little. I think even she realised how the FA had used her and her tone was almost apologetic. I accepted that, but still, I had to be honest with her. I told her frankly that I didn't believe she had done her job properly and that if she had insisted on speaking to Drew during her first investigation, none of us would be where we were.

'It isn't personal,' I said. 'I just think it's not right that as a barrister you decided not to interview one of the key witnesses.'

Katherine looked at me with wide, sad eyes.

'I wasn't given Drew's name,' she said.

I stared at her. Quite apart from the fact that I felt certain anyone wanting to identify Drew could have done so in five minutes, it seemed the FA really had ushered Katherine towards certain witnesses and kept her away from others. Still, I couldn't bring myself to accept that she was entirely without blame. There was no doubt in my mind that she was selected because she was black, and I sympathised with her for that. Yet however bad I felt for her, she was a lawyer, and as such, she was responsible for her decisions, and for not insisting on talking to Drew. Had she done so at the start; things could have turned out very differently and I found her reasons for not doing so unconvincing.

After the meeting with Katherine, I withdrew from the daily headlines. I came off Twitter, collected myself, and let the media storm blow on overhead without me. I let myself be guided by the professionals I had surrounded myself with, by my lawyer, my union and my agent. And I threw myself into preparing for the hearing. Nick Randall had recommended colleagues Gavin Millar QC and his junior Adam Smith at Matrix Chambers, a leading employment law firm. I spent four days working with them on my personal statement, and gathering other written evidence, emails, documents and reports, to submit to the hearing. I wanted my message to be as clear as possible.

I was confident I could present my case calmly, with logic and evidence. It was easy enough; I would simply tell the truth. At last I could correct all the misunderstandings, confusion and half-truths still flying around. The public would see me tell my whole story for once without it being edited or spun. I knew then that they would see I hadn't been lying.

Yet this went far beyond me. I hadn't set out pushing for transformation at the FA, but God had other plans. Now a parliamentary hearing was involved, I hoped that by sharing my story I would be able to inspire far-reaching change. There were plenty of lessons to be learned. I thought of all the players yet to come. Where could they raise concerns without fear of retribution? The FA desperately needed an independent body to investigate players' grievances while protecting them from harm. No one should go through what I had. No one should be ignored, fobbed off, intimidated. No one should have their confidential information exposed, be called a liar in public, or lose their career over a complaint.

I grew nervous as the day of the hearing approached. It felt like going into a high stakes game; I didn't want to mess up. I went over the evidence and my statement until I knew it all back to front. The evening before the hearing, I even did a dress rehearsal with Gavin and Adam, the two barristers I had been working with. I visited their chambers and they cross-examined me for ninety minutes in a kind of mock hearing. They almost did too good a job. I stumbled over a few of their questions and though I put on a brave face as I left the chambers, I burst into tears as soon as I was out of sight. I was tired, and I wanted it done. Still, at least now I was ready for anything.

I stayed that night at a hotel at Stamford Bridge so as to be closer to Westminster for the hearing in the morning. Lianne was staying there too; she had flown over from the States to give her evidence. Though I know I could have faced this alone, I was grateful to have an old friend there with me. Lianne and I had been through a lot together over our fifteen-year friendship. Still, she wasn't there as my cheerleader, she had been through her own ordeal. We were both ready to share our stories.

Later, waiting in bed to fall asleep, my mind was calm and focused on what needed to be done. I certainly knew what not to do. Mark, the FA, the players, they had all tripped over themselves in their bid to twist the facts. All I had to do at the hearing was what I had tried to do all along. Remain steady, calm, present the facts, put forward the evidence in a logical way. I was confident I could do it; I had trained my whole adult life to do just that.

In fact, in that moment, it felt like much of my life had been leading up to this point, to a final confrontation with the Goliath machine of the FA. All along, nobody had taught me how to act, because there was no right or wrong way. It was experience, life, that had handed me the lessons, the weapons; I needed to take a stand, to push through change for those yet to come.

And now I had learned yet another lesson. I had panicked at times throughout this whole affair, I had done the wrong thing, I had tried to fight fire with fire, and I had lost patience, even with those trying to help me. But life had taught me patience, it had taught me calm. It had taught me that, with the truth on side, there's no need to rush or panic. Sometimes it is far more powerful to stay silent and not rise to the bait. Now, when things go wrong, I am much less quick to react. Now I know perfectly when silence is the best response and when to calmly speak the truth.

I knew the truth I had to tell would make things difficult for the FA, yet I was no longer scared of what they might do to me. I had let go of my England career, of my job, of my settlement pay-out. Now they could never touch me. Tomorrow, I would finally move on from months of fear and hurt, frustration and confusion. Tomorrow, the record would be set straight once and for all. I prayed and I asked God to be with me. A Bible passage I had once memorised from the Old Testament, from the book of Isaiah, came into my head.

'No weapon formed against you shall prosper,' I whispered in the dark. 'And you will refute every tongue that accuses you. This is the heritage of the Lord's servants, and their vindication is from Me.'

I fell asleep with the words on my lips, knowing that I was with God. And with Him, I would be vindicated.

I was up early the next morning and met Lianne for breakfast in the hotel. My nerves were largely gone, and in their place, there was only a solid determination. Lianne felt the same, though we were both apprehensive. Here we were, two active footballers, about to face down the full force of the FA.

I was still staggered at how quickly this battle had escalated. This was the FA, the organisation that had overseen every stage of my footballing career. The body that had overseen my development as a player, that had supported and encouraged me since I was a teenager, that had put me forward countless times as an ambassador and spokeswoman. How on earth were we now at war?

'Whatever happens,' I told Lianne over breakfast, 'let's just be ourselves. We know who we are. We know we haven't done anything wrong. Our strongest weapon is our honesty.'

My agent Jo met us at the hotel later that morning, and the three of us piled into a taxi to Westminster. The committee hearing was in Portcullis House opposite the Houses of Parliament. We were early, the hearing wasn't scheduled to begin until half past two. We told the driver to drop us at the back entrance of the building to avoid any photographers that might be waiting. We went upstairs and found the chamber. The doors were still shut, so we sat down to wait in the corridor outside, chatting and going through our statements one last time.

An hour before the hearing was scheduled to begin, Nick Cusack from the PFA arrived and handed me a thick wodge of paper. I read the title: 'An Independent Investigation for the Football Association into Allegations Raised by Eniola Aluko. Part II.' So here they were, at the eleventh hour, the results of Katherine Newton's second investigation. I flipped eagerly to the conclusions page. My heart beat faster as I scanned the words.

'I have concluded that on two separate occasions, MS [Mark Sampson] has made ill-judged attempts at humour, which, as a matter of law, were discriminatory on grounds of race within the meaning of the Equality Act 2010.'

I sighed with relief. Here at last, was the ac-knowledgement I had wanted for months. An acknow-ledgement that I hadn't been lying, that Mark had made discriminatory remarks.

'However,' Katherine continued. 'That is not the same as concluding that MS is racist. In fact, I consider it fundamentally important to emphasise that I have not concluded that MS is a racist.'

I scanned the rest of her conclusions. I didn't agree with everything by any means. Katherine found I had been dropped for what she termed bad behaviour, not because of racism, or because I had raised allegations of racism. She also categorically ruled out that I had been bullied. I found this odd because she'd never interviewed me about bullying. Surely as part of a comprehensive investigation she should have questioned both parties to ascertain the facts? In our meeting, she hadn't asked me one question about the itemised list of grievances I sent to Dan, which now seemed like a lifetime ago, and she still could not itemise what she meant by bad behaviour. Still, I focused on the positives. After months of flat denials from the FA, this was a colossal breakthrough.

It was nearly time now; the corridor was filling up with people. With just fifteen minutes to go, another piece of paper was put into my hands. A letter, on FA note paper, offering a full and unreserved apology to me and Drew for Mark's conduct towards us. It was signed by Martin Glenn himself. I stared at the words on the page as their meaning sunk in. Within an hour, the FA's position had turned on its head. It didn't seem possible.

The doors to the chamber opened, and I stepped inside. I took my seat facing a panel of MPs sitting in a horseshoe at one end of the room. In the centre sat Damian Collins, the chair. I arranged my papers and poured myself a glass of water as people filed into the room and took their seats behind me.

My mind settled. I was alert and calm as the last traces of fear melted away. The FA had admitted I was telling the truth. They had admitted fault and apologised. I took a deep breath, and silently gave thanks to God. Those who had judged me, accused me, tried to silence me, had lost their way. I had been vindicated, just like the Bible verse had promised.

The chair tapped his microphone and an expectant hush fell. I waited for the panel's first question, certain that nothing could unsettle me now. I had the truth on my side. And truth doesn't panic.

EPILOGUE:

Rise Above

Doors close, others open, and life goes on. After the hearing, I stepped through one of life's many doorways and found myself in a new chapter. God, ever my guide and trusted concierge, closed the door behind me, directed me forwards, and opened a new door on to new and exciting possibilities. I've learned to be as thankful for old doors closing as I am for new ones opening. Daunting as it might seem, I've noticed that the act of closing the door on the past often propels me into life's next encounter. This was one of those moments, of closing doors, and forward momentum.

Before I knew it, I found myself in another summer, at another tournament, trailblazing another broadcasting first for women footballers. In June 2018, ITV invited me to Russia as a pundit for the men's World Cup. Together with my former England teammate Alex Scott, who was working with the BBC, I became one of the first female pundits to join coverage of a men's World Cup with a British broadcaster. Personally, it was another huge stride forward from the two Euros I had already done, and a breakthrough to rival my ground-breaking appearance on *Match of the Day* four years before.

It was a huge honour, and an even bigger responsibility. I knew from my previous experience at the Euros in France in 2016 that, as a female pundit at the top level of the men's game, I would be allowed no margin of error. I had a following now, and my opinions had won the respect of both fans and others in the media. Still, I knew there would be detractors, those who would question my right to talk about the men's game on television.

Inevitably, the questions would come. Was I there on merit, or was I there as another token diversity gesture by a broadcaster? Was I there because I was a good pundit, or because as a black female player I was a convenient box-ticking exercise? These same questions had lurked in the background since I first went on air, but this was the men's World Cup, and they were about to get much louder. In some ways, of course, it was true. I did tick all those boxes, but that only made me even more determined to do a good job. I told myself I was going to be the best ticked box ever to grace a screen.

I understood the kickback as an unavoidable part of being a trailblazer. Anyone engaged in breaking moulds is likely to encounter resistance from those who want to maintain the status quo. And, as always, I found the best answer was to perform in the hope of quickly establishing a new norm. So that's what I did, I focused on performing, and looked forward to the day when it would be entirely normal to see female football pundits at a men's World Cup.

Once again, I knew preparation would be everything, and I threw myself into the work. I enjoyed preparing for games behind the scenes just as much as being live on air. A month before the first World Cup game kicked off, I asked my agent Jo to get a schedule of the games I would be working on. Then I did my homework, practising my analysis in the mirror, and pinning down my opinions on the teams, their tactics, players and managers, as if my life depended on it.

By the time the tournament kicked off, I had digested enough information to be able to communicate fluently and naturally when the cameras were on. At times my pursuit of perfection took on slightly ridiculous proportions. At one point, ahead of the opening game between Russia and Saudi Arabia, I caught myself panicking about the correct pronunciation of the Saudi Arabian players. But I knew I had to keep to my high standards and push on. I didn't know any other way.

Once I got into the studio, I was glad I had done so much background work. Being prepared meant I felt at home with the other ITV pundits, footballing legends such as Ryan Giggs, Gary Neville, Roy Keane, Slaven Bilić and Henrik Larsson. It was obvious right away they weren't under the same pressure as I was to perform. Viewers were used to seeing them on their screens, and their reputations as iconic footballers went before them, so they could afford to relax. That was just the way things were.

The games started, and I settled into a productive daily routine. Every morning I rose early to get in a pre-breakfast gym session with fitness guru Ryan Giggs. Gary Neville joined us most days, as did former Manchester United player Patrice Evra. I had to pinch myself every time I got a text telling me it was 'gym time' from Ryan Giggs, a player Sone and I had imitated in our back garden as kids. It was a daily reminder of how far I had come. I guess you never know when you will meet your heroes, let alone get to work alongside them.

After breakfast, I spent the rest of every morning listening to the latest podcasts for updates on the World

Cup teams, before heading to the studio for the show. Throughout the tournament, for each show I made sure I could always offer something new, a unique view, or piece of analysis. That meant a lot of hard work, and I even attended matches on my days off to gain another perspective on the teams. My efforts went down very well; I got great feedback from ITV and from fans on social media.

Of course, not everyone loved what I was doing, there was always a bit of criticism online. Here and there, I got some nasty comments based on my race and gender, but most of it was objective and constructive, and I made sure to take it on board. Pundits can be an acquired taste, and some people said my delivery was too heavy on statistics and came across as over-prepared. I needed to relax a bit, they said. I took it on board, and with help from some constructive feedback from family and friends, I tweaked my punditry style a little.

I felt the criticism was largely a positive thing. I wanted to be held to the same standards as any other pundit. After all, if Roy Keane was getting criticised for his punditry, then it was only right that I should be too. I didn't want to be applauded just because I was a woman, as much as I didn't want to be shouted down for the same reason.

Despite my efforts to be treated as any other pundit, there was one incident that brought my gender into the spotlight. On the third day of play, I was on air with Patrice Evra, analysing a group stage game between Costa Rica and Serbia. Patrice had been friendly towards me behind the scenes, but I sensed he was a little confused as to who I was. It wasn't the biggest surprise then, when Patrice greeted my opening analysis of Costa Rica's chances with a loud, patronising clap. I smiled through it, but it was desperately awkward. We cut to a break, and Mark Demuth, controller of ITV sport, approached the studio table.

'Patrice,' said Mark, firmly. 'You don't need to clap Eni.'

Patrice looked surprised.

'I clapped because I think she's good,' he said. 'She knows a lot.'

It was toe-curlingly awkward. I know Patrice felt he was being complimentary, but sometimes even the best intentions don't come off as planned. The game began, and as my phone was always off in the studio, I didn't register until afterwards that social media was exploding with outrage. On Twitter, users were united in condemning Patrice's applause as sexist and condescending.

'Would he clap a male colleague's analysis?' wrote one Twitter user. 'Was he surprised because he didn't expect more of a woman?'

There were thousands of tweets in the same vein. Suddenly, Patrice clapping me was a big story, with newspapers running the incident separately, alongside their World Cup coverage. Jo's phone started ringing off the hook with journalists asking for me to comment.

At the end of the show I felt no real emotion towards Patrice except awkwardness. On air, it was easy to focus on the game; I had prepared plenty to say about Costa Rica's strikers and the team's overall performance. But once I came off air and saw the reaction, I had a decision to make. I could respond to the incident, or I could stay silent.

I was torn. I felt the weight of others' expectations as to how I should react. I felt pressure to comment on behalf of anti-sexism campaigners, particularly given the stance I had taken against racism during the incident with the FA. At the same time, I knew that responding to the noise on social media or talking to journalists about Patrice would only dial up the volume on the story even further. I didn't want anything to distract from the job I had prepared so hard to do. From the other side, there was subtle pressure to pose in a picture with Patrice for social media and act like it had all been a big misunderstanding. But I knew that wouldn't work either. I didn't want to come across as excusing casual sexism or insulting viewers' intelligence.

It was a fine line to tread, so in the end, I decided to rise above the noise and stay silent. The world is a noisy place, full of kneejerk reactions, but I've learned silence is often the best response. It's in my nature to speak up for women and against sexism, but I can't always fulfil the expectations of others. This wasn't the time or the place: I couldn't afford to be in a sideshow about Patrice Evra, I was at the World Cup in Russia to do a bigger job. Many people rushed to my defence, and I appreciated that, but ultimately, I knew the best defence was to keep performing. To keep doing the kind of job that prompted Patrice to clap me in the first place. It was the right choice. Within two days, starved of the extra fuel of my reaction, the story ran out of gas.

The World Cup rolled on, and quickly became what for England was without doubt one of the greatest tournaments of all time. I was glad at last to see the conversation around female pundits moving on. Increasingly, the discussion was less about whether a pundit was male or female, and more about whether he or she was any good at the job. I was enjoying the work more than ever and as always, focused on delivering strong, fresh, well-informed opinions. I felt especially engaged when people disagreed with me; it meant they were listening to what I had to say.

For me personally, the World Cup was deeply cathartic. The excitement, thrill and passion helped scatter the last of the stress and negativity of the previous years. I didn't worry too much about running into anyone from the FA. I had told the truth at the hearing, and I had felt liberated and empowered ever since. I'd be damned if I was going to walk around with my head down.

The same couldn't be said for the FA leadership. The hearing didn't go well for them. In his closing comments, chair Damian Collins questioned whether Dan Ashworth, Greg Clarke and Martin Glenn were the right people to take the organisation forward, though in the end, nobody stepped down. At the end of the hearing, Greg Clarke approached me, shook my hand and said he wanted to meet with me. That never happened either, but I appreciated the gesture.

Nevertheless, some positive changes occurred after the hearing. Within a few weeks, I was approached by UK Sport to help with their review of the FA's whistle-blowing policies. I called for the FA to set up a safe procedure for players to raise complaints without having to go through members of staff often compromised by conflicts of interest. If I had been able to talk to an independent body, I said, maybe my grievances could have been dealt with in a normal way and matters wouldn't have got so out of hand.

UK Sport and the FA launched a new whistle-blowing and grievance policy in January 2018. New codes of conduct were also issued for players and coaches and an additional training programme was introduced for national coaches supported by Kick it Out. I hope these new structures, along with an increased awareness and a culture shift within the FA, will be enough to prevent players going through what I endured. We won't know for sure until something happens to test them.

By the time I went to Russia, my relationship with the FA had already come a long way. Their official apology at the hearing was soon followed by the outstanding second tranche of the settlement payment. To my surprise, I was also offered another central contract with England. I turned it down. I felt it would be wiser to move on with no strings attached. Emotionally, I had already let go of my England career, and I preferred to be financially independent from the set-up. I felt more empowered that way and letting go felt like the right thing to do.

Don't get me wrong, it wasn't easy to turn down a £30,000 annual contract to play for England. But, as so often happens when you let something valuable go, you are rewarded with something of even greater value.

The ITV World Cup offer, which was worth more than the central contract, came in just three months later. By letting go and closing one door, I had allowed another to open. Some will call it karma or fate, I call it God's will.

It was God's will that I went to the World Cup and learned yet another lesson: how to rise above, move on, and forgive. In Russia, I came face to face with the FA leadership for the first time since the hearing. It was all down to a mentor of mine, former Arsenal vice-chairman David Dein. David was at the World Cup, together with my commercial agent and friend Misha Sher, flying between games in his private plane – which is also know as 'Dein Air' – and meeting with FIFA executives. Ahead of England's second group game against Panama, David invited me to fly with him between stadiums. I had already accepted when he told me that Martin Glenn and Greg Clarke were also going to be his guests on the plane. I took a deep breath. I had been saying to myself and to others for months that I had moved on and forgiven all the mistreatment I had suffered at the hands of the FA. It was time to put my words to the test.

I appreciated David's attempt to heal relationships and rebuild bridges. He and I agreed it was vital for the benefit of all concerned for me to get back on to a normal footing with the FA. That said, I didn't exactly relish the prospect of sharing an eight-seater plane with the very people I had faced down at a parliamentary hearing seven months before. I needn't have worried; it was very civil. Mum had taught me all I needed to know about diplomacy from a young age. I climbed aboard, shook hands with both Martin and Greg, and made my way to the back of the plane. Thankfully, I didn't have to make any awkward small talk. I had a bad cold, which meant I slept through the whole flight.

We landed in Nizhny Novgorod, a city east of Moscow, and made our way to the newly built stadium. David led us into the VIP section, which was full of FA people chatting with top FIFA officials. A few eyebrows were raised as David and I walked in with Greg and Martin. It was an unexpected and uncomfortable moment for me, but David grinned widely and began shaking hands with a charming charisma which put me immediately at ease.

Robert Sullivan, the FA's director of communications, left a group chatting in one corner and came over. My stomach squirmed a little as he approached. We hadn't met in person before, but I knew that the previous summer it had been Robert's job to spin the story to make me look bad in the press, in effect the FA's only defence strategy. It was his job to make me look bitter, or like I was just out for the money, or that I was a snowflake who couldn't take a joke. He was the one that had fed the press unpublished extracts of Katherine Newton's initial report, sections that I hadn't been allowed to see, to make it seem like my England teammates hated me. I held him partly responsible for the loss of my England career, and now here he was, standing in front of me, holding out his hand. There was a lot to forgive.

'Hi Eni, I'm Robert,' he said, as if I didn't know who he was or what he had done. 'I'm sorry for everything that happened,' he went on, without specifying what he was apologising for. 'It got out of hand, didn't it? I wanted to come over and apologise. I hope there are no hard feelings?'

There was a pause, and for a moment, time stood still. The confrontational and impulsive part of me was dying to say something. I wanted to ask Robert why, if he really was sorry, he hadn't apologised during the seven months since the hearing. He had my email address, didn't he? The timing was embarrassing. Coming now, in full view of all these FIFA executives, the VIPs of world football, I couldn't help but feel the apology was more than a little contrived. It was hollow.

I took a deep breath and battled to let it go. I so wanted to move on, and I knew that holding on to hurt wasn't going to get me anywhere. I was enjoying life; I was focused on more positive things now. Here was the perfect opportunity to leave behind all the nastiness of the previous year and move relations on to a higher level. I smiled and took his hand.

'It's fine, Robert,' I said. 'Thanks for coming over.'

Then I changed the subject to talk about England's line-up against Panama.

A similar thing happened at England's last sixteen game against Colombia. It was a huge game, England's first knockout match of the tournament. I decided to get there early, take my seat, and watch the teams warm up. As I sat in the stands, soaking up the incredible atmosphere, I posted a selfie on social media.

Seconds later, I felt a tap on my shoulder. It was Dan Ashworth; he had also come to apologise. I smiled, shook his hand, and quickly steered the conversation on to talking about the game. As with Robert, an email after the hearing would have gone a very long way to healing things between us. But better late than never, I suppose. If individuals in the FA wanted to show good will towards me in public, then that was something to be welcomed. I knew these gestures were more important for them than they were for me.

Far more significant for me was the chance to put into practice everything I had learned about forgiveness. It was a powerful word; one I had often heard in church. In striving to let go of the pain I felt, I remembered teachings in the Bible about Jesus' humility and forgiveness in the face of suffering, and ultimately, as he faced his own death. It was a standard I always looked up to, though, of course, I was unlikely to ever achieve it.

There is no manual for these things, but here God had once again guided me to a place of learning. Here was a lesson, an important test, staring me in the face. To pass it, I had to forgive Robert and Dan for the pain and hurt they had caused me. I knew the theory from church, but it wasn't until I was confronted with my adversaries that I truly learned how to forgive.

Through that process, I learned that the act of forgiveness had more to do with me than it did with them. I was the one who had to actively let go of the pain and rise above it. However awkward, I'm grateful for the impromptu meetings in Russia. They were an important step in my personal development and gave me confidence that I was able to forgive and move on.

But there was one test left to come. In January 2019, Mark Sampson put out a statement breaking the silence he had kept since the day of his dismissal. Almost five years after making the Ebola comment, Mark felt it was the right time to offer an unreserved apology for his racially discriminatory remarks to me and Drew, remarks he previously insisted he had never made. Mark then gave a wide-ranging interview in the press, in which he said his biggest regret was that our complaints weren't handled with the humility and respect they deserved. He also said he had worked hard since then to educate himself as a white male.

The day the interview and statement came out, I turned off my phone. I didn't want to spend the day dealing with the inevitable bombardment of calls from journalists. I wouldn't know what to say. Unlike the encounters with Robert and Dan in Russia, Mark's apology was indirect, and in some ways that made it more difficult to deal with. One thing I did know was that Mark didn't care about me or Drew. If he had, he would have apologised to us directly, in an email, a call, or a message. Instead, we were left to read about it in the newspaper.

I hadn't been waiting for Mark's apology, or needed it, but the timing seemed weird. He had lots of opportunities to express regret while the matter was under the glare of the public eye, but he chose not to. Mark said he had waited to speak because he was bringing a claim of unfair dismissal against the FA, a claim which was ultimately settled in his favour. But I wasn't so sure. It felt more like Mark was engaged in a public relations exercise, an attempt to rebuild his damaged reputation in preparation for a new management role.

Seeing Mark's words in print made me furious all over again. I realised then that the anger I had felt towards him hadn't gone away, it had only fallen dormant while I moved on to the next chapter of my life. Now it had woken up. Everything came flooding back. I couldn't help but feel disgusted by Mark's actions. All along, he had chosen to act in what I felt was the most cowardly way. First, he point-blank denied making the comments, then he tried to detract from his mistakes by painting me as difficult and over-sensitive.

The anger was still there. I felt he had ruined my international career, and Drew's too. I hadn't played for England since that day in May 2016 when Mark visited Cobham. It hadn't mattered that I finished as the league's top scorer. And Drew hadn't played for England since the incident with Mark in China the year before. We had lost our England careers, and then the system had gone into overdrive to protect Mark by any means necessary. It still hurt, and it was hard to let go of it all.

Then it clicked and I understood: this was the biggest test of all. Here was an apology, however convoluted, however indirect, and I was being asked to forgive. This time there was no World Cup excitement, no England game or VIP box to soften the confrontation. It was up to me. Was I going to stay angry at Mark for ever? I had to face forgiveness head on, I had to let go of my anger, not for Mark, but for my own sanity and peace of mind. This time I couldn't shake hands, smile, and make small talk. This time I would have to find another way to rise above it.

For me, once again, the best response was silence. I turned down interview requests from journalists wanting my reaction to Mark's apology. I was tempted to say something, but I didn't want to risk expressing the anger I felt in public. That, I felt, would be to fall victim to what others expected of me. It took some effort, but I have now let go of what Mark said and did. I've found it is possible to train yourself to forgive, though I admit that forgetting might be harder. Mark's apology pushed me to exhume all that dormant anger, all those hurtful memories, and finally let them go. I'd like to think that if I encounter Mark again one day, in footballing circles somewhere, I'd be able to show I have risen above it all and wish him well. After all, everyone deserves another chance to move on and learn from the past.

Getting a bit of distance from England also worked wonders. My time away from the national team has given me space to experience more of the world and soak in new cultures, more than I ever could have done as an England player. I've been busy ticking off my travel bucket list with trips to Africa, a continent I believe awakens the soul like no other. I took a safari to the Masai Mara National Reserve in Kenya to witness the great migration of wild animals from Tanzania. I also spent a Christmas in Cape Town, South Africa, and returned many times to my beloved Lagos. I feel the draw of the city I was born in, the familiar heat, the vibrant creative energy. It's a fascinating place, with a flourishing fashion and culinary scene, that along with cutting-edge development is seeing Lagos rise as the Dubai of West Africa. There is still so much for me to explore, both in Nigeria and in the rest of the African continent.

I've also taken a far bigger step outside of England. At the end of the World Cup, I flew straight into a new life. After six years, two league titles, two FA cups, and a Golden Boot, I left my beloved Chelsea for a new challenge. Though I was gutted to leave, it seemed like all the signs were pointing to a move. I had not started many games for Chelsea in the previous season and discussions with the club about a new contract were sluggish. Even my communication with Emma had become distant as she focused on her key players and the team's bid for another title, for the FA Cup and for progression in the Champions League.

And so, I started feeling restless. I wanted another journey, another challenge. I wanted to keep learning, growing, moving, both on and off the pitch. I knew I had a lot more to offer in this later phase of my career and felt driven to push myself further. I didn't want to fizzle out on the bench; I wanted to go out on a high, playing excellent football at a world-class club. I yearned to step outside my comfort zone and explore a new language, culture and way of life. I was intrigued by the idea of playing in Europe.

In December 2017, I flew to Paris to meet with Bruno Cheyrou, sporting director of Paris Saint-Germain Féminines. I first met Bruno on a UEFA master's course I started the month before. I was keen on the idea of moving to Paris. I dreamt of learning French while playing for a big European club with a proud history.

During our meeting at the impressive PSG offices, Bruno said he was interested in bringing in a player with my kind of experience, but that he wanted to wait another month before making a final decision. I went away feeling positive that it would happen, but it wasn't to be. The following months, before I heard anything more, speculation broke in the BBC about my potential move to PSG. That was all it was, speculation, with no real substance. PSG were unsure, and suggested we revisit discussions in the summer. I knew then that the move wasn't the one for me, but change was coming, and I trusted that God had something else in mind.

In the summer of 2018, I visited European giants Juventus, and loved what I saw. Juventus was just what I was looking for: a new women's team that was just a year old, but with a historic name and an ambition to match. Just like Chelsea had been all those years ago, Juve was hungry and had a cabinet waiting to be filled with trophies. I was also impressed by the way Juventus treated their players. That summer, the club also signed Lianne, welcoming her in for rehabilitation from her troublesome knee injury. That they had shown faith in an injured player I felt spoke volumes about the club's ethos.

I signed with Juve, and after the World Cup, I moved into a spacious, high-ceilinged Renaissance-style apartment in central Turin. It was the perfect place to turn over a new page and begin writing a new chapter. Not that I'm on holiday here in Italy. Playing for Juventus has been very hard work, and I'm grateful to have taken the step outside of my comfort zone.

From my first pre-season training session, I realised my body would have to adjust to cope with the higher training demands. I would have to get used to endurance-based running and working out on machines I had never seen before such as VersaPulley strength training machines. The sports science here is meticulous, they even record lactic acid levels in real time and give us detailed nutrition programmes to trim body fat down to the optimum level.

It hasn't been easy, but all the hard work has been paying off. My game continues to improve under my exacting, technical-oriented coach, Rita Guarino, whose complicated passing drills have pushed forward my touch, concentration levels and appreciation of space. I've been in great scoring form and got my first hat-trick for the team against Roma within a few months of arriving.

It was the start of a wildly successful year that exceeded my expectations. As I write this I've just come to the end of a challenging season at the helm of the competitive and growing Serie A *femminile* league. It's been fascinating to watch the Italian women's game flourishing, with top teams Fiorentina, AC Milan and Juventus all taking points off each other at various times in the season. In March 2019, a record crowd of just under 40,000 fans watched us beat our rivals Fiorentina when we played at the Allianz Stadium for the first time, smashing the previous record crowd of 14,000.

It was an unforgettable game, and one that turned out to be decisive in our ultimately successful title bid. A week after we lifted the league trophy, we completed the double, winning the Coppa Italia after defeating Fiorentina 2–0. I finished the season as Juventus's top scorer, with fourteen goals in the league and sixteen across all competitions.

It was mission accomplished, both for the team and for me personally, the kind of success that made every minute of hard work, every difficult day, entirely worth it. In the words of Roman general Julius Caesar: *'veni, vidi, vici'*. I came, I saw, I conquered. Next stop, going further in the Champions League. We want to become one of the best clubs in Europe.

My punditry career is moving on too. I worked my second World Cup as a pundit after securing a contract with American broadcaster Fox as an analyst for the 2019 Women's World Cup in France. It was a wonderful experience working with a top US broadcaster and I was excited to engage with a new audience. It was an exhilarating tournament, as the women's game reached more fans around the world than ever before.

Women's football has been on a thrilling journey, not only in Italy and the UK, but around the world. At last, our game is now coming to the place I always dreamed it could, with sell-out stadiums, global female-specific ad campaigns from major brands, and broadcasters showing women's games on a weekly basis. And as the game's profile continues to soar to new heights, so do conditions for players. The fight for better player welfare and gender equality continues in other national teams.

I've been impressed by recent collective actions of Norwegian, Danish, and US teams to secure better pay and professional conditions. I've looked on with respect as Norway's Ada Hegerberg has stood firm, sacrificing a place at the world cup in pursuit of a personal cause. And I've closely followed developments in Australia and New Zealand over the past year, as national players rose up to rid themselves of managers they accused of creating a culture of fear and bullying. It seems female players are feeling increasingly unafraid to stand up to change their footballing environment, and that should be celebrated at every opportunity.

In another way, being at the World Cup this summer also presented a personal challenge. There is still some healing to be done between me and some players on the England team. Mistakes were made on both sides. For my part, I took a wrong step just after the hearing, when I gave an interview to the BBC that, looking back, I think only opened old wounds. My intentions were pure. I wanted to encourage England players to show more solidarity with their teammates, especially when it came to matters of racism or sexism. To this day, I can't help but feel concerned that none of the players spoke out firmly against discrimination, despite having many opportunities to do so.

One example of the kind of action I'd like to see more of has come from the US team. Their player Megan Rapinoe, though white herself, has chosen repeatedly to take the knee during the national anthem in protest against police brutality towards people of colour in the United States. This summer, she went one step further, after footage was released in which she took a vocal stand against the anti-immigrant and divisive politics of US President, Donald Trump. It was an electric moment that once again showed female football players in their best light: unafraid, unapologetic, defiant, and willing to take a stand to drive through change.

What struck me is that Megan hasn't been alone. Though her teammates didn't join in they have come out publicly to support her right to protest. That, at the end of the day, was all I expected. A nod of mutual respect, an acknowledgement from the team that the issue I was raising went beyond them or me or Mark. Say the issue had been around homophobic comments directed at a player, I'm sure the team would have showed more solidarity. But back when I said that to the BBC, it came across in a way I hadn't anticipated, as disappointed and accusatory, when in fact I had wanted to bury the hatchet and move on.

Last November, the FA WSL league announced that striker Nikita Parris had broken my record as the highest scorer in the league's history. I hadn't spoken to Nikita since she celebrated her goal with Mark the night before he was fired, but in that moment, I felt nothing but pride for both of our achievements. I wrote to congratulate her on Instagram, and when she wrote back, I could tell she was pleased and surprised to hear from me. It felt good to reach out and helpful to celebrate Nikita's success, to hand on the baton, and to let it go. I'm sure these moments, with the FA, with Mark and with Nikita, are life's way of teaching me how to let go of hurt, how to move on, and how to forgive.

And life's lessons don't stop coming. When I look back, I know I haven't learned every lesson perfectly. There are some of life's teachings that I've forgotten, and will have to relearn, sometimes over and over again. But I've made my peace with that, because

I know that learning never ends. And I look forward now to the rest of the masterclass, to all the wonderful, surprising, and sometimes painful lessons life still has to teach me.

Playing with Sone and the boys back on the estate, I didn't have the faintest clue what was to come. In my wildest dreams I couldn't have predicted any of it: a first-class Law degree, six major trophies, three World Cup appearances, three Euros, the American league, the Olympics, the one hundred caps for England. But God saw it all, laid out before Him, He had a plan for me.

And so, when I look to the future, to the lessons yet to come, I put my trust in God's guiding hand, the hand that gave me talent, gave me football that set me on this fascinating, surprising, and ever-winding path. And when I fail, when things go wrong, I know it will be part of His plan. Through crushing defeats and euphoric wins, through storms and trials, I will emerge one day, stronger, wiser, with another lesson learned.

I hope the lessons I have laid out here help you on your journey through life as they have me on mine. If you take only one thing away, let it be that the path to success isn't linear and that there will surely be losses along with the wins. All of life's twists and turns, especially the failures, contain a lesson. If I've learned anything, it's that the game of life is about getting things wrong, going back, and trying again. Don't be disheartened; listen to what life is teaching you. Because learning never stops, and they don't teach this.

LIST OF ILLUSTRATIONS

School award for showing good character; a certificate for 'super behaviour and a good attitude in school', author's own

The only girl in the school team; back to back with Sone at the Birmingham Youth Academy, author's own

First class honours degree in Law from Brunel University, author's own

***

Scoring in the 2005 FA Cup final. Charlton beat Everton 1–0 to win the trophy; top and middle Julian Finney/Getty; bottom Adam Davey/EMPICS Sport/Press association

In action in the USA, for Saint Louis Athletica, Atlanta Beat and Sky Blue FC. Former St Louis coach,

Jorge Barcellos, top left Scott Kane/Southcreek Global/ ZUMApress/Alamy; Barcellos, Bill Barrett; Beat, David Todd; Sky Blue, Howard C Smith, ISI Photos

Confirmation of my first England call-up, author's own; England v France, 2004, Julian Finney/Getty; Celebrating with parents, James Prickett

World Cup qualification secured, Julian Finney/Getty

***

100 Caps for England, FA social media composition; receiving armband and running on, photographer unknown

Disappointment against Manchester City, 2014, top The FA/Shutterstock; bottom Simon Stacpoole/ Offside

Women's Super League Champions, top Darren Walsh/Chelsea FC/Getty; bottom Chelsea/Getty

Dressing room with the FA Cup, 2015, Ian Tuttle/ Shutterstock

Headline montage; Mark Sampson, Martin Rickett/ PA Images; DCMS hearing, PA Images

Celebrating the Coppa Italia with Juventus, 2019, Juventus FC; shoot for the 2019/20 Juventus kit, Julia Puder/Addidas

FOOTBALL BEYOND BORDERS

Football Beyond Borders (FBB) is an education charity that uses the power of football to educate and inspire young people from disadvantaged backgrounds. Following the publication of *They Don't Teach This*, Football Beyond Borders, Eniola Aluko and Vintage teamed up for a series of workshops as part of FBB's educational project inspired by lessons from the book. Read on for a few of the creative writing responses from the FBB girls group.

When I walk into the class,
They Don't Teach This.
They call me lazy. Do you know
What that means sis?

I'm a role model,
Like a gold medal.

Listen.
Yes you may be different
But we're all equivalent.

Jessica Milambo
Age 16

———

They call me lazy, they don't want to see my success.
They say I can't do it, but do you know what that means?
They don't teach you to how to love yourself,
And what you're capable of,
But you need to remember what you are made of.

You can do anything you put your mind to, which I learnt
From a famous role model,
Who I look up to.

So if they don't teach you,
You teach it to yourself.

Make it come true and show them
That you can do anything
That you put your mind to.

Yusra Orfeye
Age 15

———

They don't teach them to think before they speak,
They don't teach us our true value and worth.

They don't teach me to believe in myself,
They want me to be lighter, but I've been this way since birth.

Aaliyah Yusuf
Age 13

———

BE YOUR BEST SELF

Judgement I let faze me.
I even wanted to change me.
My mind always echoed who am I meant to be?

Depression, anxiety in society.
They cause a variety of problems
Not just me,
But everyone who doesn't believe in themselves.

But I realised who I am and who I am meant to be
My name is Jemima Agbega,
I wasn't proud of my family tree,
Since I'm French and Congolese,
But FBB embraced me,
Then I was free
And it taught me to be me.

My voice has been heard,
I'm spreading and flying like a bird,
I'm not always angry,
That's just how society…
Portrays me…
I'm on my journey.
Judged by appearance.
I'm always called ugly

But it's my mindset
So don't fret
Cause I know that I am blessed, so…
Clap for the heavyweight champ, 'Me',
But I could never do it alone, you see,
Because being my best self
Is not having to do it by myself,

Cause I can't be shining,
Whilst everyone is hiding,
Because being my best self,
Is knowing that I have tried to help,
Everybody else.

So be your best self
No matter who you are
Cause sis you're a star!

Jemima Agbepa
Age 13

———

Find out more about Football Beyond Borders and the work they do
at www.footballbeyondborders.org

INDEX